DRAWING ACADEMY

PERSPECTIVE DRAWING

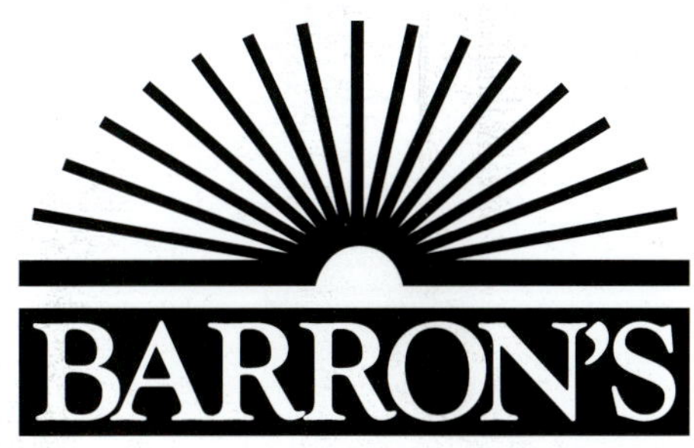

Original title of the book in Spanish: *La Perspectiva en el Dibujo*
© Parramón Ediciónes, S.A., Primera edición: Septiembre 2006
Published by Parramón Ediciónes, S.A.
Barcelona, Spain

Text: Gabriel Martín Roig
Exercises: Carlant, Almudena Carreno, Gabriel Martín, Esther Olivé de Puig
Photography: Nos & Soto

Translated from the Spanish by Michael Brunelle and Beatriz Cortabarria

All inquiries should be addressed to:
Barron's Educational Series, Inc.
250 Wireless Blvd.
Hauppauge, NY 11788
www.barronseduc.com

ISBN-13: 978-0-7641-6050-9
ISBN-10: 0-7641-6050-8

Library of Congress Catalog Card No.: 2007925085

Printed in Spain
9 8 7 6 5 4 3 2 1

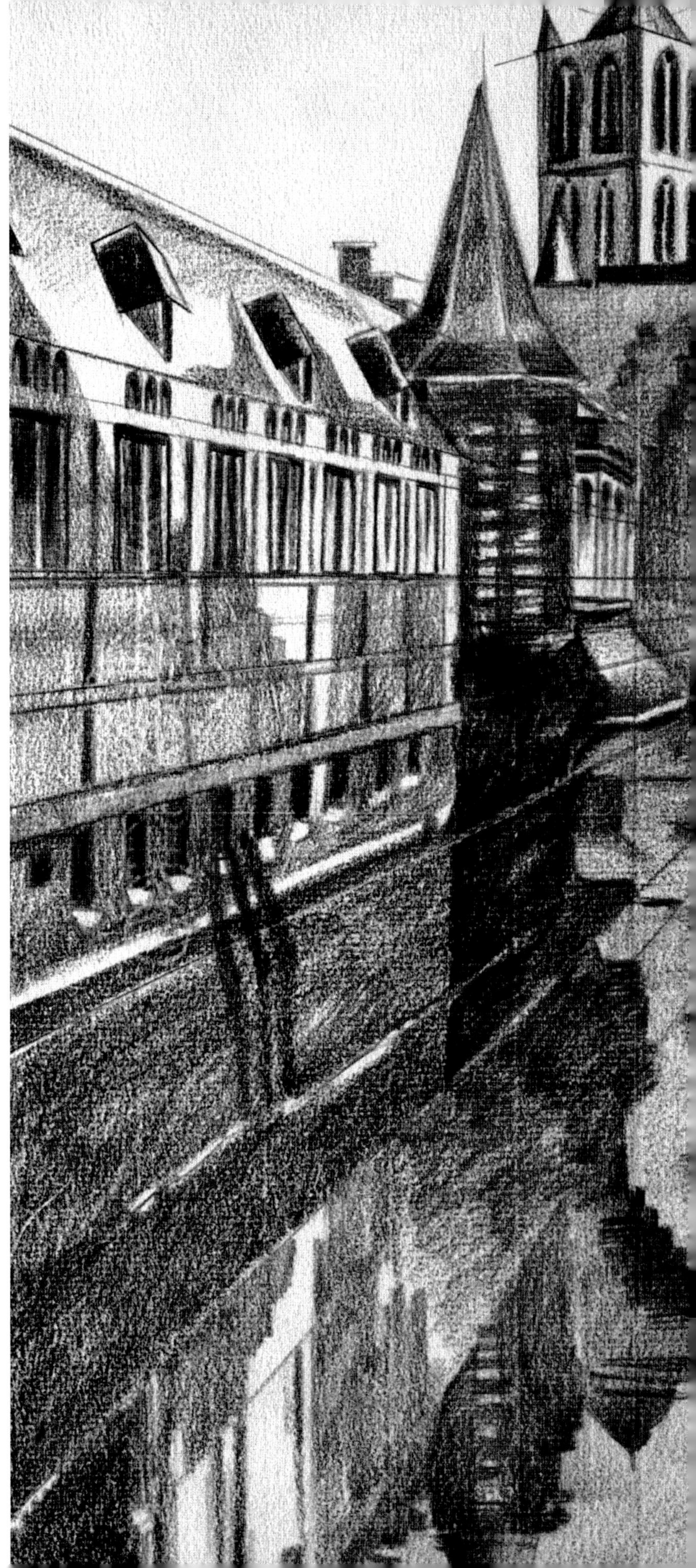

CONTENTS

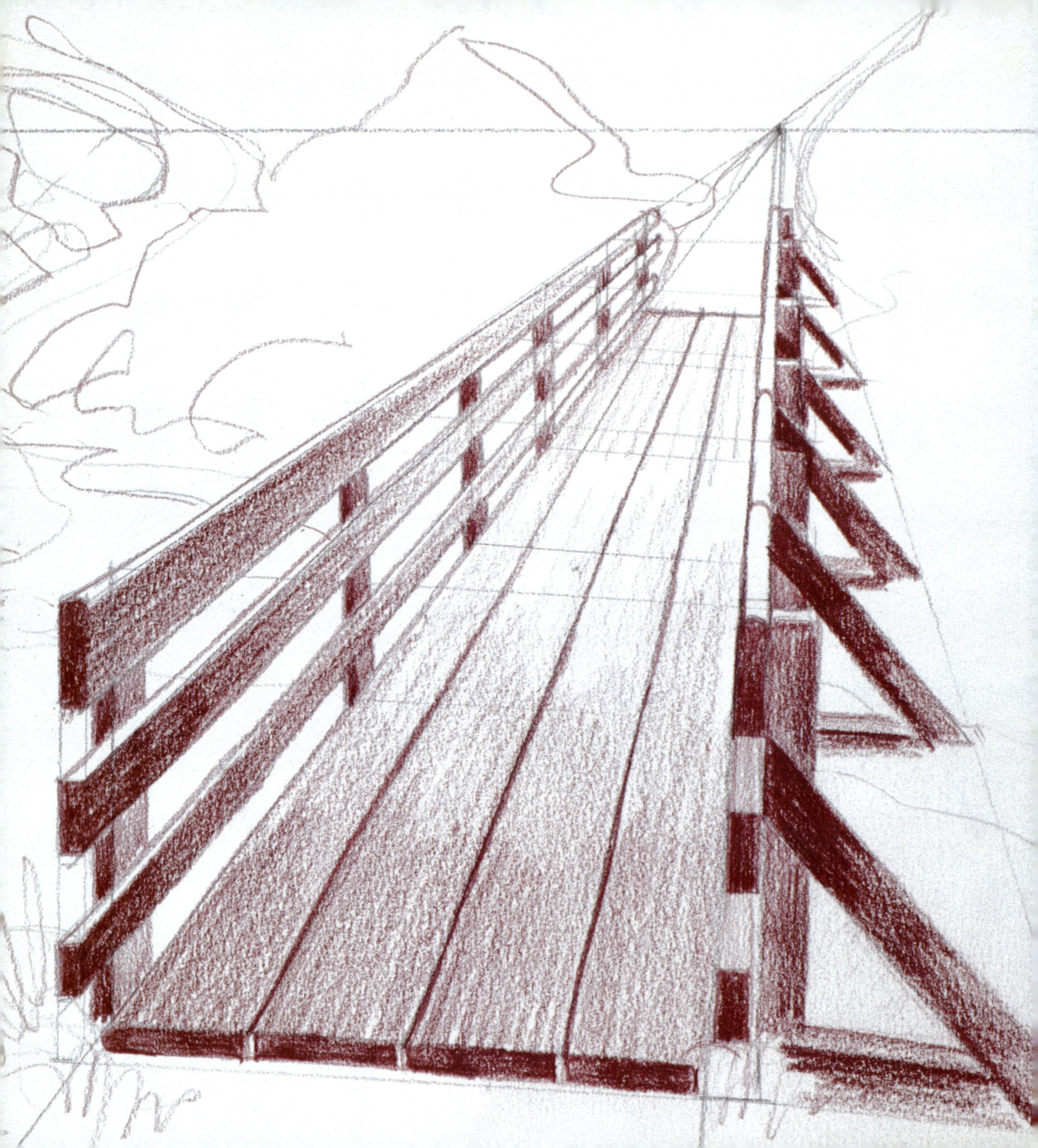

INTRODUCTION

For centuries, artists studied the effect that depth had on images and described it in books. Despite their analytical efforts at illustrating space and depth in their drawings, they admitted that they had made mistakes and that the final representation was not fully convincing.

Since it is impossible to flatten the objects onto the surface of the paper, they had to create a new system that could codify and simplify spatial representation and convey visual correction to the viewer.

With this in mind, the first studies of linear perspective attributed to the architect Leon Battista Alberti and the sculptor Filippo Brunelleschi made their appearance in Florence at the beginning of the fifteenth century. In their treatises they demonstrated that space could be articulated mathematically to recreate the feeling of depth. This was argued from the standpoint of geometry using the concepts of projection and section.

The system quickly became a success because, when put into practice, it produced a result that looked like the image perceived by the eye. In other words, it mimicked the way that the eye sees space and objects in daily life.

Since then, the study of perspective has been a requirement for anyone who wants to draw accurately; yet, even though this method produces results that are close to reality, it is a fabrication, a simplification, an adaptation. It is obvious that between perspective and the eye there are certain formal analogies, but mathematical correction and exactness exist only in the drawing, not in the real model. Although perspective is an extraordinary tool, it is a convention; if we project the perspective lines meticulously over photographic images, we will notice that the geometric measurements do not always coincide with the real model.

PERSPECTIVE AS A TOOL FOR DRAWING. To represent a model, which in real life has three dimensions, on a sheet of paper that has only two, we must use perspective. Perspective is very helpful when we need to organize the space and to structure depth.

LINEAR AND INTUITIVE PERSPECTIVE. When we wish to represent depth when drawing from nature without the rigorous parameters of mathematical perspective, we apply it intuitively, that is, "by eye," without the use of geometric rules.

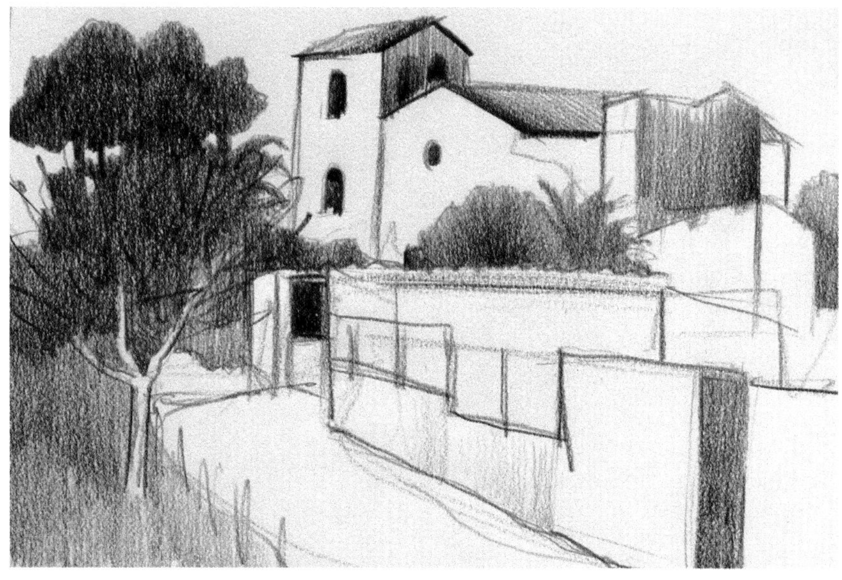

Pencil drawing of a landscape executed with intuitive perspective.

HORIZON LINE. Before drawing in perspective, the artist has to establish the eye level or horizon line. This is an imaginary line located at eye level when we are looking forward. If the painting is divided into two areas separated by a horizontal line, the one below is considered the land and the one above the sky.

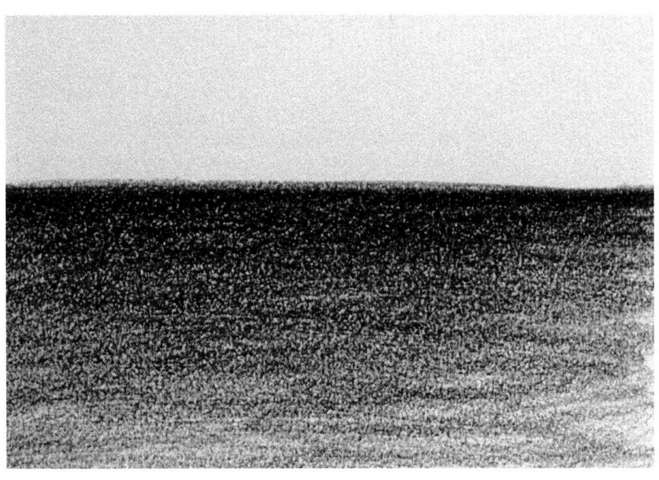

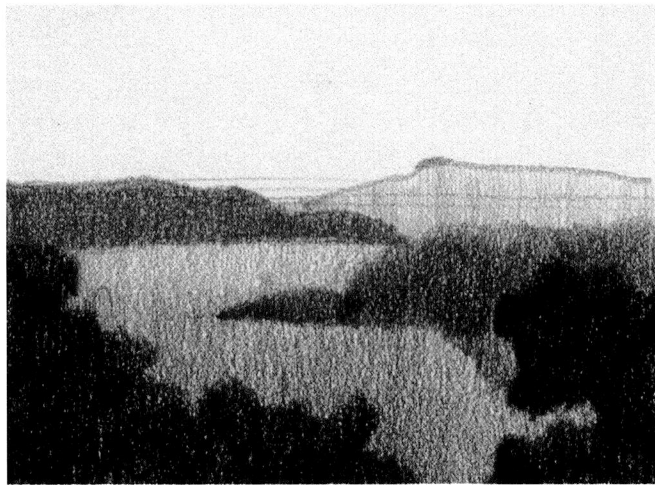

When we divide the paper with an imaginary line, the lower part is usually considered the land, while the area above is the sky.

THE HEIGHT OF THE HORIZON LINE CHANGES. The horizon line is not constant; it changes according to the position of the viewer. To create a painting that has great depth, we choose a very high horizon line. A low horizon line removes the emphasis from the land and puts it on the sky.

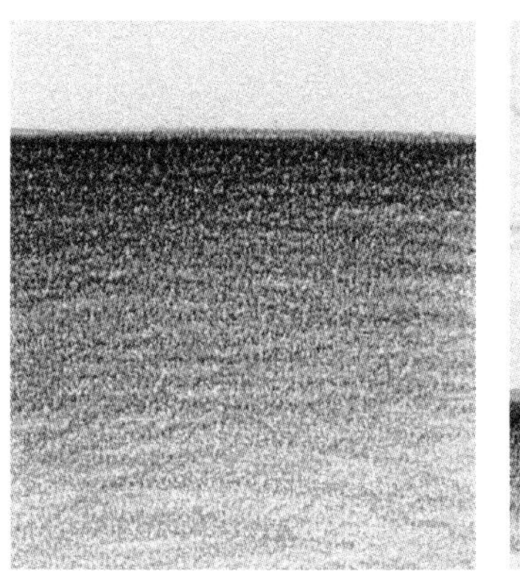

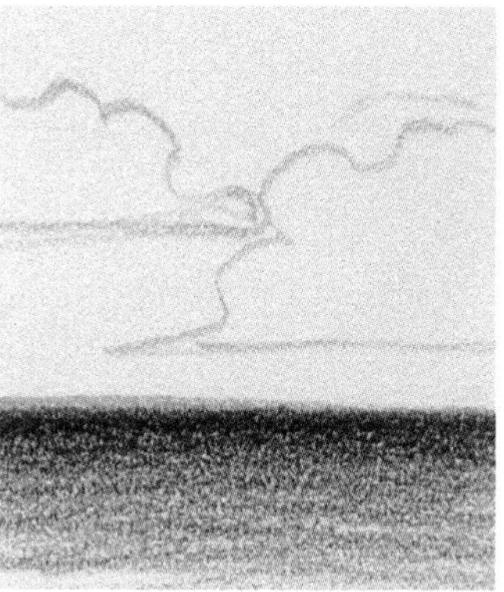

A high horizon line emphasizes the terrain, while a low horizon line gives greater importance to the sky.

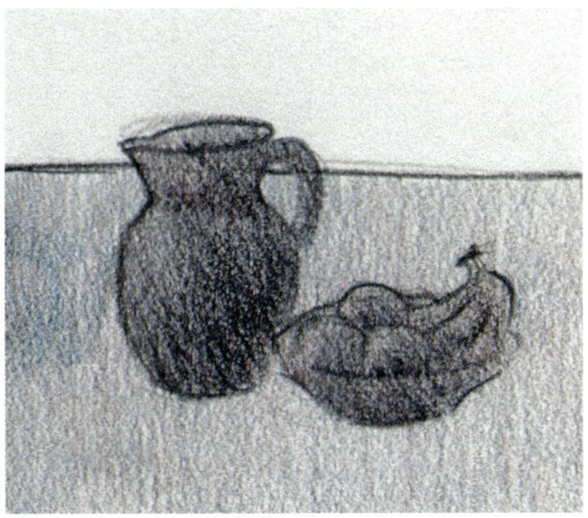

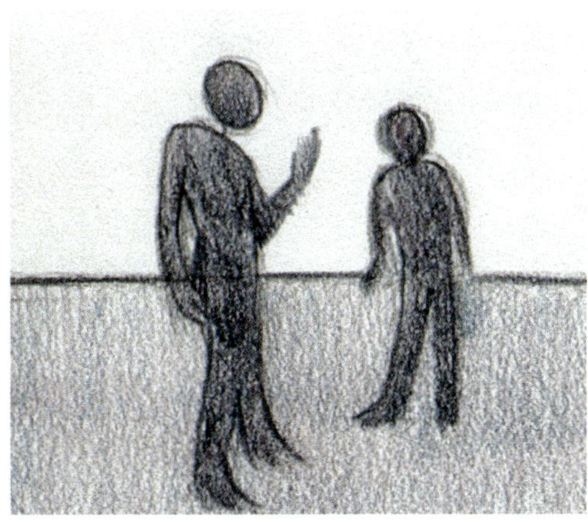

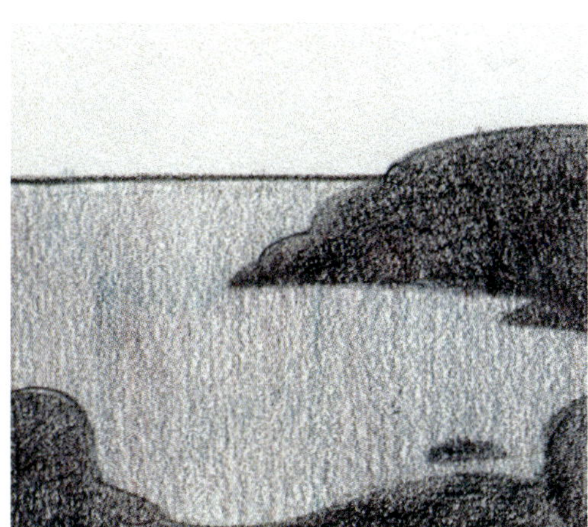

Each theme dictates its own natural horizon line.

EACH THEME HAS ITS OWN HORIZON LINE. Each genre has its own perspective, which helps to structure the space. In still lifes, the horizon line is usually above the subject because the chosen point of view is almost always high. In representations of full body figures, the horizon line divides the painting in two. In seascapes and flat landscapes, the perspective horizon is the same as the real horizon. If the landscape has mountains, the horizon line is somewhat below the upper edges of the mountaintops.

LINES AND DEPTH. The effect of depth in a drawing increases when we draw lines that move away from the edges of the painting and converge at the center of the paper; they immediately create an illusion of depth. When these lines converge on a fixed point on the horizon line, they are called vanishing lines.

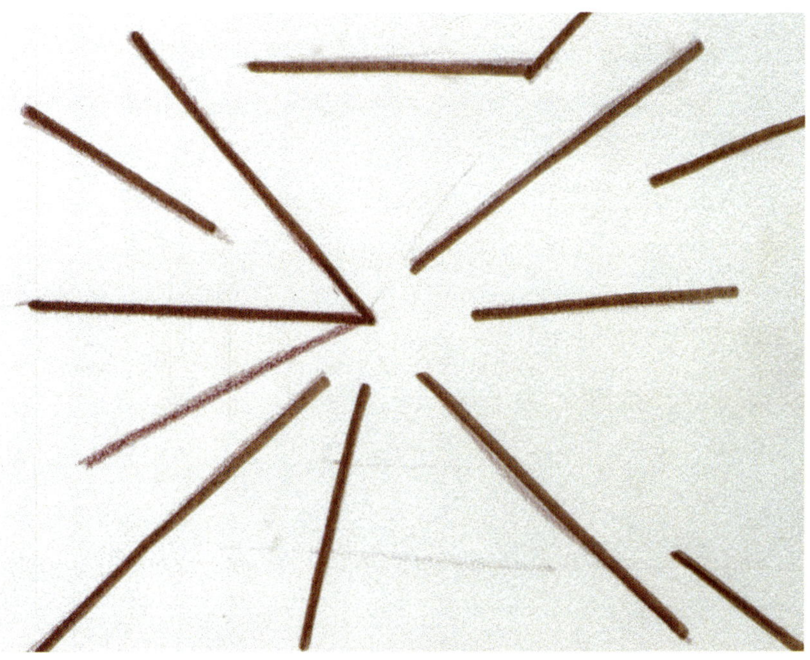

When various lines converge at a common point on the horizon, the effect conveyed to the viewer is one of psychological distance.

CREATING THE SPACE. Knowledge of perspective is without a doubt very useful for setting up and constructing space and depth. In geometric or linear perspective, a series of diagonal points and lines project the object toward the background of the drawing, but there are other compositional approaches that should not be ignored.

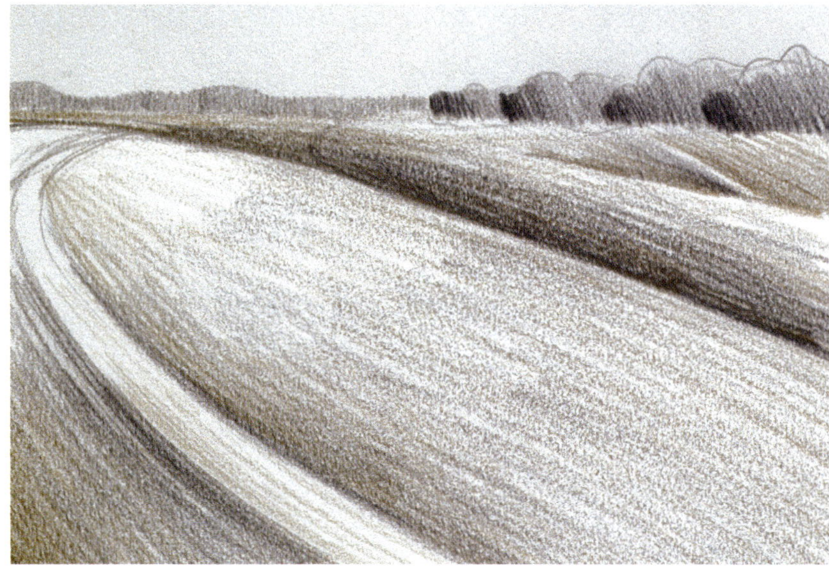

The diagonals that cut through the plane of the drawing are the first indicators of distance.

DIAGONALS THAT SET THE SCENE. The perspective effect is easily achieved if the landscape has a diagonal element that arranges the objects from front to back. This diagonal can be a riverbank, a hill, a fence, or any other linear element that cuts through the composition.

POSITION IN THE VISUAL FIELD. An object drawn higher or lower on the surface of the paper is perceived the same way by the viewer as one seen on a horizontal surface. As the object moves farther away from the foreground, the viewer has to move his or her eyes up, or lower them as he or she approaches it.

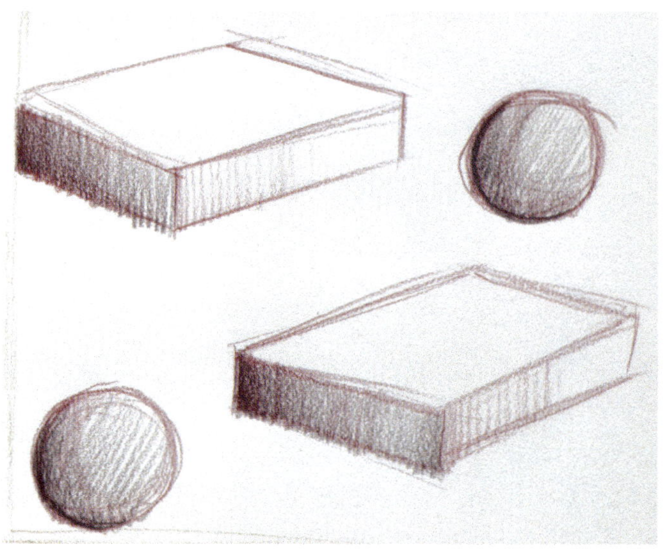

Psychologically, the same object placed at a higher level on the paper appears to be farther away.

SUPERIMPOSED OBJECTS. The objects that are closer to the viewer conceal the ones located farther away; therefore, when we draw some figures over others, we create an immediate feeling of depth. As a result, the contours of the most distant elements are interrupted by the figures placed in front of them.

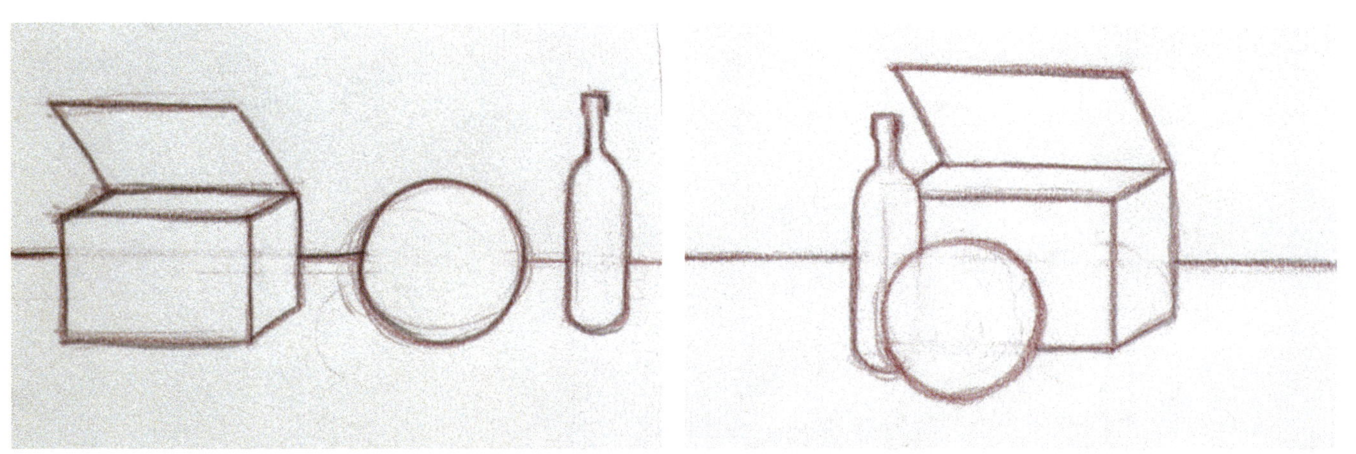

Superimposed objects convey a sequenced feeling in the distance. When they are shown separately, they look like they are on the same plane and thus lose any reference of depth.

DIFFERENT SIZES. If two figures of similar size are placed so that one is farther away than the other, the former appears smaller to the viewer. In a drawing in which different size objects are involved, a familiar element, such as the human figure, helps convey the depth and size of the space represented.

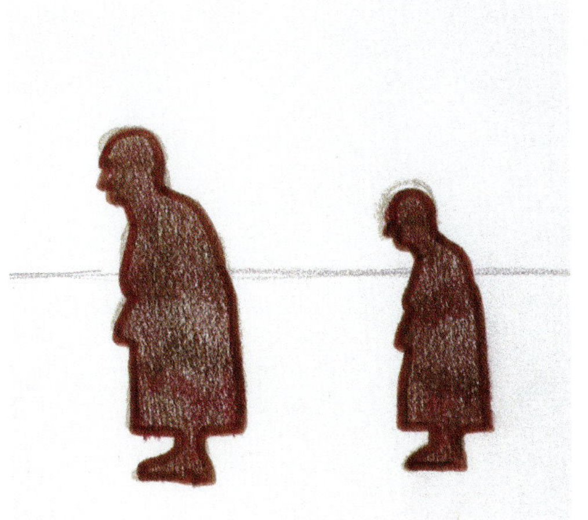

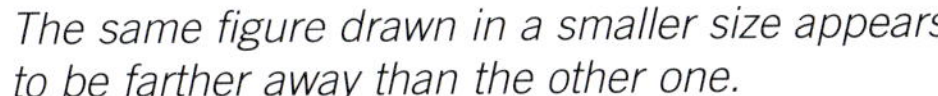

The same figure drawn in a smaller size appears to be farther away than the other one.

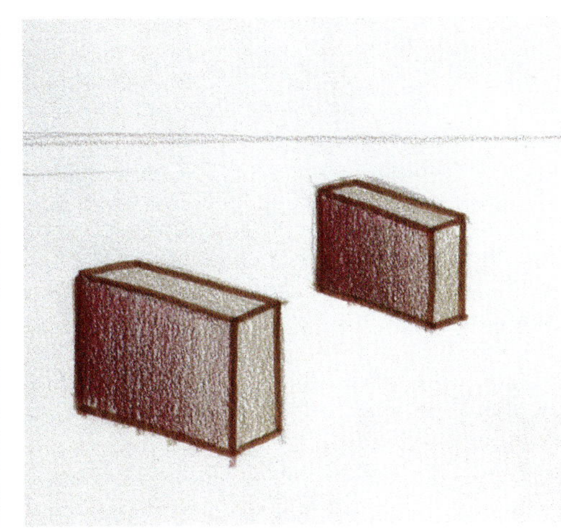

This effect is even more pronounced if the smaller object is placed higher.

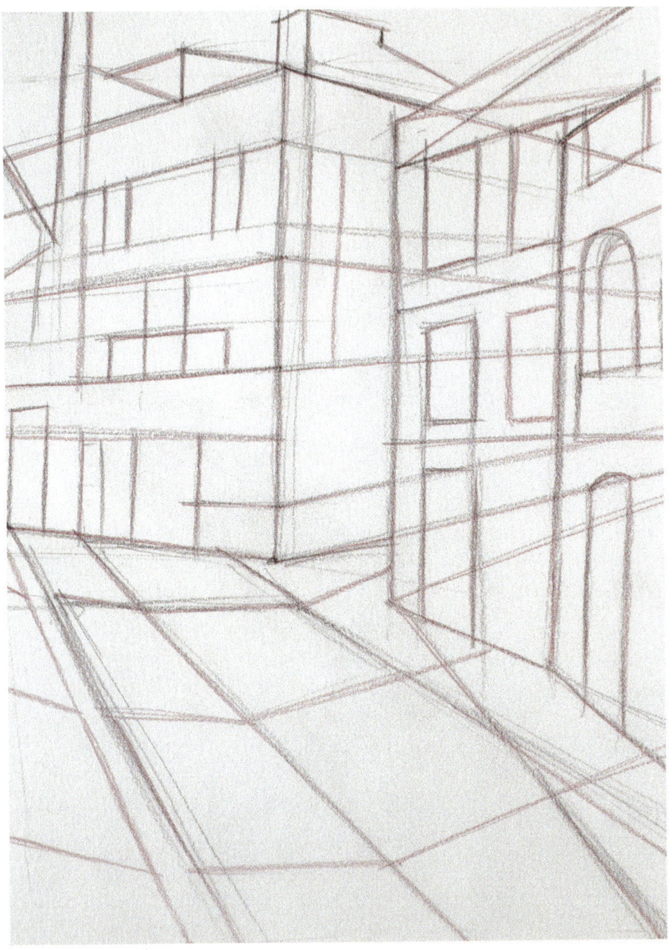

AVOIDING TOO MANY GEOMETRIC STRUCTURES. In addition to the compositional methods shown so far, there are many more complex geometric approaches that help create a feeling of depth. It is important to be aware of them without overusing them, unless the work involves an architectural project. Putting too much emphasis on technical rules will result in a drawing that lacks creativity and spontaneity.

It is important not to abuse the rules of perspective. Using too many lines is confusing, cumbersome, and makes the drawing less appealing.

Linear Perspective

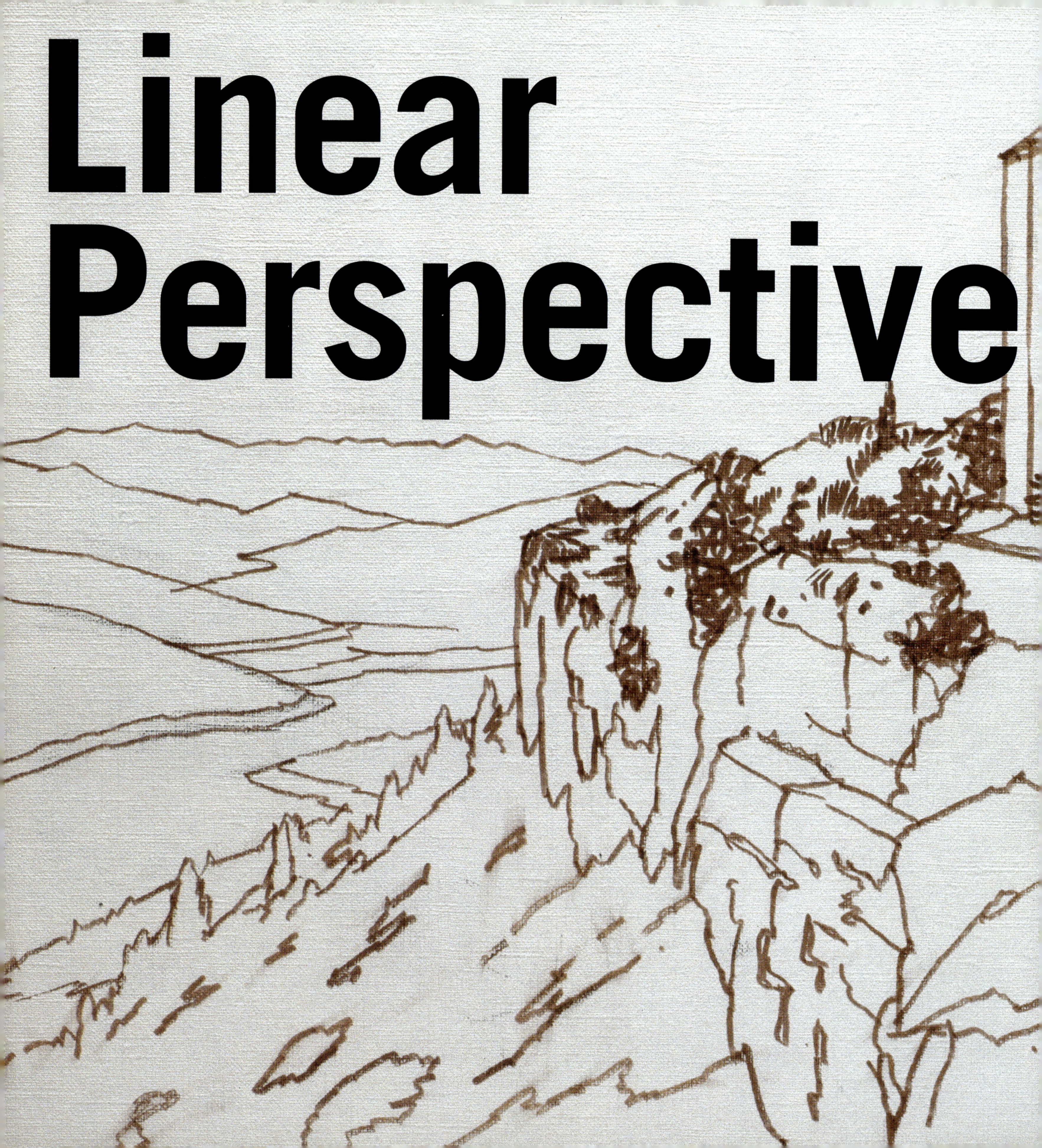

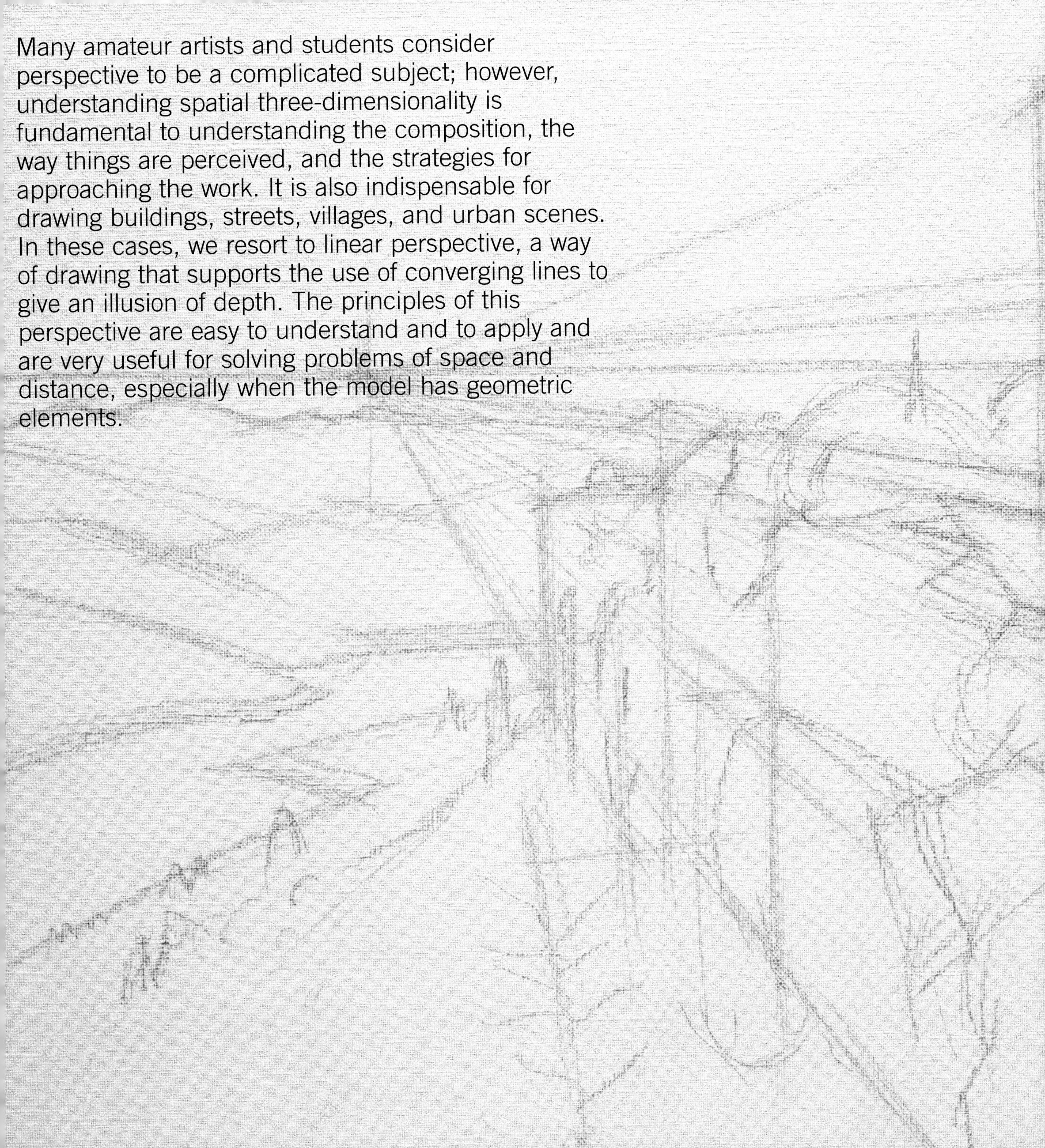

Many amateur artists and students consider perspective to be a complicated subject; however, understanding spatial three-dimensionality is fundamental to understanding the composition, the way things are perceived, and the strategies for approaching the work. It is also indispensable for drawing buildings, streets, villages, and urban scenes. In these cases, we resort to linear perspective, a way of drawing that supports the use of converging lines to give an illusion of depth. The principles of this perspective are easy to understand and to apply and are very useful for solving problems of space and distance, especially when the model has geometric elements.

LEARNING BY DOING

CENTRAL PERSPECTIVE. This projection in perspective is derived from conical perspective, with a single vanishing point. It is used to explain the use of the vanishing lines in expressing the distortion of the space in the distance. Exercise by Gabriel Martín.

1.1

IT BEGINS WITH A SQUARE. To draw a small street with a strong effect of depth, we look for the center of the perspective, the point where all the lines that define the bases of the walls and the inclination of the roofs converge. Once we have located this point, we draw a square around it.

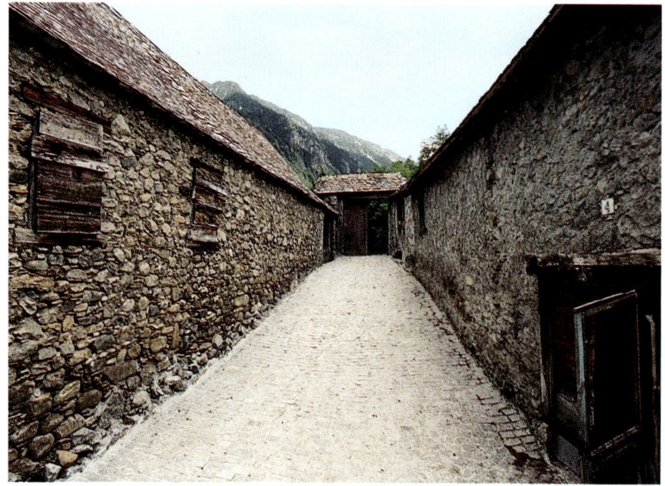

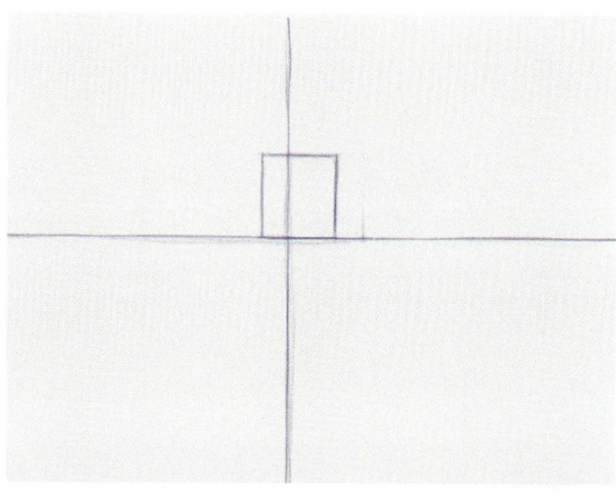

We mark the center of the paper. We see that the lines of the street converge at a point that is somewhat higher, which is located exactly in the center of a square; this can be used to represent the door that is located in the background.

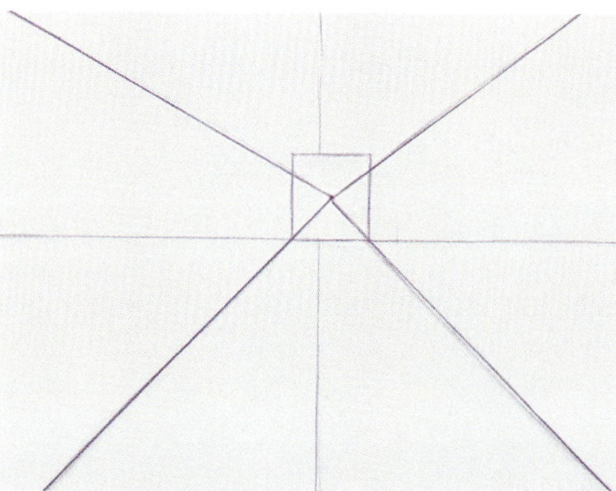

From the point located in the center of the square, we extend four diagonal lines that represent the vanishing lines of the walls. These vanishing lines are the basis for understanding the space distorted by perspective.

We can use a ruler or a triangle to draw the vanishing lines.

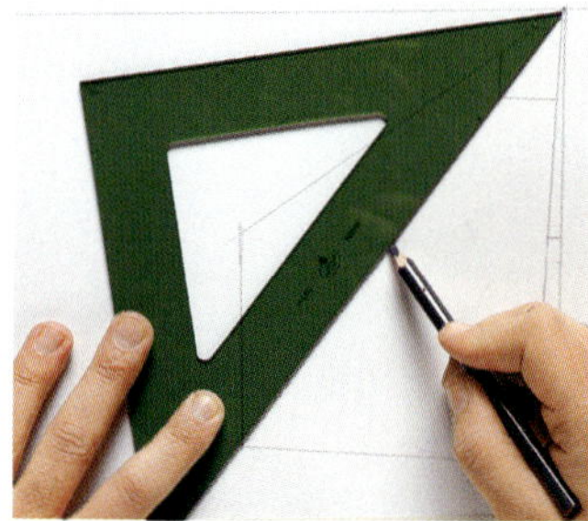

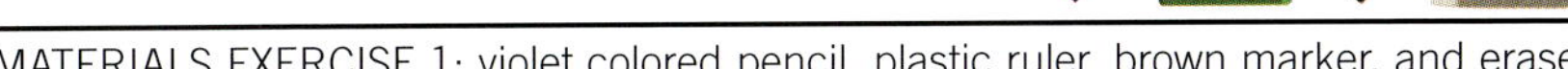

MATERIALS EXERCISE 1: violet colored pencil, plastic ruler, brown marker, and eraser

1.2

DOORS AND WINDOWS. With new perspective lines we draw the main openings on the walls. Rectangular and square shapes for doors and windows also appear distorted by the effect of perspective.

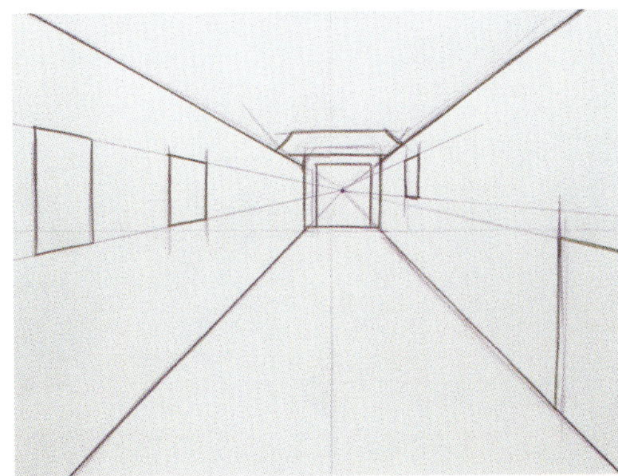

The roof and the frame of the door in the background are sketched in. New vanishing lines are projected from the same central point to define the positions of the door and the windows.

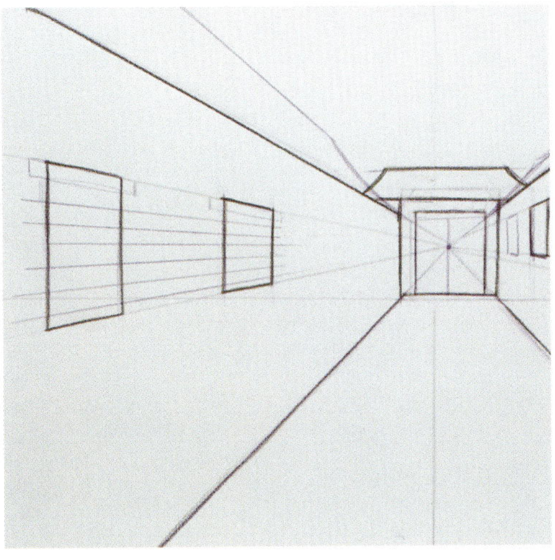

New diagonal lines that are projected from the same central point define the angles of the boards that cover the windows more accurately. With a new line we define the profile of the roof.

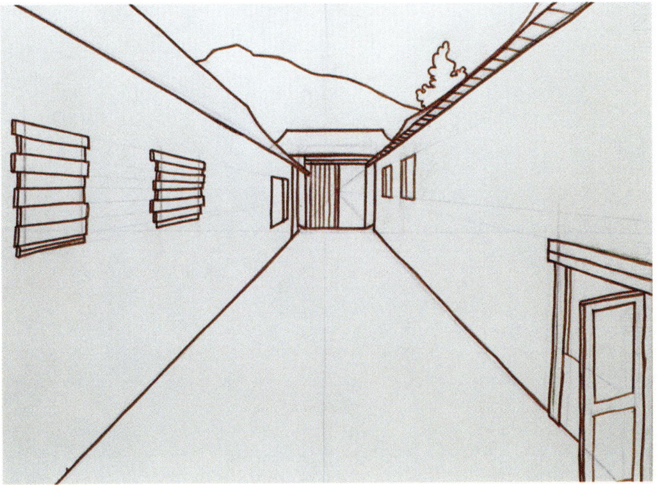

Finishing the drawing is simple. With a brown marker, we redraw the lines based on the previous perspective lines and then clearly define the doors, windows, and the outline of the mountain in the background. All this is done freehand.

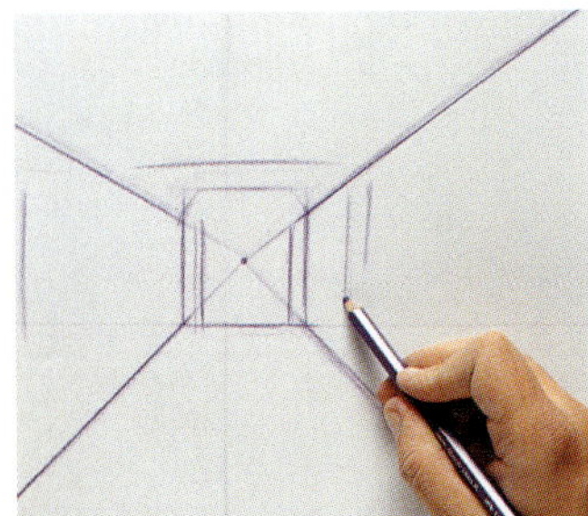

The vertical lines for the windows can be drawn freehand. These lines must always be perpendicular and parallel.

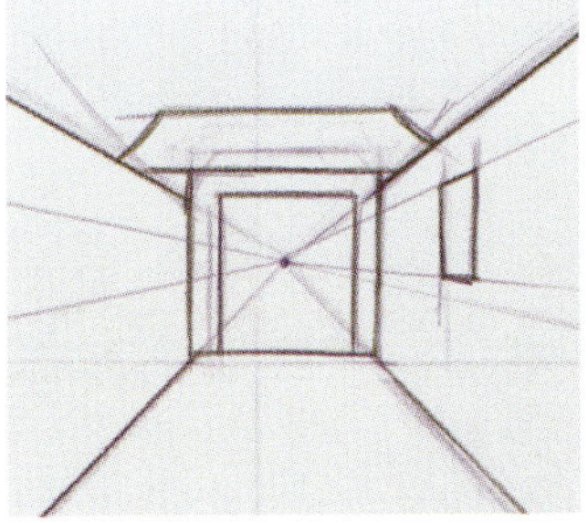

Central perspective is characterized by an array of vanishing lines from a point situated in the center of the drawing.

LEARNING BY DOING

A WOODEN BRIDGE. We leave central perspective to draw a simple object that has a single vanishing point, which is located far away. The object is a wooden bridge that has a quadrangular structure, which is very distorted by perspective. Exercise by Gabriel Martín.

2.1

A GLASS BOX. To make the work easier, we think of the bridge as if it were a rectangular glass box, so the far sides and the angles are visible. In other words, we approach the structure of the bridge as if it were transparent.

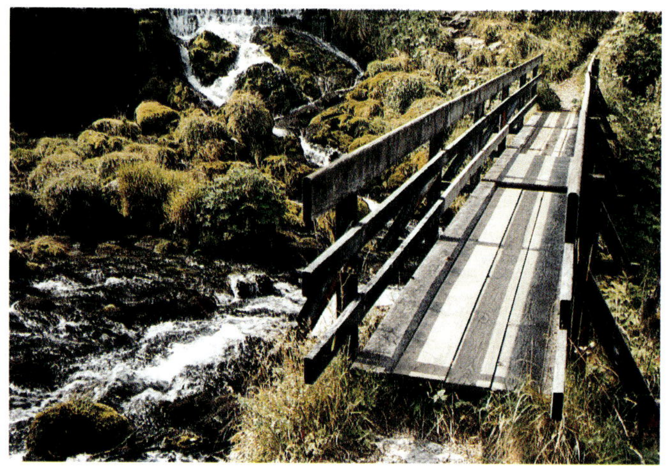

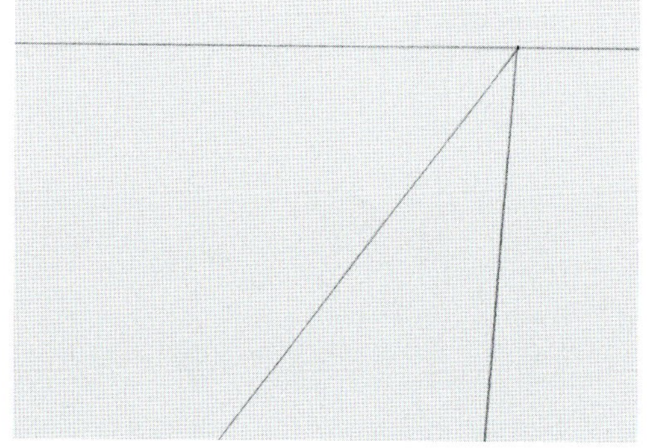

We draw the horizon line, which is placed very high on the paper. Then we locate a vanishing point from which two diagonal lines that define the base of the bridge are projected.

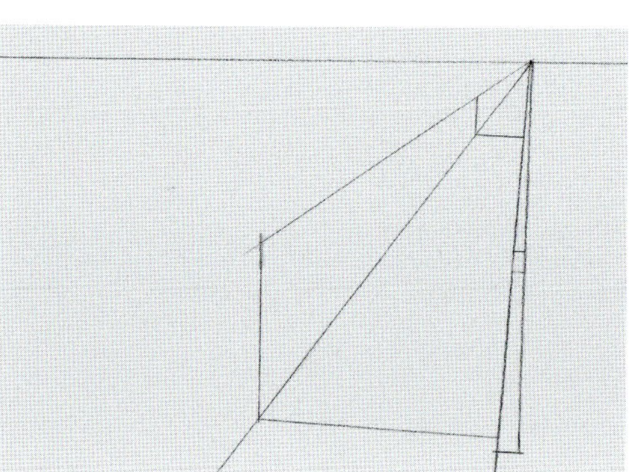

We construct the box for the bridge by imagining two square shapes on the foreground and the background. These are the parameters that establish the length of the wooden structure. We connect the top corners of the squares with the vanishing point.

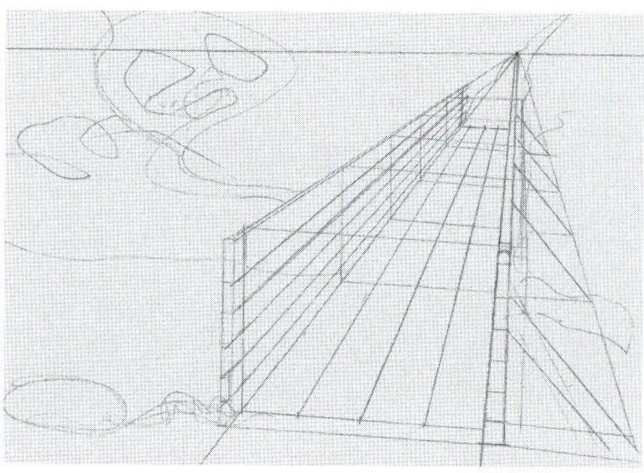

We divide the base of the square in the foreground into four equal parts. From these sections we project three new diagonal lines toward the vanishing point. We repeat the procedure with the left handrail, although this time we divide it into six parts.

The divisions that mark the crossbeams on the handrail should not be the same, because the width of each crossbeam is different.

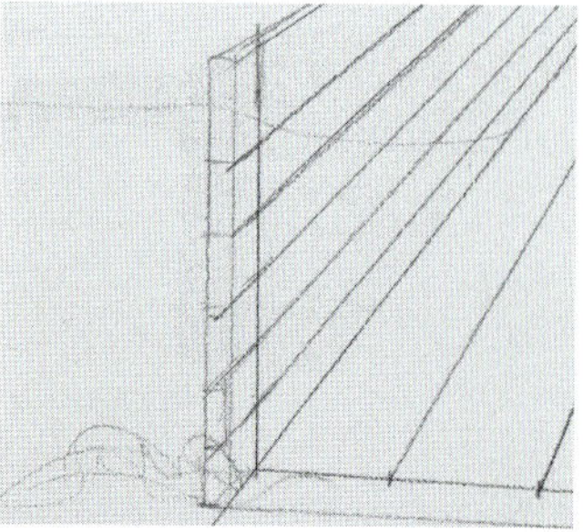

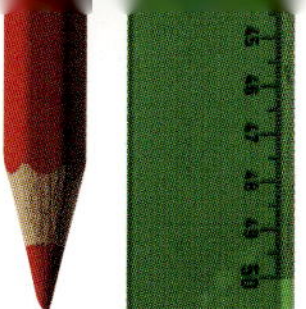

2.2

LINE AND TONAL PERSPECTIVE. We reinforce the line drawing with additional darker pencil lines, further defining the forms and creating the feeling of depth with tonal gradations. Then, we incorporate the element into its surrounding landscape by applying medium-intensity shading.

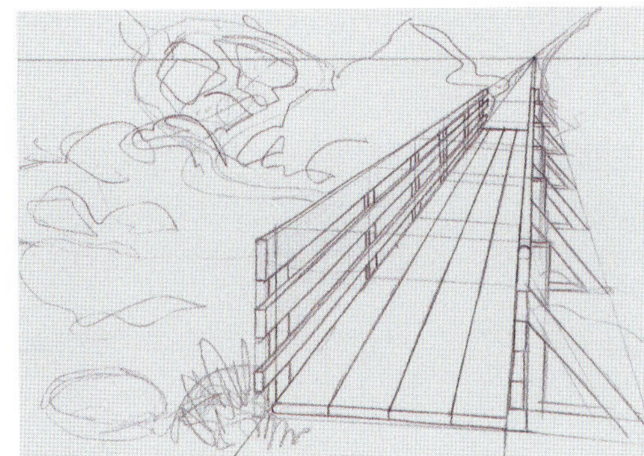

With the colored pencil used to draw the perspective, we go over the main contours and outlines of the bridge to define its structure. The main lines of the surrounding landscape are drawn with soft, spontaneous lines

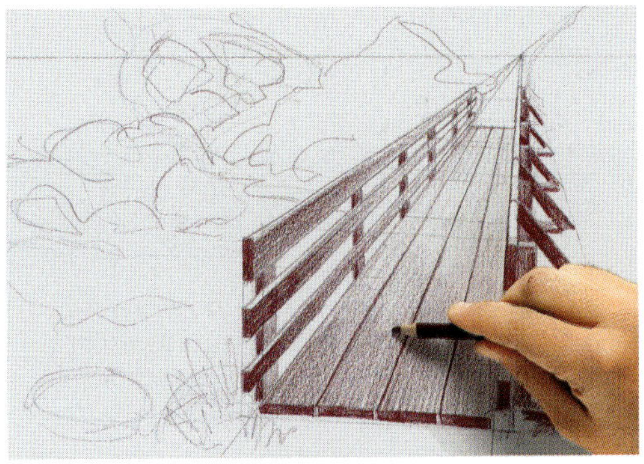

To further reinforce the effect of depth, we apply tonal gradations to the wooden walkway, darker on the foreground and lighter as we move farther away. The crossbeams of the handrail are also shaded the same way.

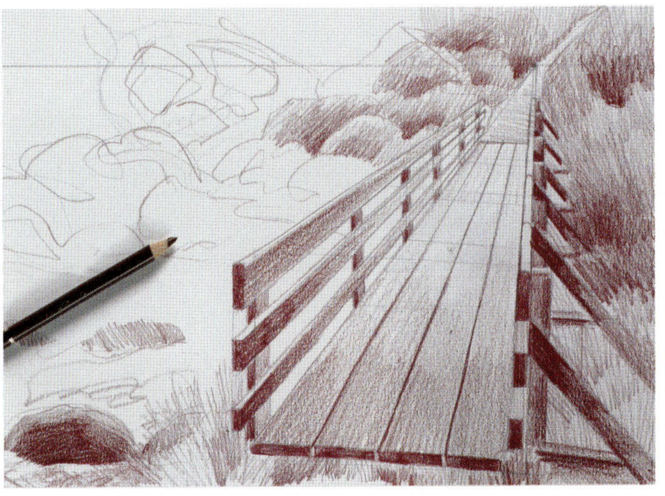

Finally, we incorporate the bridge, which until now has been treated as an isolated element, into the landscape around it. It is enough to draw the areas of vegetation and to apply graduated shading.

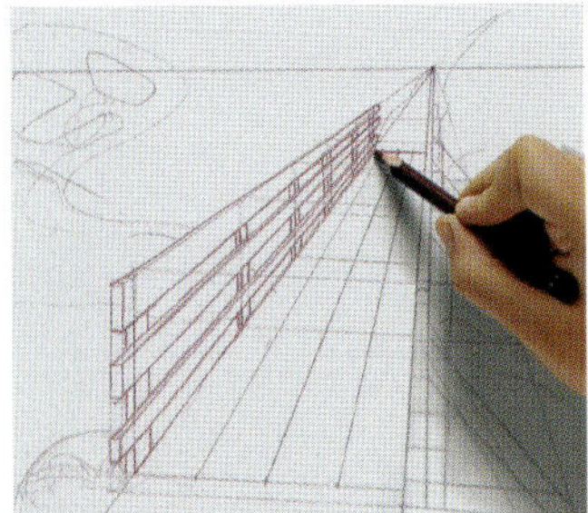

We define the profile of the object in perspective by going over the lines previously drawn with a ruler. It is not necessary to use the ruler again.

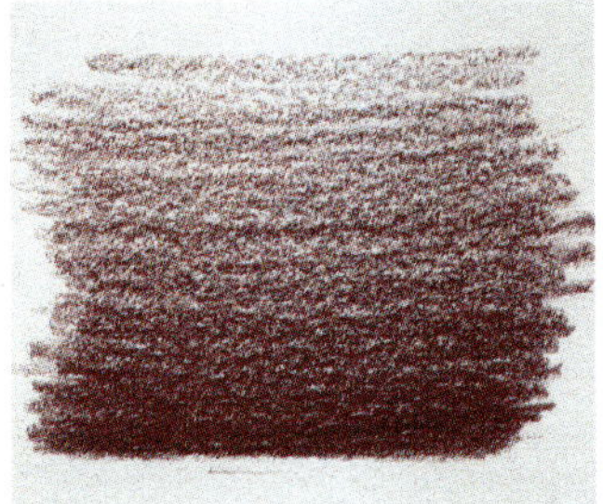

Adding gradations to a drawing done using linear perspective strengthens and enhances the effect of depth in the model.

A SINGLE POINT. The object's angled lines always point toward some point on the horizon called the vanishing point, which is the place where all the lines of the drawing converge.

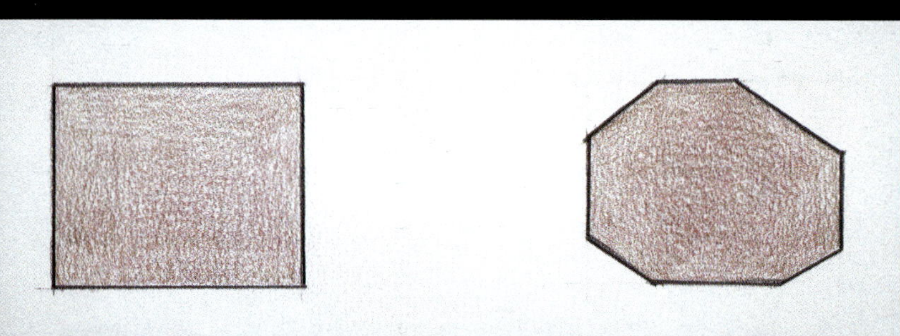

VANISHING LINES. The vanishing lines are very useful for distributing the space or the objects in space. With diagonals, it is possible to suggest the depth of the object represented, which becomes narrower as it moves farther away from the viewer.

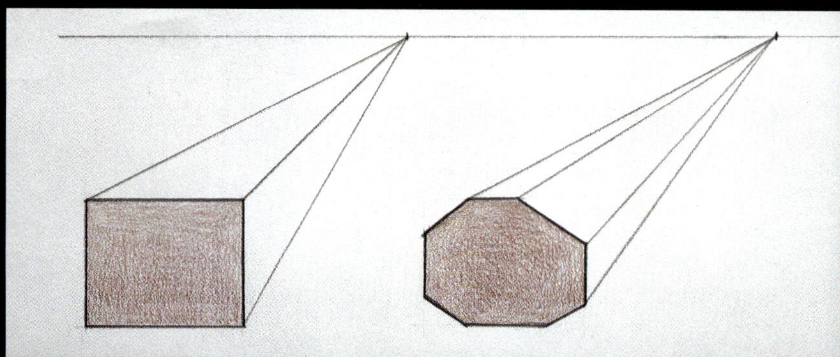

When the objects that we are representing have a side that is parallel to the drawing's surface, perspective is constructed with lines that connect the corners of the objects with a point on the horizon line.

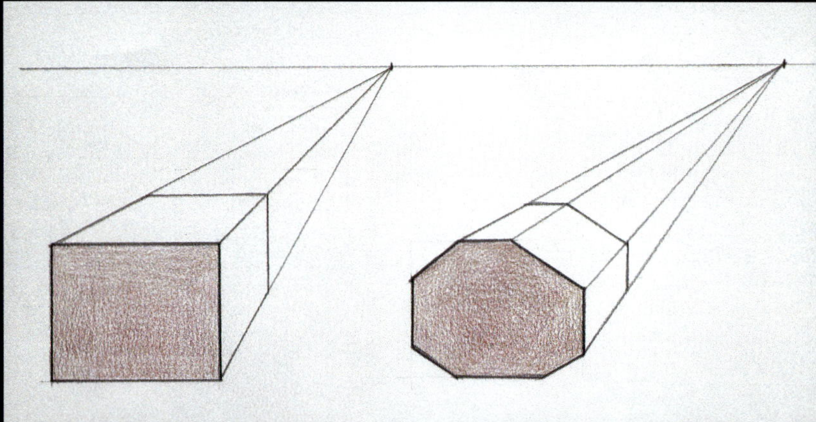

Vanishing lines help project the flat geometric figure into three dimensions.

TRAIN TRACKS. A classic example of parallel perspective is the drawing of train tracks. They get closer together the farther away they go, until the lines converge at a point on the horizon.

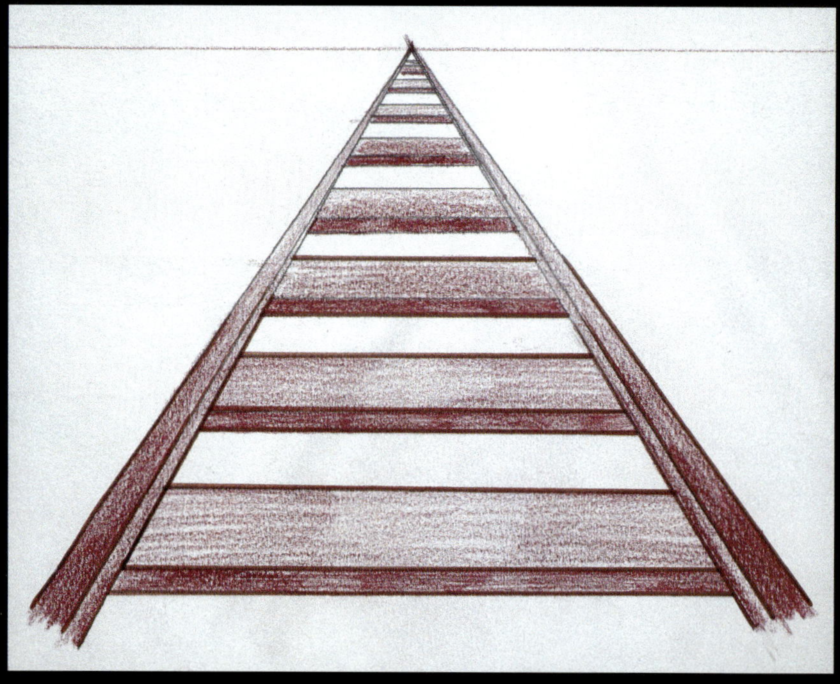

When we think about oblique perspective with a single vanishing point, the classic example of the train tracks always comes to mind.

VANISHING LINES AND PARALLEL PERSPECTIVE. Parallel perspective is used when one side of the model in front of us is parallel to the drawing's plane. Diagonal lines move away from the viewer, starting at the sides of the figure represented, and seem to meet at a point in the far distance.

ABOVE AND BELOW THE HORIZON LINE. When we look at objects around us, we see only the tops of some of them and the bottoms of others. This is due to the fact that the former are below the horizon line and the latter above. When we see neither the top nor the bottom part of the object, it is because it is located on the horizon line.

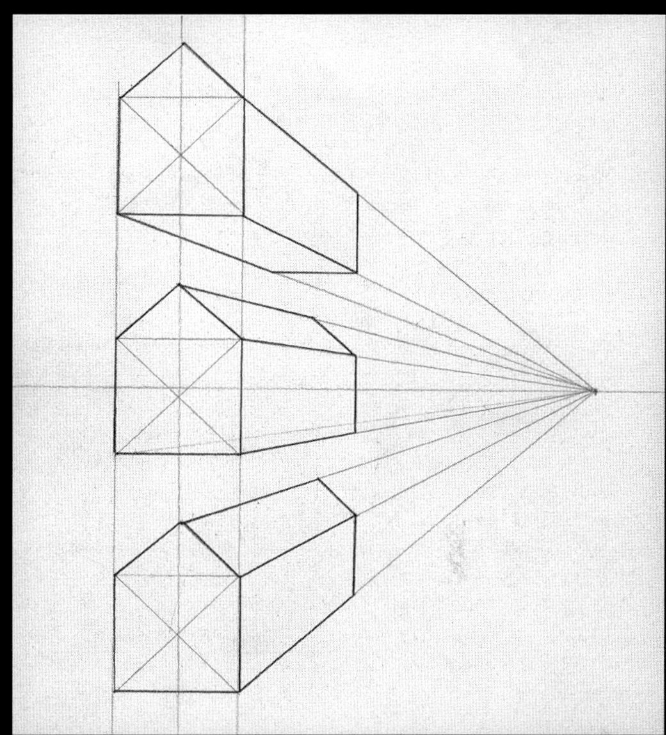

It is very helpful to draw the same building above and below the horizon line to see how the position of the artist affects the representation.

A TILED FLOOR. This is drawn with a linear one-point perspective; the vanishing point has to be located in front of the viewer, above eye level. The lines of tile joints must then simply go from left to right, parallel to the surface of the drawing.

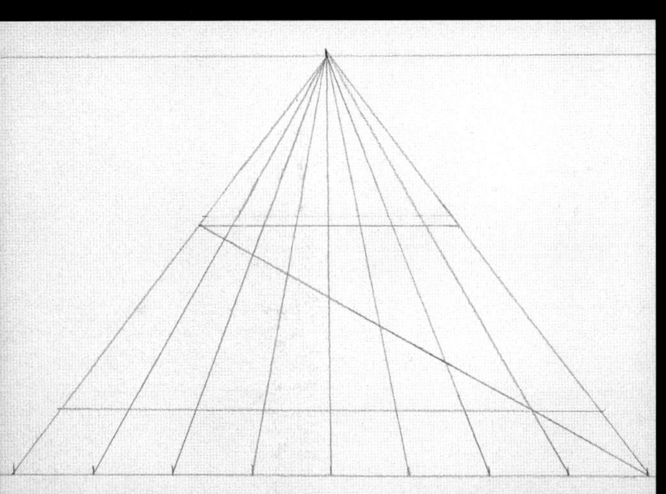

We divide the floor's base line into eight equal tiles. We connect each point with vanishing lines that converge at the vanishing point on the horizon. One diagonal line that runs across the edges of the squares is used as a guide to draw the rest of the tiles.

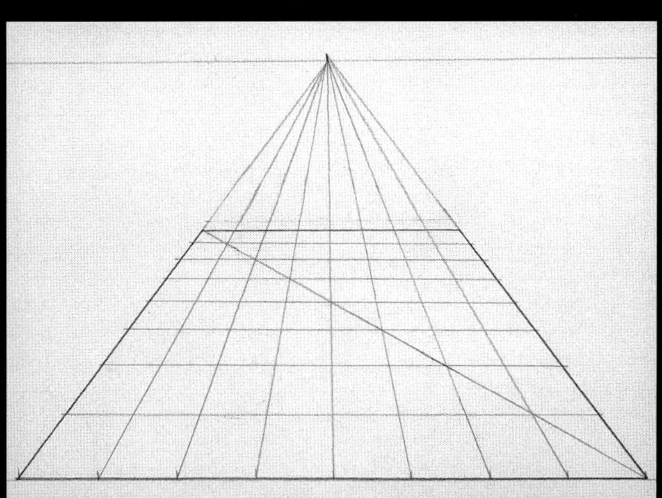

Every point where the crossing line cuts through each of the diagonals is used as a reference to draw a horizontal line parallel to the base line. This way, the floor tiles gradually become smaller as they move farther away.

LEARNING BY DOING

DRAWING BOXES. We develop the previously explained cone of vision, this time with a model that is a little more complex: a chapel on top of a rugged boulder. To construct this architectural element we use boxes and cubes drawn in perspective. Exercise by Carlant.

3.1

PROJECTING GEOMETRIC SHAPES. The successful outcome of the exercise rests on the ability to translate the volumetric forms of the chapel and the rocks into simple geometric shapes whose constructive lines converge at a point located on the horizon line.

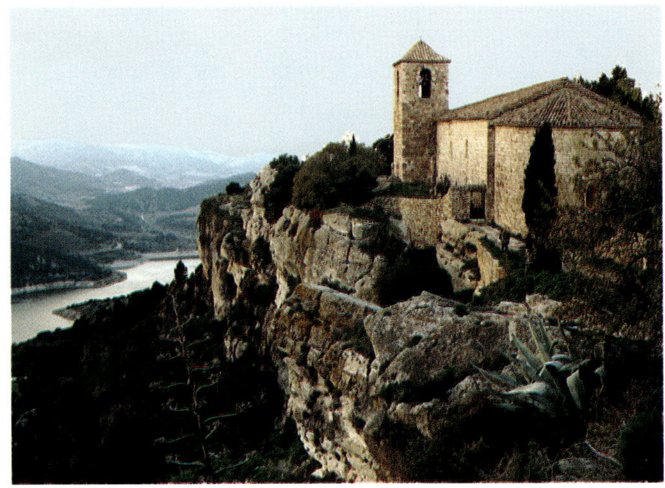

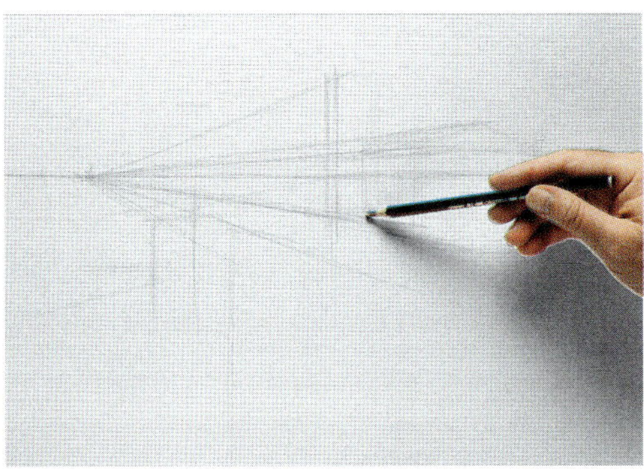

We draw the horizon line. On it, we locate a point from which diagonal lines will emerge, which will be used to construct the boxes that form the body of the chapel.

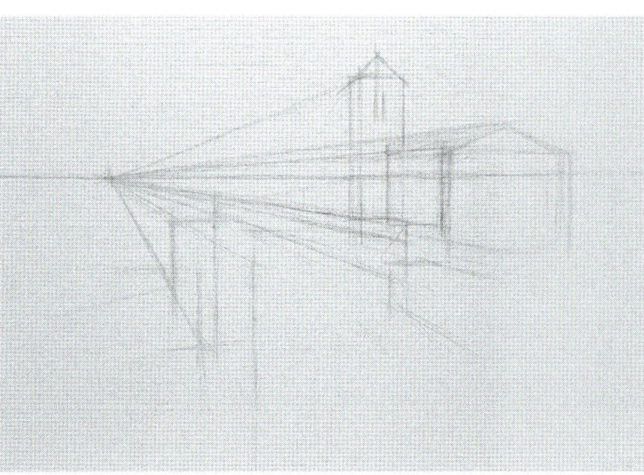

The chapel's bell tower is created with a rectangular body, the nave with a cube, and the apse with a cylinder. This rectangular design in perspective is also used for the rock formations.

When the model is located on a high elevation with respect to the surrounding landscape, the perspective horizon has to be placed necessarily above the real horizon.

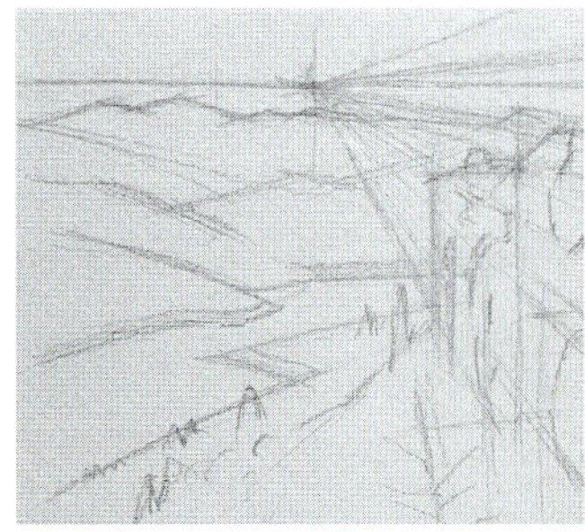

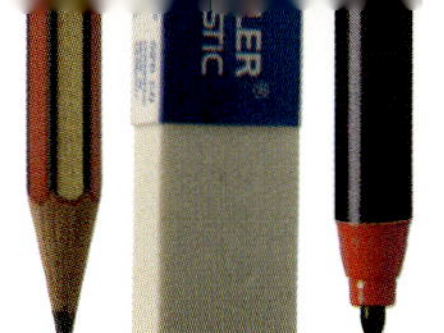

3.2

ADJUSTING AND OUTLINING. When the "blocking in" phase is completed, the outlines are drawn more precisely and the landscape's organic elements are added; this means describing the shapes of the rocks and the vegetation.

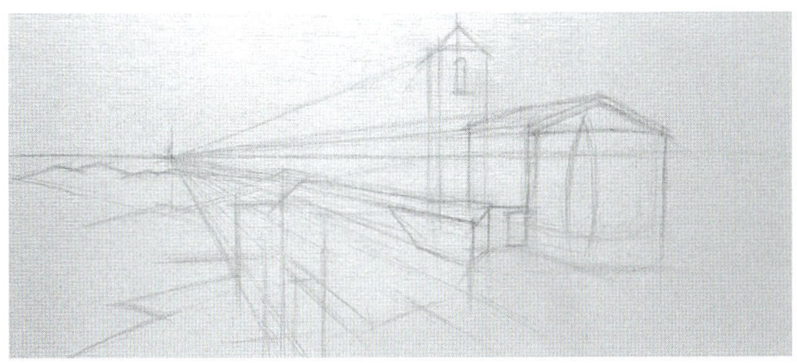

We go over the lines that describe the outline of the chapel again with a graphite pencil. We draw new lines over the previously sketched lines to define the shapes of the mountains and the placement of a few of the trees.

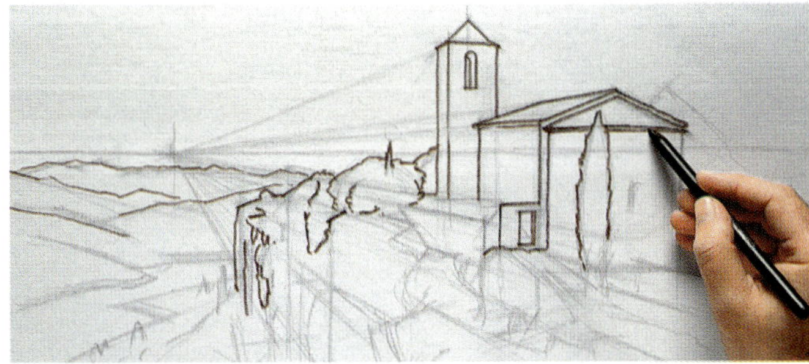

The sketched lines of the rock formations give way to more organic shapes. We focus on the irregularities of the rocks and vegetation-covered areas. To finish, we define the drawing by going over the outlines with a brown marker.

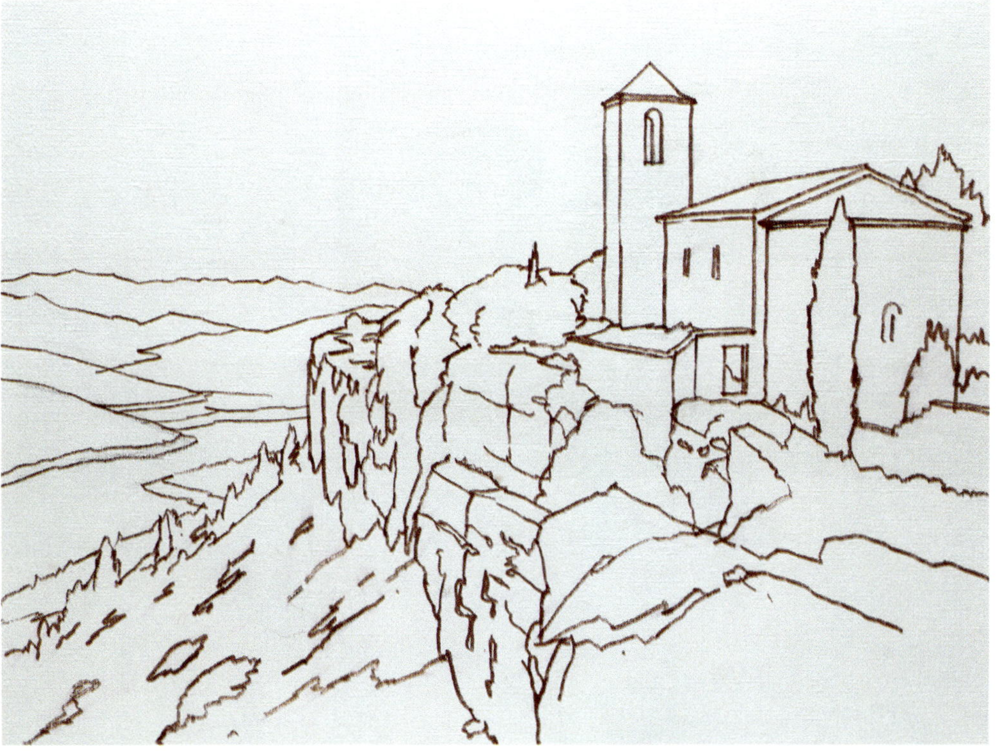

The pencil lines are erased to avoid confusion in the final drawing. The finished drawing is simple, not overly decorated, the shadows and details are clean, and it has a strong feeling of depth. The vegetation has been treated very simply.

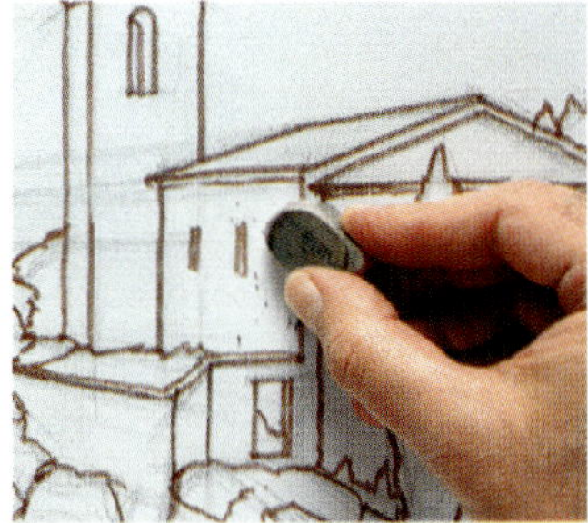

The lines are erased at the end, after waiting a few minutes for the marker to dry completely.

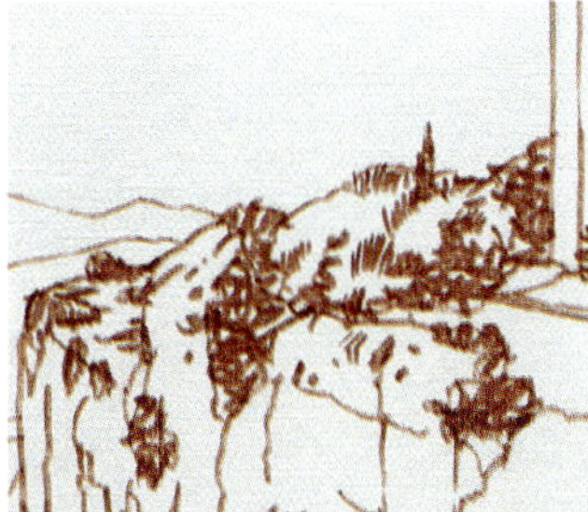

To introduce tonal elements in the drawing, we paint the areas of vegetation with a brown marker and short, loose lines.

LEARNING BY DOING

FAÇADE WITH WINDOW AND DOOR. This is another exercise with conical perspective. This time the elements we are going to draw do not require a volumetric projection but rather the representation of a flat surface moving away from us. We will work with forms that look flat and are slightly distorted to conform to the perspective of the façade. Exercise by Carlant.

4.1

DISTORTED SQUARES AND RECTANGLES. It is obvious that perspective makes regular geometric figures look distorted to create the effect of depth and distance in the drawing. Following this principle, we establish the basic lines and the degree of distortion of the door and window.

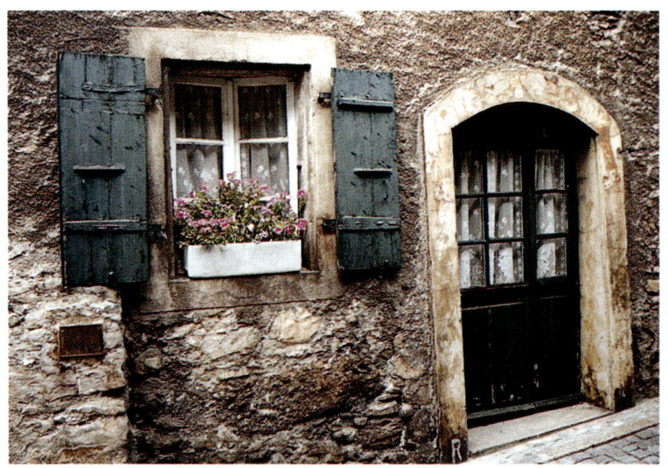

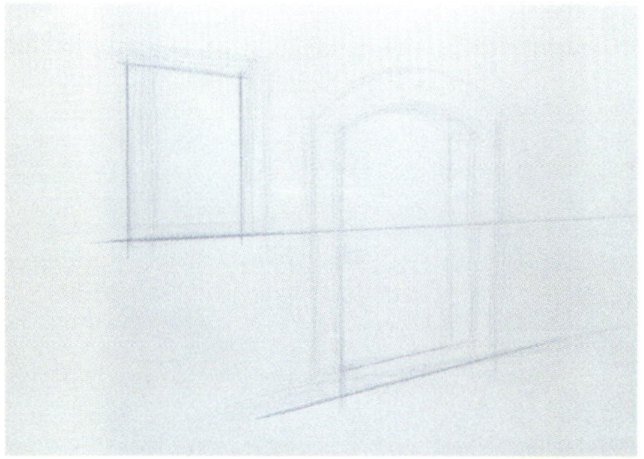

For this model, which has little depth, it is not necessary to draw a horizon line, especially since the only vanishing point is outside the paper. Therefore, from this imaginary point we draw the diagonals that define the base of the door and the top and bottom parts of the window with a ruler.

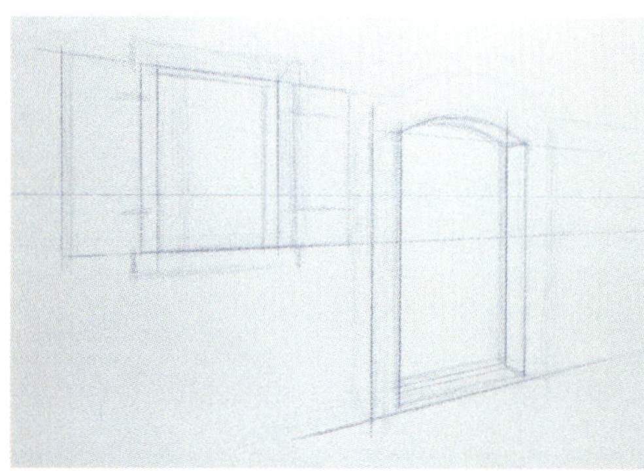

The same lines that define the window frame are used to represent the shutters, especially if we keep in mind that all the vertical lines are perpendicular to the edge of the paper and parallel to each other. The flat arch of the doorway is drawn freehand.

If it is difficult to draw the door's flat arch, first, we draw a straight line and we use it as a reference to draw a rounded line that is more symmetrical and graceful.

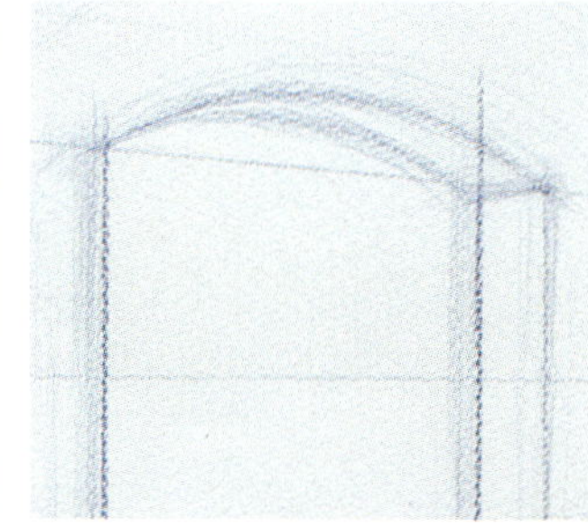

For this first phase it is important to draw very lightly with a pencil, so that it will be easy to erase any mistakes at the end of the project.

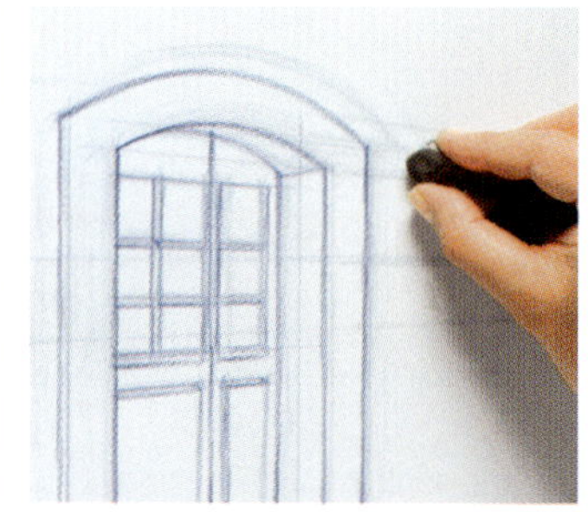

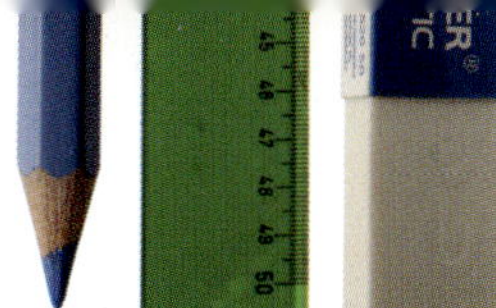

4.2

MANY SQUARES. The perspective approach does not pertain only to the basic structures. The door and the window (shutters, glass, frames) contain many quadrangular shapes that should also be drawn according to the rules of perspective.

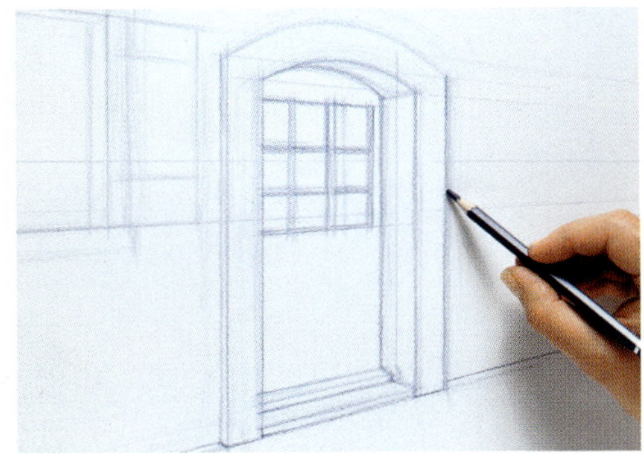

We go over the perpendicular lines of the door with darker lines. The door panes are drawn by projecting new perspective lines that establish their shape and correct distribution.

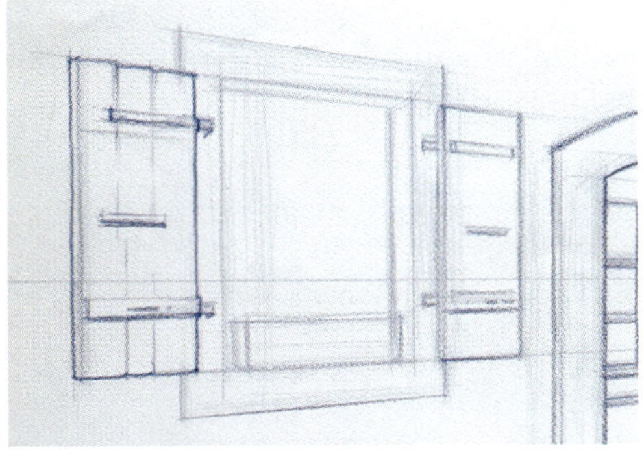

We extend the vanishing lines for the window frame to represent the shutters. The window flower box is drawn with a new vanishing line. Once the structure is completed, we shift our attention to the shape and details of the wood of the shutters.

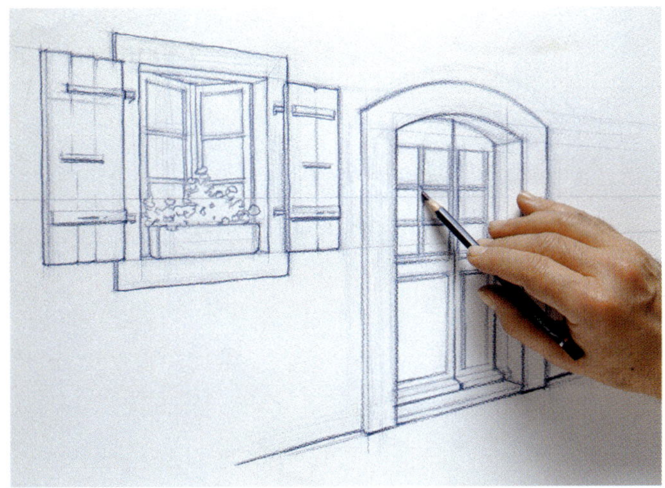

We sketch the vegetation in the window box and finish the window and the glass. We redraw the lines of the doors with soft lines, which give the architecture a sturdy feeling.

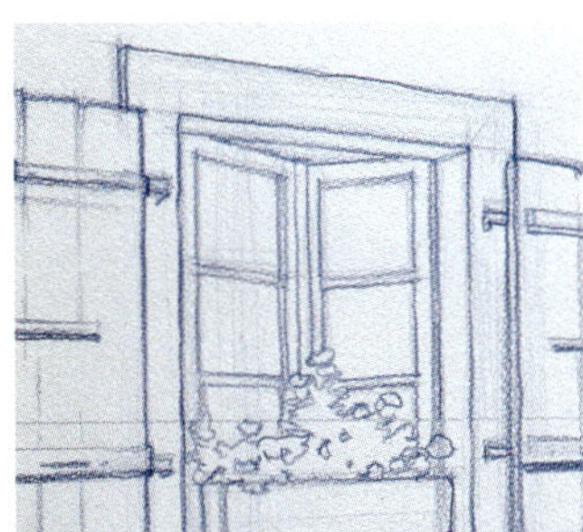

Since the windows are slightly open, they are drawn completely differently from the perspective approach of the rest of the drawing. That is, they should not be constructed with the same vanishing lines that have been used to project the façade.

TWO POINTS INSTEAD OF ONE. The oblique view of the model forces us to draw the objects in two-point perspective. The one-point perspective is static and formal and does not conform to the way we actually see the objects. Therefore, by using a 45° angle on each side of the line of view, we can locate the vanishing points where the top and bottom sides of the cube converge.

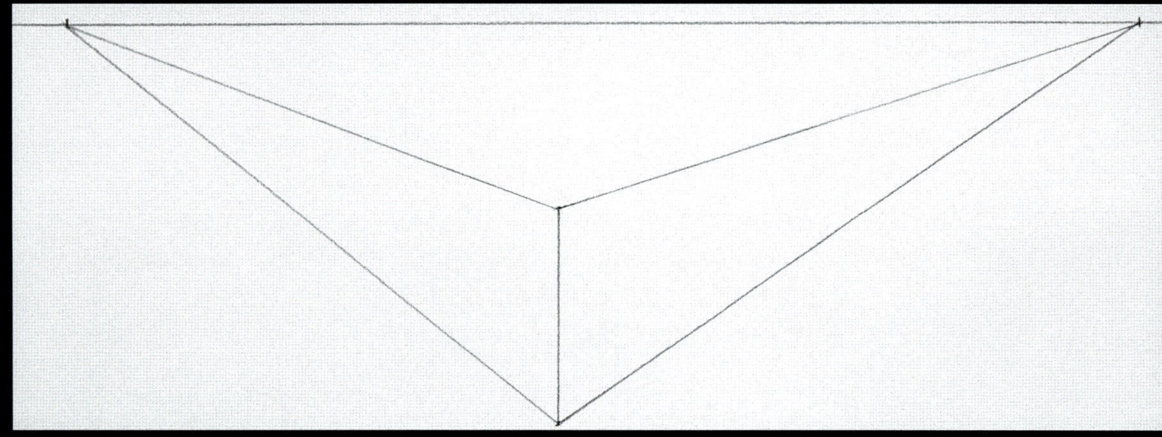

To draw a cube with oblique perspective, we take an edge of the square as reference. From each side of the straight line we project two diagonals to two vanishing points located at either side of the horizon line.

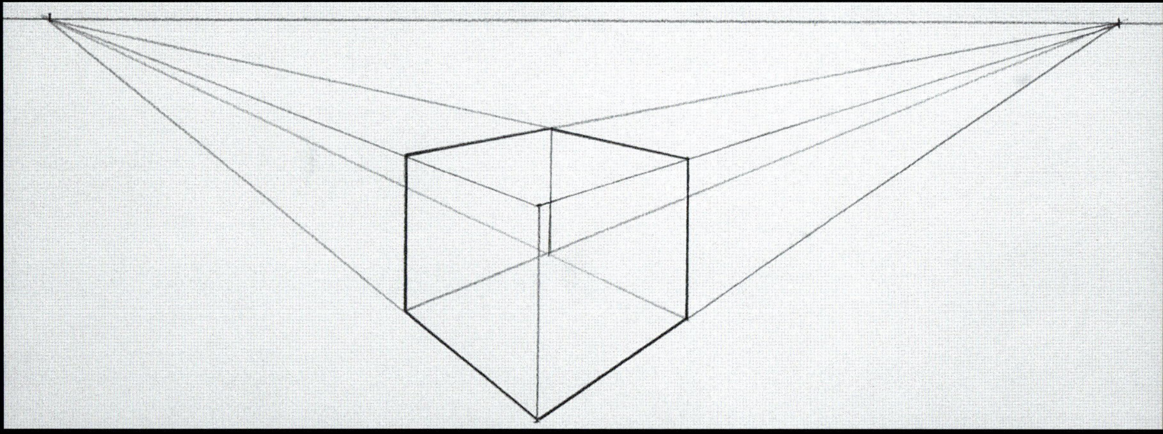

New vanishing lines are added to project the other sides of the cube, which we draw as if it were transparent.

DISTANCE TO THE VANISHING POINTS. The distance of the vanishing points with respect to the object plays an important role in its representation. The closer the points are to the model, the more distorted it will appear. It is important to place the vanishing points at a distance, otherwise the images will look distorted.

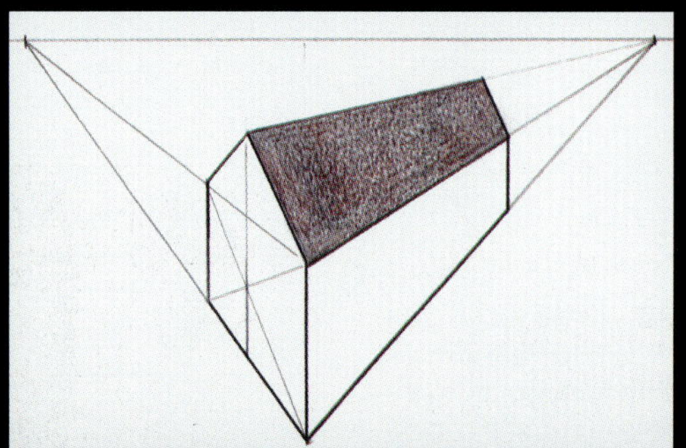

The vanishing points located near this house make the image look distorted or forced.

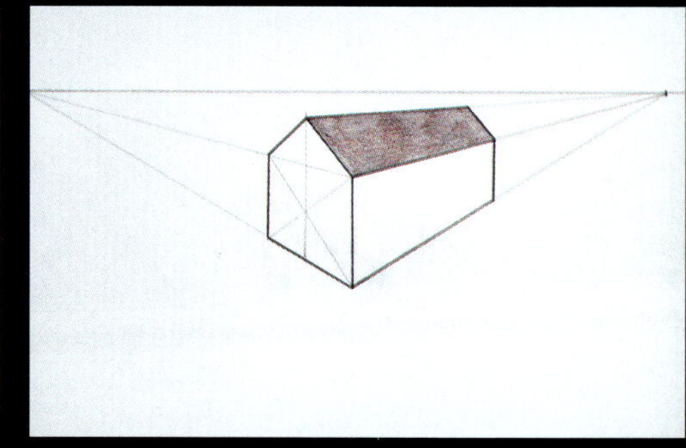

The same house, drawn with the vanishing points farther away, looks much more natural and closer to the real object.

OBLIQUE PERSPECTIVE. Whether in landscapes, interiors, or cityscapes, objects rarely look appealing if they are placed parallel to the plane of the drawing. They are almost always placed at an angle to the picture plane.

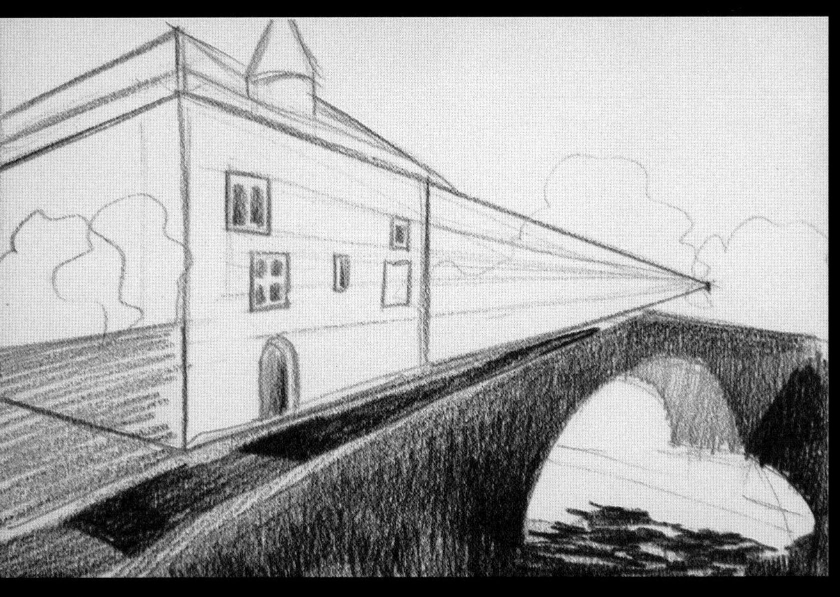

Oblique perspectives are very useful for drawing buildings where the corner moves forward to the viewer.

If we reverse the direction of the diagonals that project the two vanishing points, the corner that we are drawing moves away from the foreground.

A GRID FOR CITYSCAPES. Faced with the challenge of drawing a cityscape, when the groups of houses look chaotic, we use a grid with two-point perspective that resembles a tiled floor based on two vanishing points on the horizon. The different groups of houses, decreasing in size as they approach the horizon, are placed on this grid.

To make a grid we draw diagonal lines from the two vanishing points.

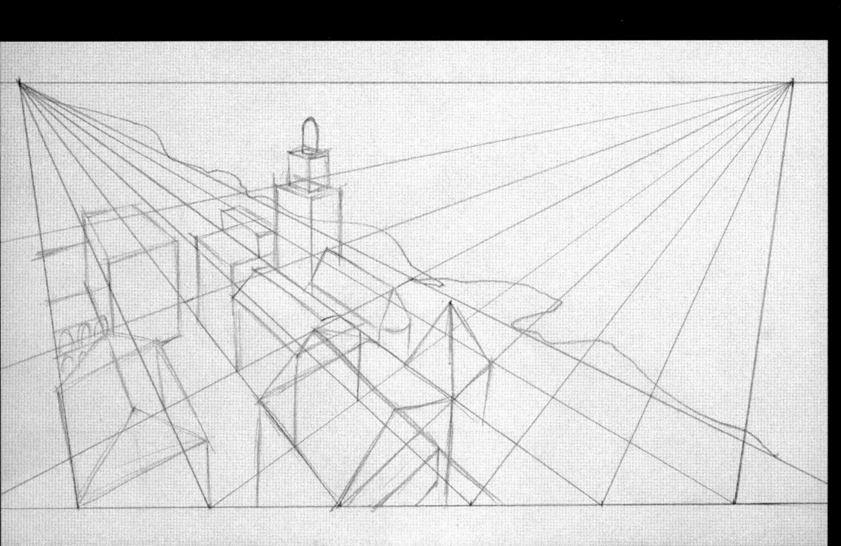

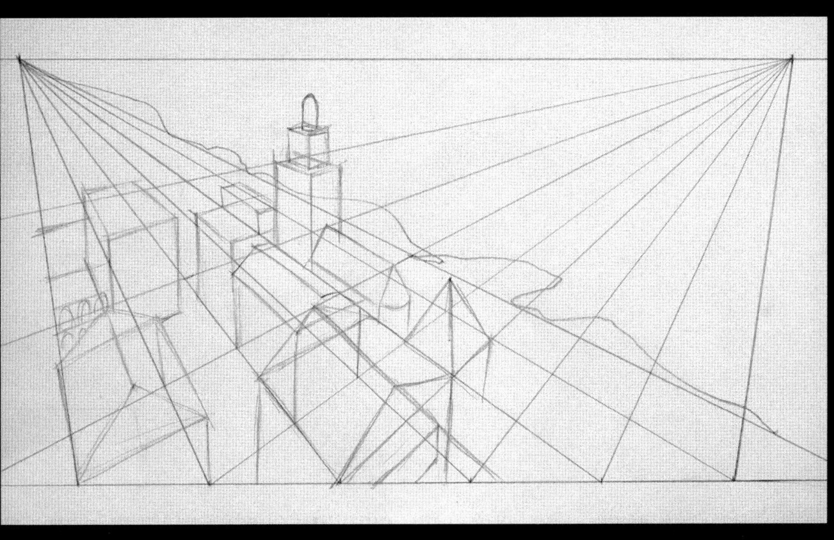

Using the grid as a guide, we begin arranging the buildings in an orderly fashion. We just need to project them as if they were geometric shapes.

LEARNING BY DOING

DRAWING AN INTERIOR. The exercises that we have done so far involved one-point perspective, very simple configurations in which all lines converge at a single point on the horizon. Now, we are going to work with two-point perspective to draw an interior, even though the treatment is less rigorous and the perspective used is quite intuitive. Exercise by Almudena Carreño.

5.1

WE BEGIN WITH THE CORNER. After constructing a few boxes according to the rules of oblique perspective, it is very easy to erect a vertical line of any size at the corner of the room to create an interior. The originality of this drawing resides in the fact that we focus on the room's angle and disregard the horizon line.

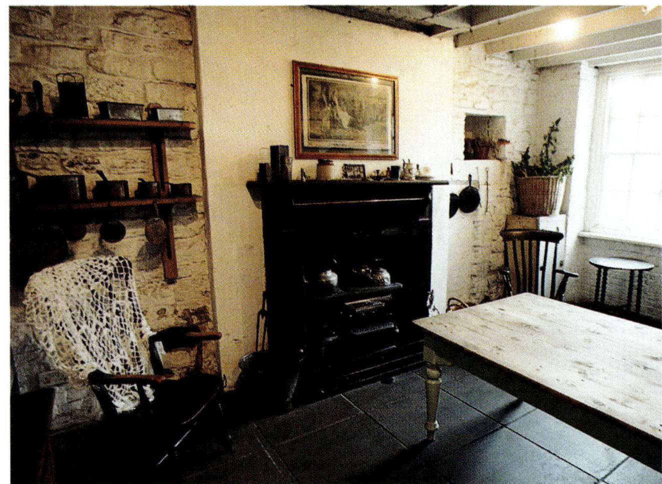

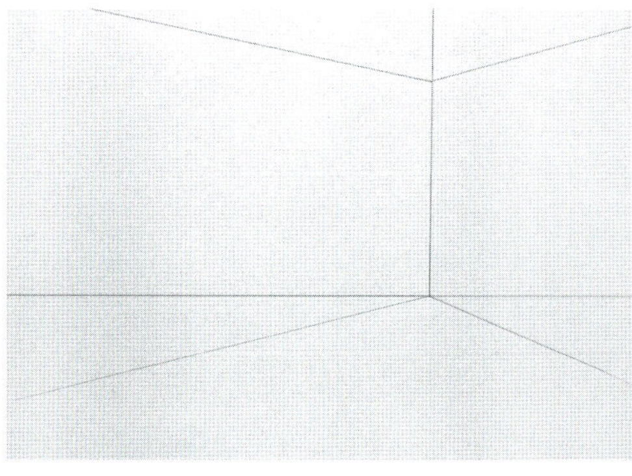

The starting point is a vertical line that represents the corner of the room. Two diagonal lines are projected from the upper and lower parts to define the ceiling and the floor.

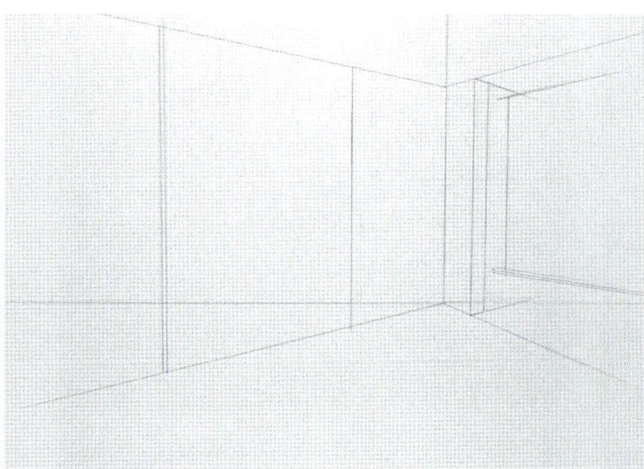

We cut through the two walls with vertical lines to establish the chimney and the window. All the lines must be parallel to each other. The placement of the lines is done by eye.

When executing the drawing, it is important to keep in mind that one of the vanishing lines of the walls is located outside the drawing.

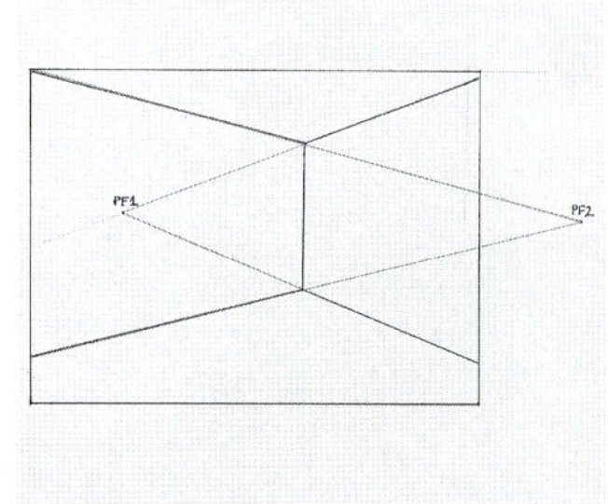

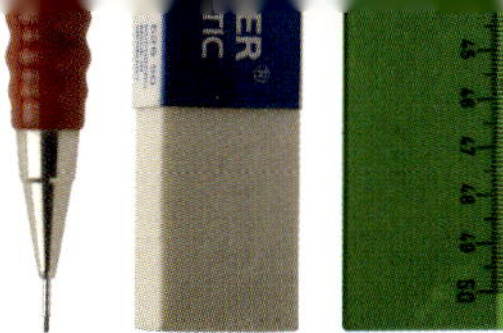

5.2

DRAWING THE FURNITURE. This should not pose any problem, since the pieces of furniture are regarded as simple geometric shapes drawn in perspective. The vanishing lines for the furniture converge at the same vanishing point used to construct the interior walls.

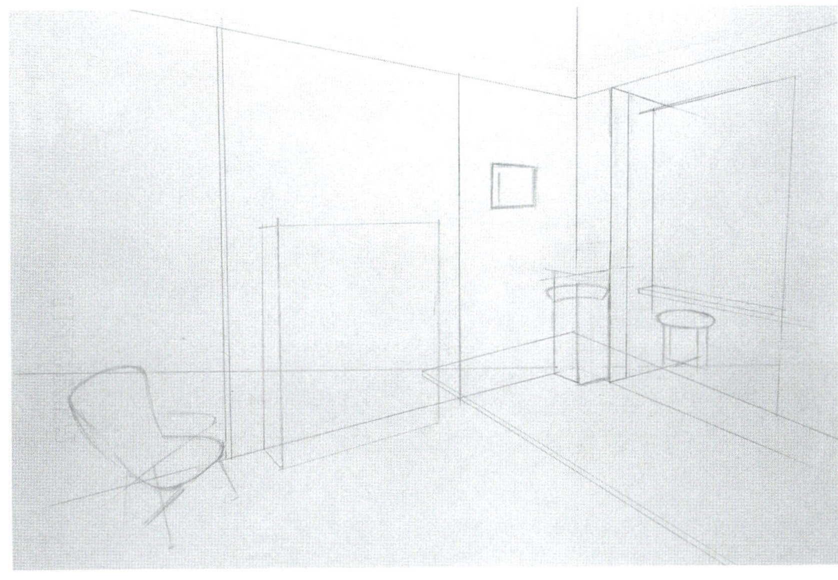

We sketch a preliminary structure for the furniture using vanishing lines. The effect of perspective is much more pronounced on the table in the foreground. The chair, with rounded edges, is drawn by eye.

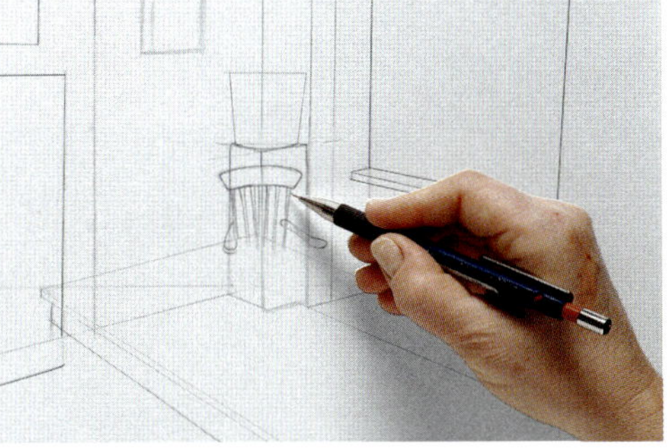

The furniture pieces have a specific number of vanishing lines. Where the furniture is parallel to the walls, it shares the vanishing points with the latter—for example, the paintings on the walls, the shelves, or the hearth. Once the basic lines are established, each piece of furniture is drawn in more detail.

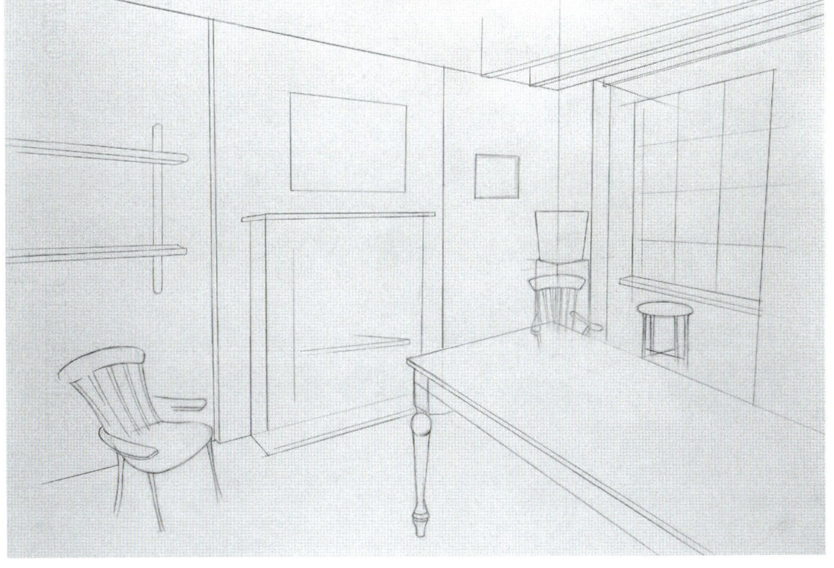

If we analyze each element individually the project is not difficult. The furniture should not be copied exactly, rather, an approximation should be drawn using geometric shapes in perspective.

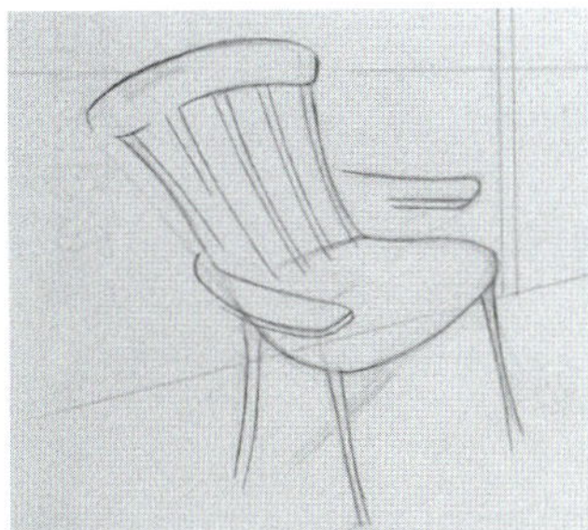

Most of the furniture pieces are not as complex as they look. They are based on cubes, drawn in perspective, connected to each other and at the same time combined with others.

LEARNING BY DOING

THE CORNER OF A HOUSE. Here we take on a different challenge involving oblique perspective. It consists of the corner of a house; the difficulty stems from the vanishing points, which are very far away from the plane of the drawing. This requires working with a large board that makes it possible to extend the field beyond the paper's edges. Exercise by Carlant.

6.1

ADDITIONAL PIECES OF PAPER. The first difficulty resides in the fact that the vanishing points are located on the drawing board, far away. To solve this, we attach two additional sheets of paper on each side of the drawing for the vanishing points.

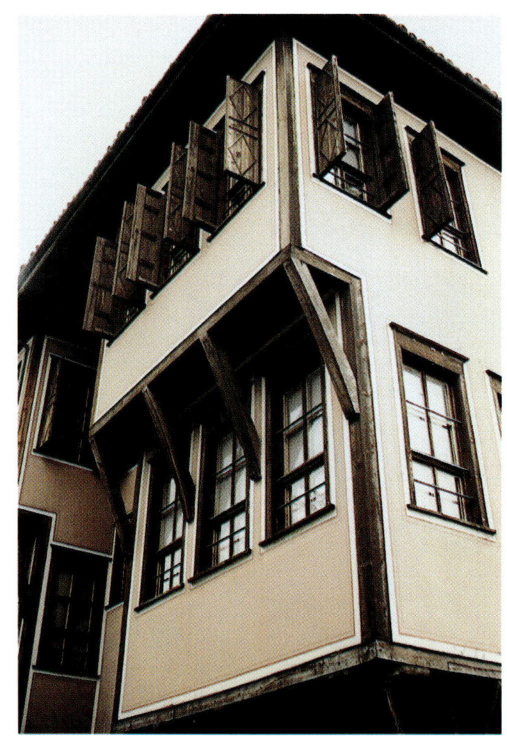

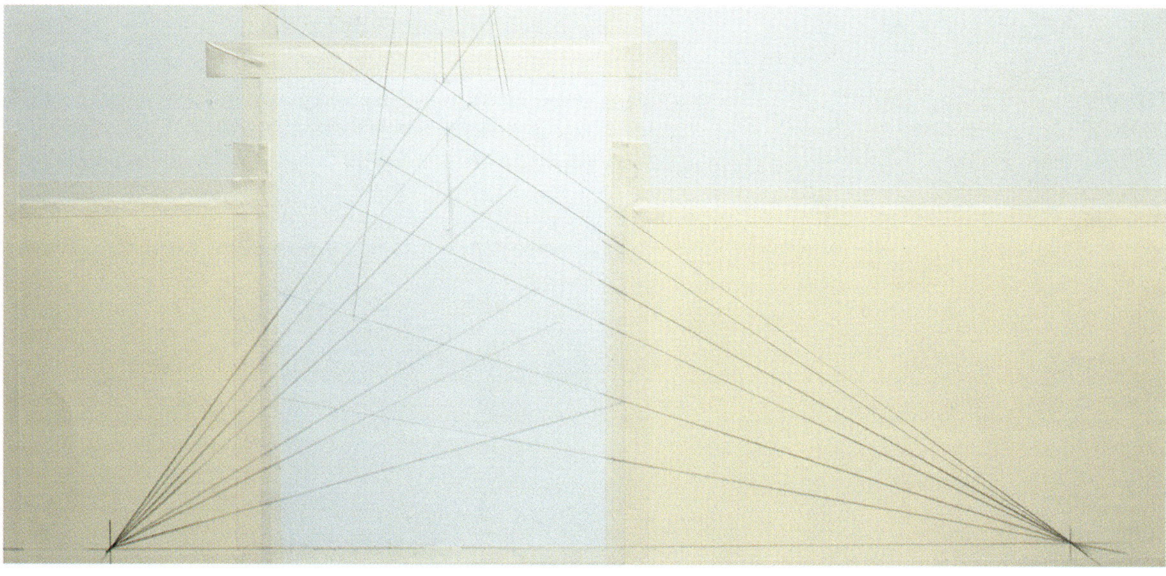

With two pieces of paper we extend the work surface, making the vanishing points visible. From each one of them we project the diagonals that define the angle of the building's walls and the placement of the windows.

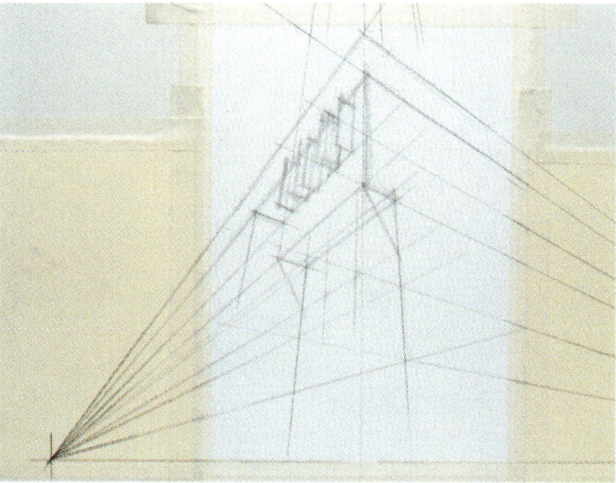

The lines go into the drawing on both sides, defining the height of the roof, the window shutters, and the base of the gallery. The architectural structure is completed by drawing the vertical lines. They are not completely parallel because they converge slightly as they move upward.

Before we begin to draw, we locate the vanishing points. In this case, we project the diagonals from the photograph using a ruler or a measuring tape.

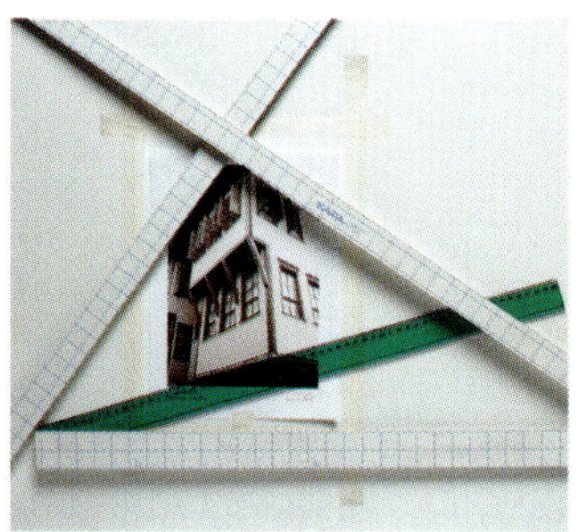

All the window shutters are open symmetrically to make it easier to draw them with vanishing lines.

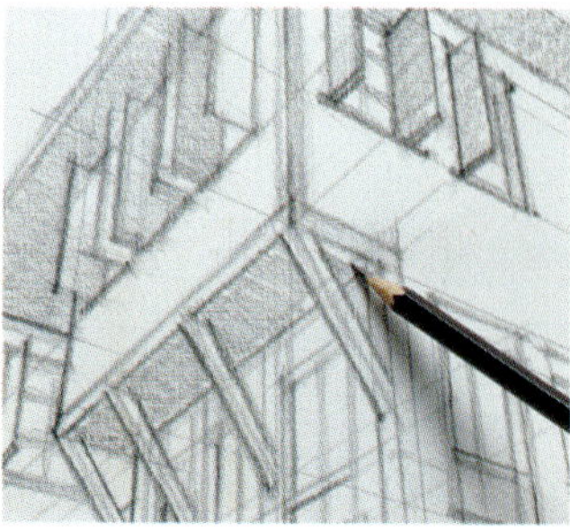

6.2

THE ARCHITECTURAL ELEMENTS. These are not drawn freehand like we did in other instances; they are constructed more rigorously with vanishing lines. In this drawing, all the elements are subject to the effects of perspective.

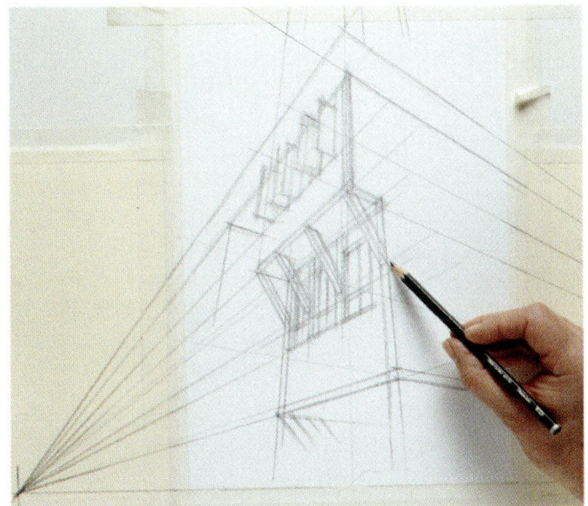

We reinforce the rectangular structure of the building by going over the outlines. We draw the shutters and the windows with perspective lines. They should narrow as they recede into the distance.

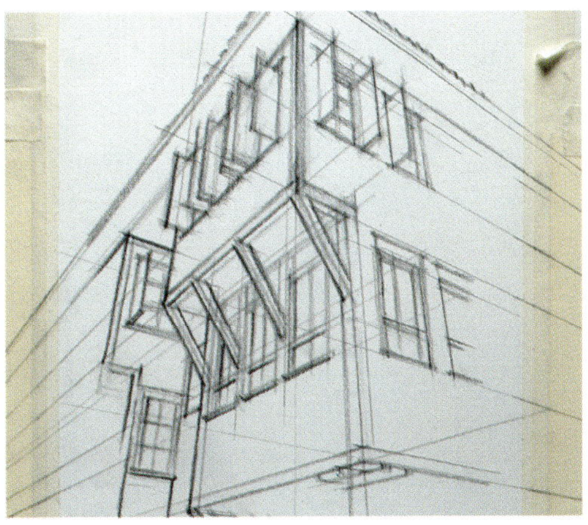

The line drawing concludes with the construction of the wood beams that support the gallery. These narrow with perspective, and the distance between them is decreased. We finish the remaining windows that conform to the vanishing lines.

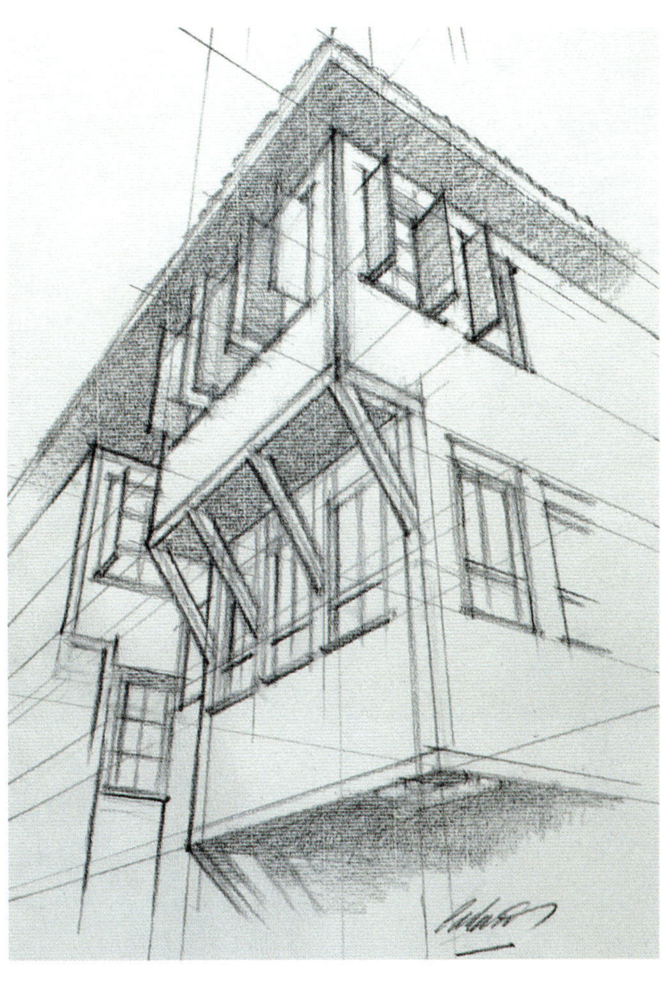

We finish the drawing with evenly applied shading. Perspective explains the effect of depth and the volume of the building, but the shading creates contrast and emphasizes some areas against others.

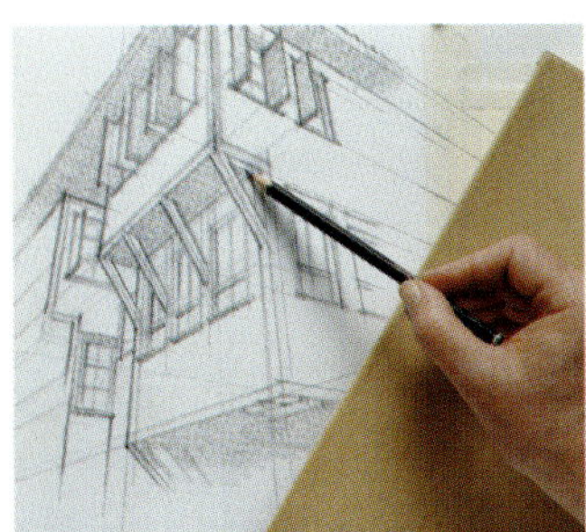

The shading is applied very gently; the pencil is held at the end to avoid applying too much pressure.

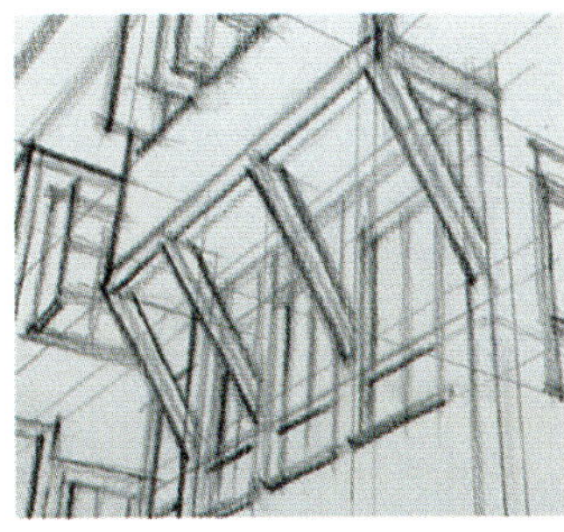

The diagonal wood beams that support the balcony are also drawn in perspective. The way these are arranged reminds us of train tracks vanishing in the distance.

LEARNING BY DOING

CASTLE WITH RECTANGLES AND CYLINDERS. It is very common to encounter circles and cylinders in perspective when drawing architectural elements and urban scenes. In this exercise, we approach them not only from the perspective point of view, but also emphasizing the angular distortion of the camera lens.

7.1

DEFINING THE ANGLE OF VISION. In the following subject, it is important to define the angle of vision prior to drawing the cylinders involved. The analysis of the model shows three cylindrical towers located at different heights, an element that affects the shape and angle of its walls.

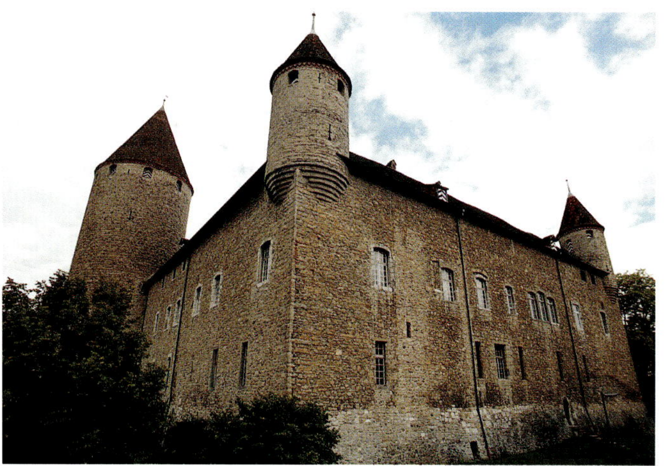

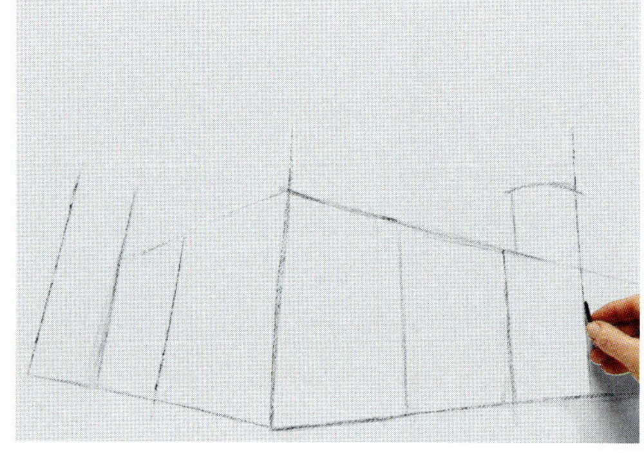

We begin drawing with a charcoal stick, approaching the body of the building in perspective at an angle, with two vanishing points located outside the drawing's plane. We subdivide this surface with diagonal lines for the walls and then establish the positions of the towers.

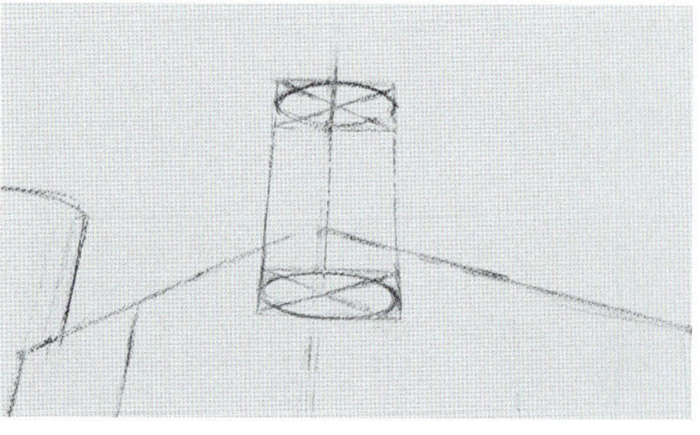

To draw a cylindrical tower in perspective, we resort to a rectangle. We draw an ellipse in perspective for its top and bottom areas. The cylinder is drawn by connecting both ellipses.

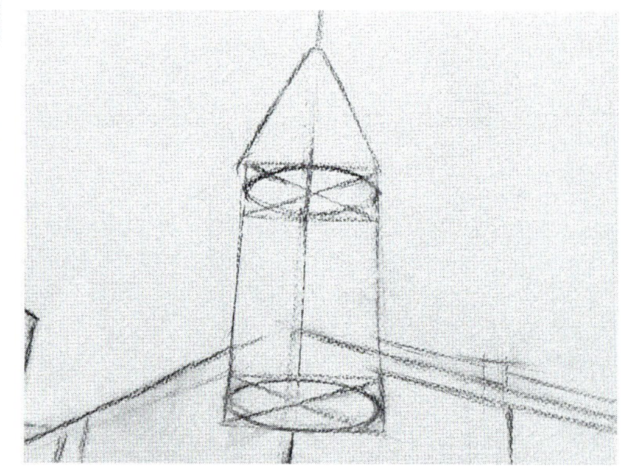

The diagonals that cut through each ellipse provide a center point that we connect with a line. If we extend the line, we project the tip of the tower's pointed roof. We do the same with the other towers.

The angular effect distorts the buildings and makes them look as if they were pyramids.

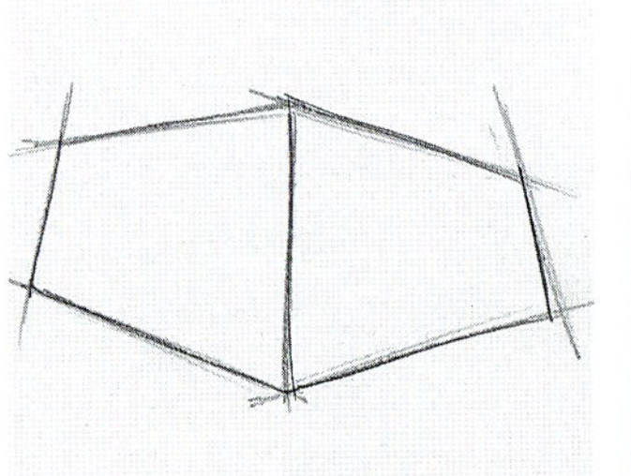

The work combines some parts done with a ruler and others drawn freehand.

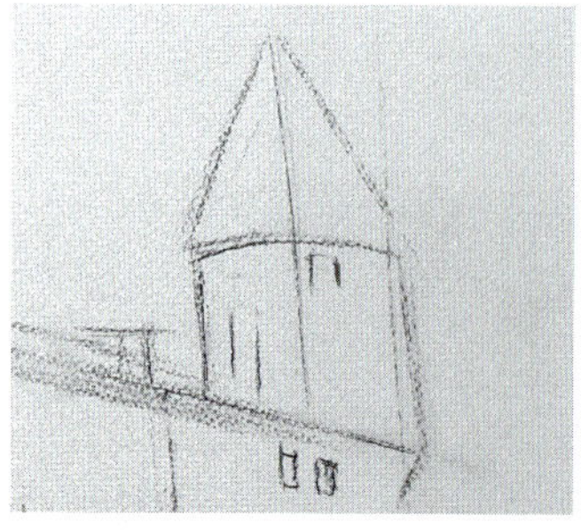

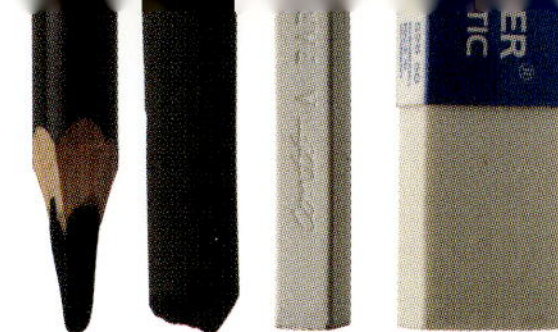

7.2

THE ARCHITECTURAL FEATURES. We introduce the structure of the castle over the basic drawing created with simple geometric shapes projected with angular perspective; we project the windows, roofs, and the other important features.

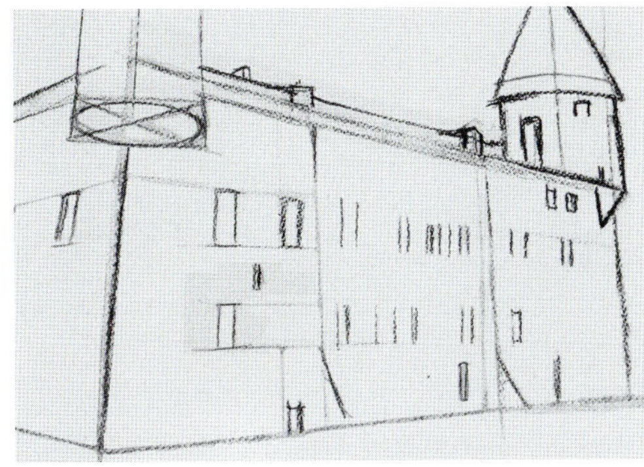

From the vanishing points located at either side outside the drawing, we project the lines that will define the windows. These become smaller as they move away from the closest edge of the building.

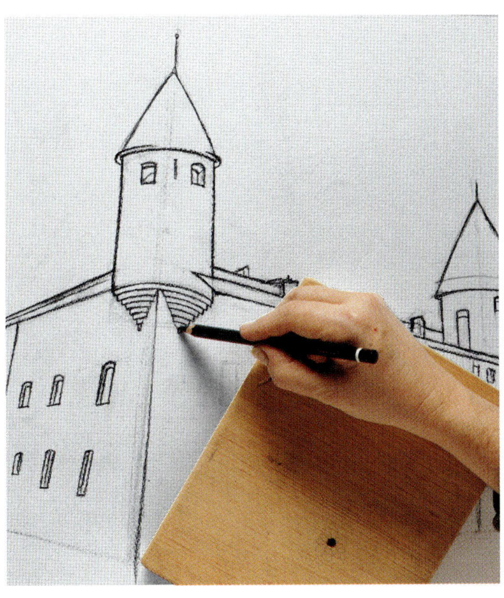

We outline and draw each architectural element with a heavy line, paying attention to the construction details. Since charcoal lines erase easily, we rest the hand on a wooden board.

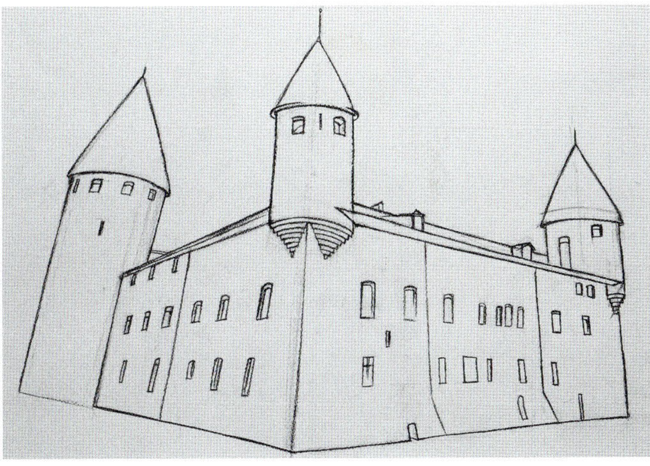

After improving the quality of the line, the castle looks solid, with clear outlines. This is the time to erase any sketched line that is still visible.

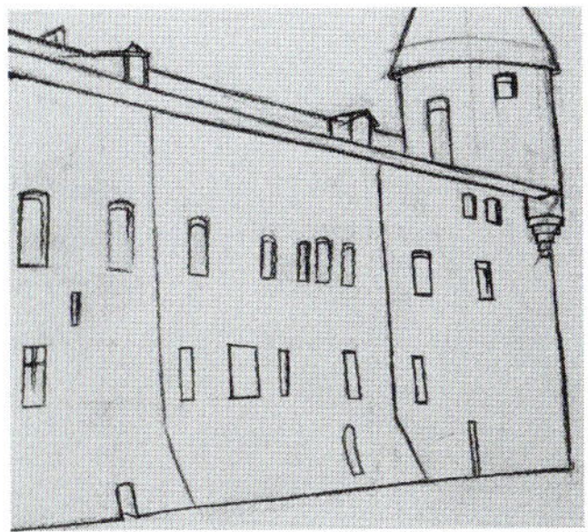

When we draw the lines of the façade, we indicate that the upper surface of the wall is exactly vertical, and the slanted lines show that it is wider at the base.

7.3

INSTILLING PERSONALITY. The shading phase is decisive in this perspective representation because it provides personality and warmth to a drawing that is dull, technical, and lacking imagination. The shading adds an artistic quality.

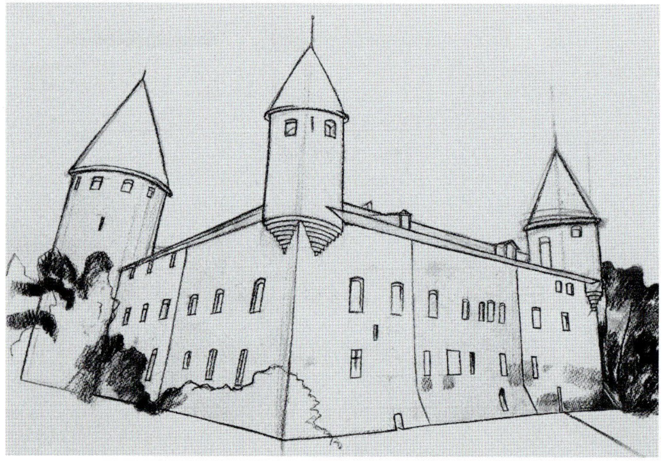

We sketch and darken the areas occupied by trees in the foreground, which later are going to end up covering part of the building. The shading is applied with a stick of charcoal held sideways.

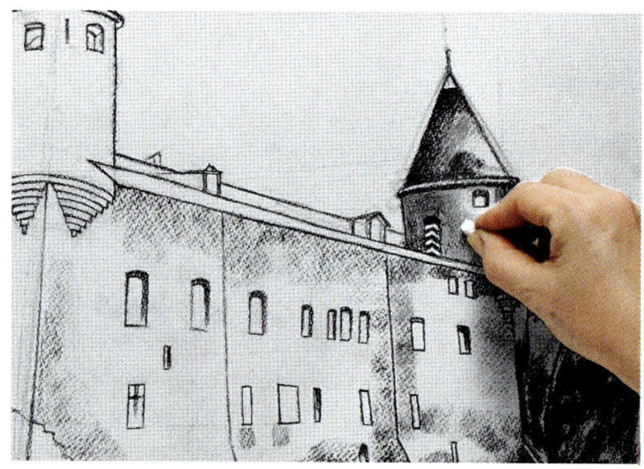

We shade the walls of the building without applying too much pressure on the stick of charcoal. Gradations and nuances are created on the shading by going over the gray areas with a stick of white chalk.

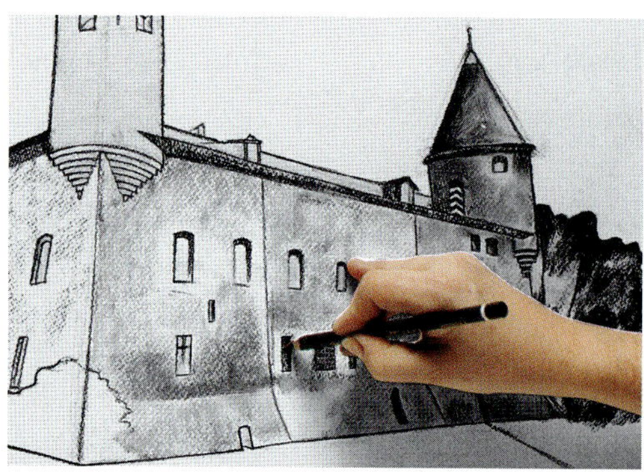

We apply charcoal, lightened with white chalk, on all the walls of the castle. The windows require more detailed attention, so we go over the shading again with a charcoal pencil.

When shading is applied with the side of the stick, the paper darkens very fast. The more pressure that is applied, the darker the shading will be.

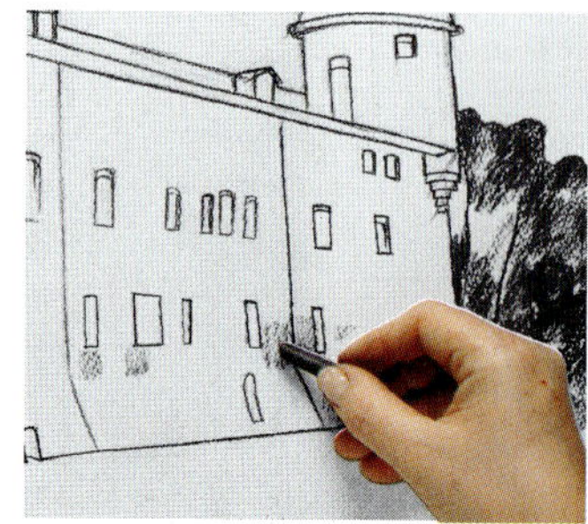

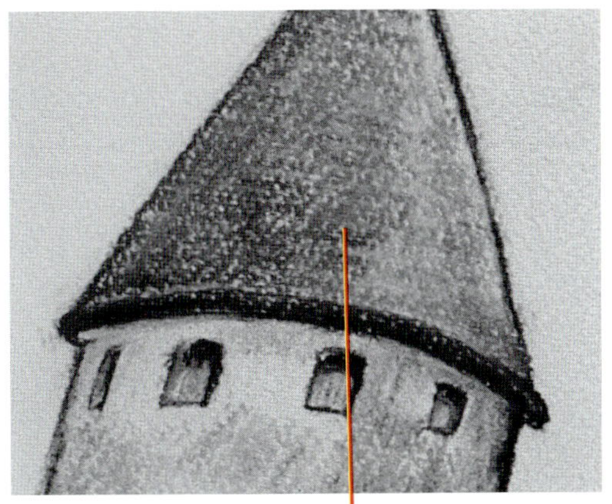

The effect of the tonal gradation is the one that best describes the volumetric effect of the cylindrical and conical shapes of the towers.

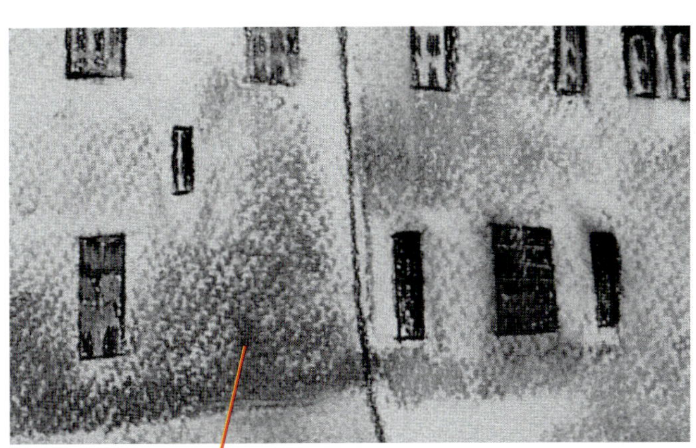

The shading on the walls is applied irregularly. This is necessary if we intend to convey an uneven look to the surface of the stones on the wall.

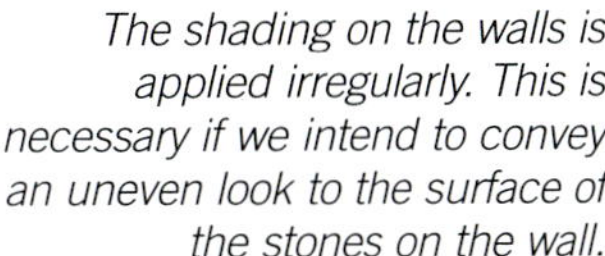

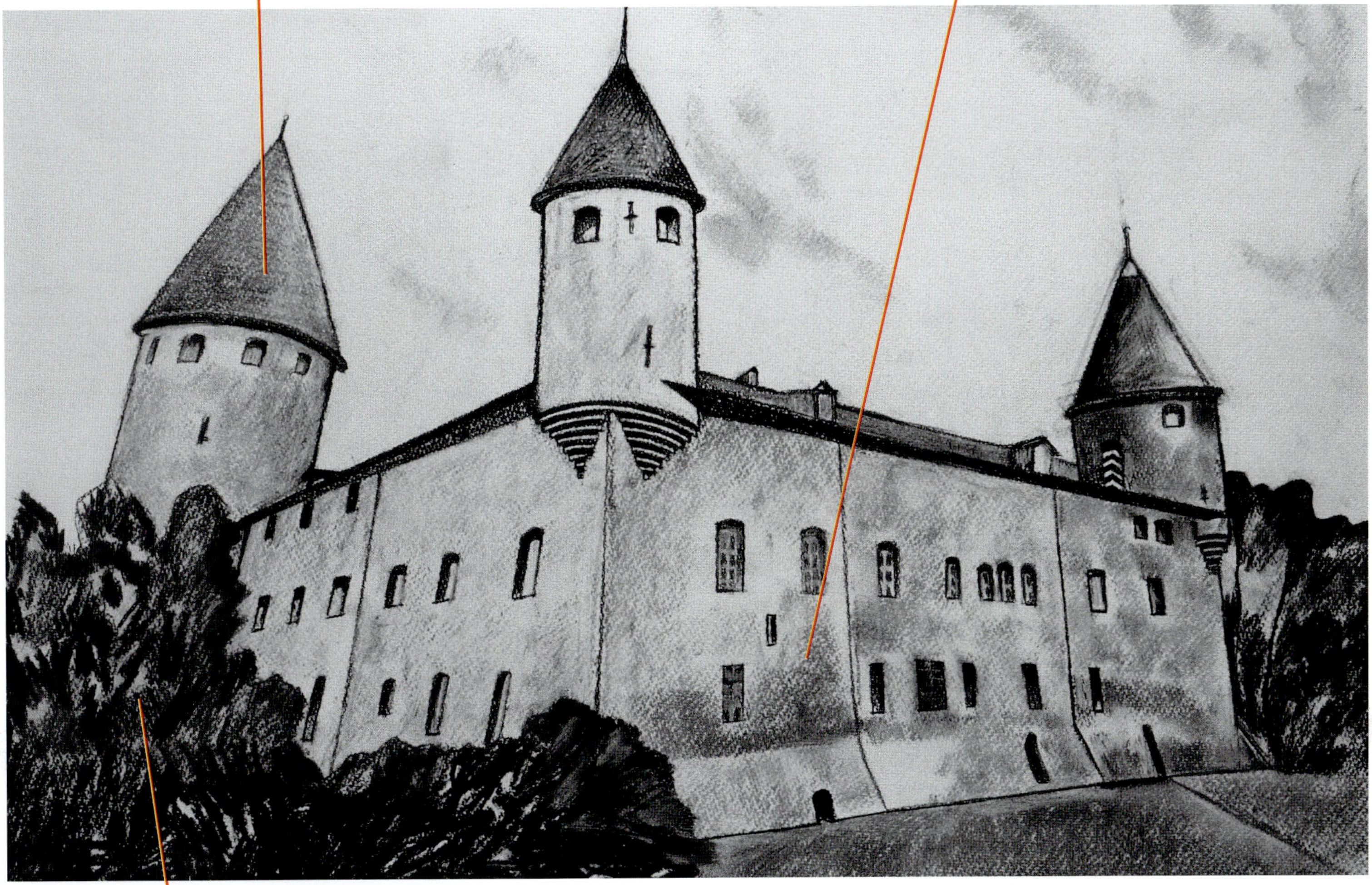

The vegetation in the foreground is drawn very spontaneously, covering existing parts of the castle. The grass is a medium tone, blended with the hand. A few shaded areas in the sky indicate the presence of clouds.

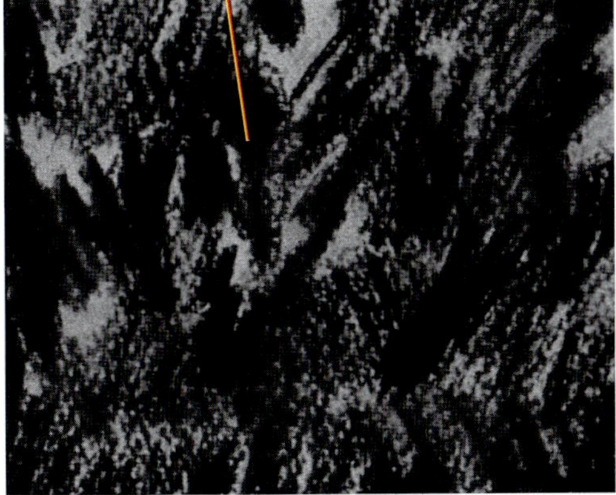

The approach used for the vegetation in the foreground is very vigorous and somewhat abstract. The top lines are drawn heavily to cover the ones located below and to create strong contrast with the background where the castle is located.

CIRCULAR SHAPES IN URBAN SETTINGS. Hardly any circular shapes can be found in natural settings, as opposed to urban scenes, where these are very common. Most of the time we see the objects from top to bottom; therefore, the circular shapes turn into ellipses.

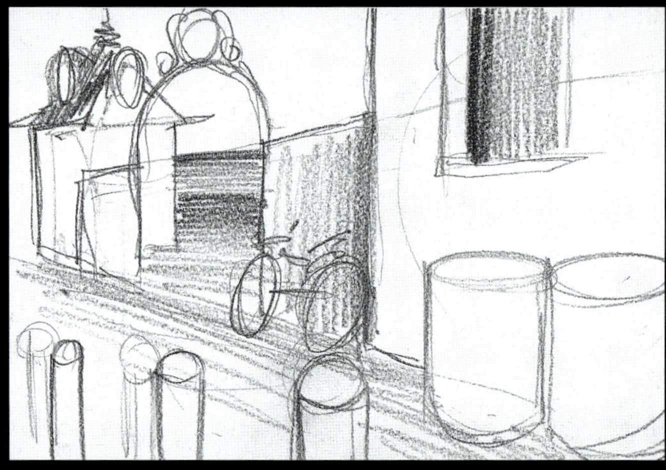

Many circular shapes in perspective can be found if we look around urban scenes.

DRAWING A CIRCLE. Inside a square we draw horizontal and vertical axes. With the help of these axes we draw the circle freehand, as carefully as possible. If we want to show the circle in perspective, we simply lower the square that contains it.

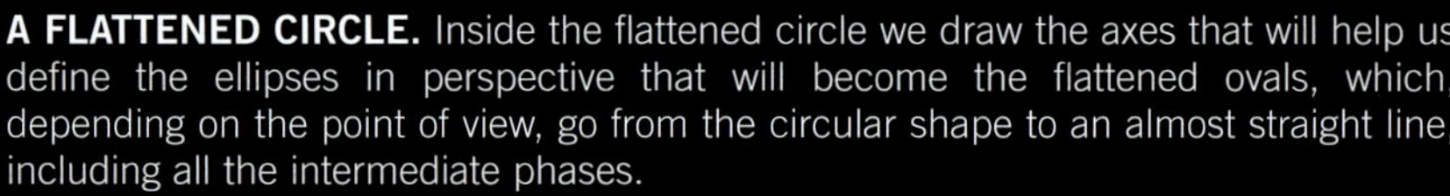

A FLATTENED CIRCLE. Inside the flattened circle we draw the axes that will help us define the ellipses in perspective that will become the flattened ovals, which, depending on the point of view, go from the circular shape to an almost straight line, including all the intermediate phases.

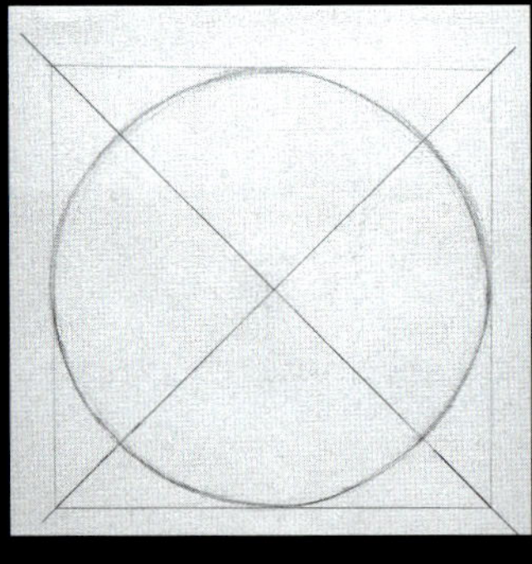

We draw the two diagonal axes of a square. From here, we draw a circle freehand with the edges barely touching the sides of the square.

We draw a square in perspective. We draw the diagonal axes and the ellipse very carefully, trying to make its sides touch the four sides of the square.

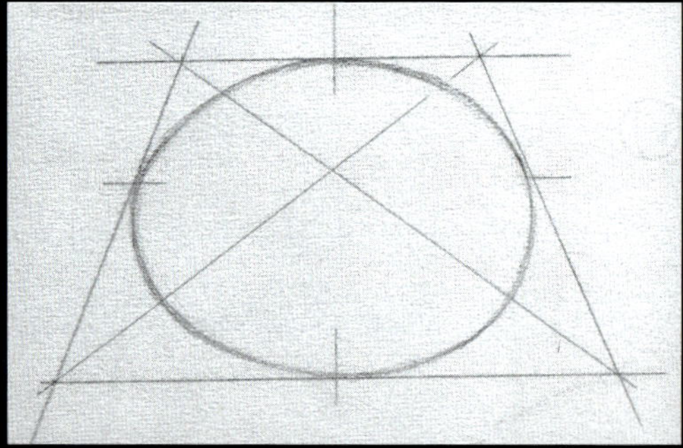

AVOIDING POINTS AND BULGES. Two mistakes should be avoided when drawing an ellipse inside a square in perspective. No matter how narrow the ellipse is, it should never end in a sharp point. Also, we should avoid bulging and unattractive curves.

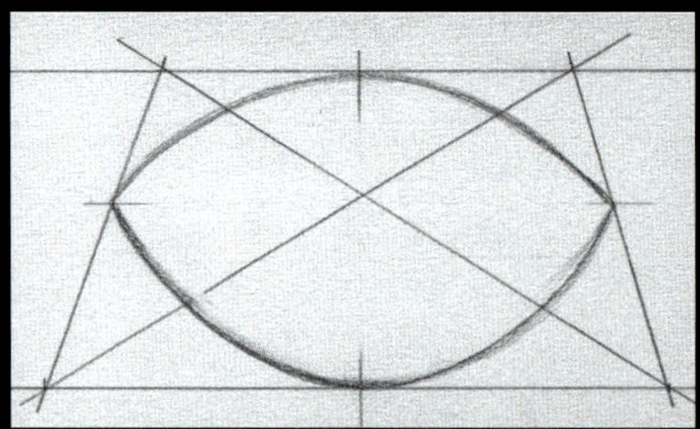

The curves of ellipses should be soft and must never end in sharp points as shown in this drawing.

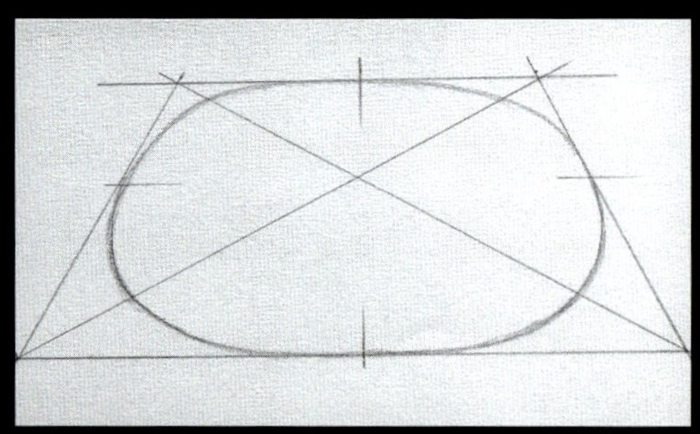

If the curves are not properly controlled, the ellipse can look bulging, somewhat square rather than round.

CYLINDERS, ELLIPSES, AND CIRCULAR OBJECTS. Until now we have talked only about rectangular shapes, but we cannot ignore circular and cylindrical ones, because many of them can be found everywhere.

DRAWING CYLINDERS. To draw cylinders, we can use the technique for drawing ellipses. To do this, we draw two parallel ellipses and we connect their sides with two straight lines. The result is a cylinder. Then we erase the sketched lines, leaving the cylinder.

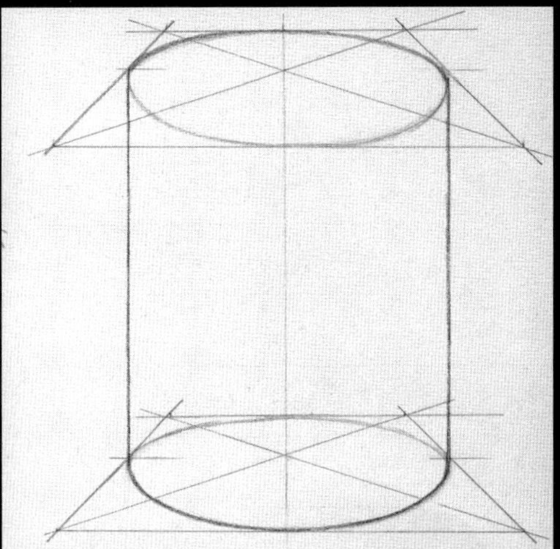

A perfect cylinder is created by drawing two ellipses, one above the other.

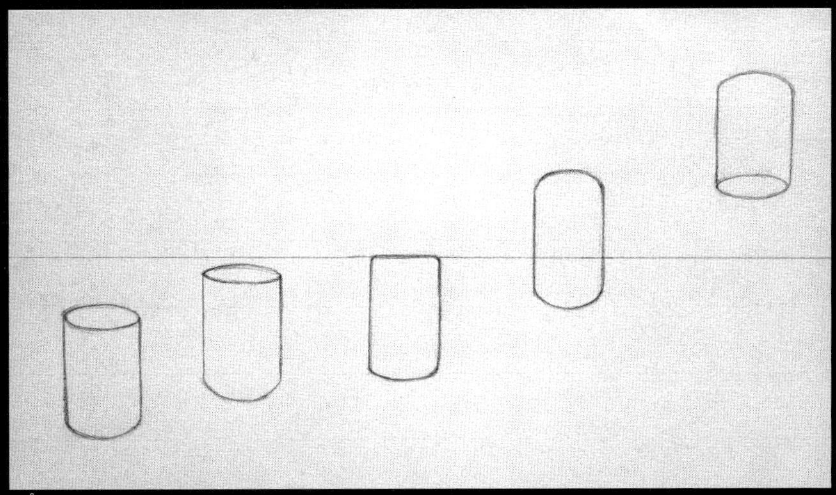

The shape of the cylinder is determined by the perspective of the ellipses and the point of view. Notice how the cylinder changes according to its placement above or below the horizon line.

DRAWING OBJECTS INSIDE THE CYLINDER. Once we become proficient at drawing ellipses, we can draw any round object without a problem.

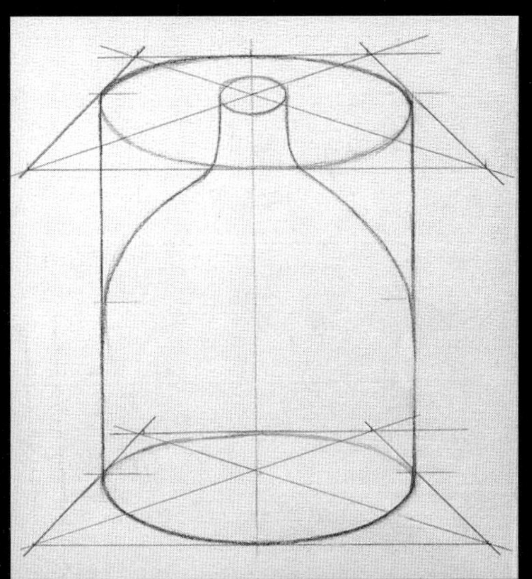

Cylinders are a good resource for drawing round, conical, or cylindrical objects in perspective.

VANISHING POINTS OUTSIDE THE DRAWING. The problem that arises with having a large distance between the two vanishing points on the horizon line is that both could fall outside the confines of the drawing. If this is the case and we want to construct the drawing exactly, we attach two sheets of paper with masking tape to the left and right of the drawing; then we can draw the horizon line and locate the vanishing points.

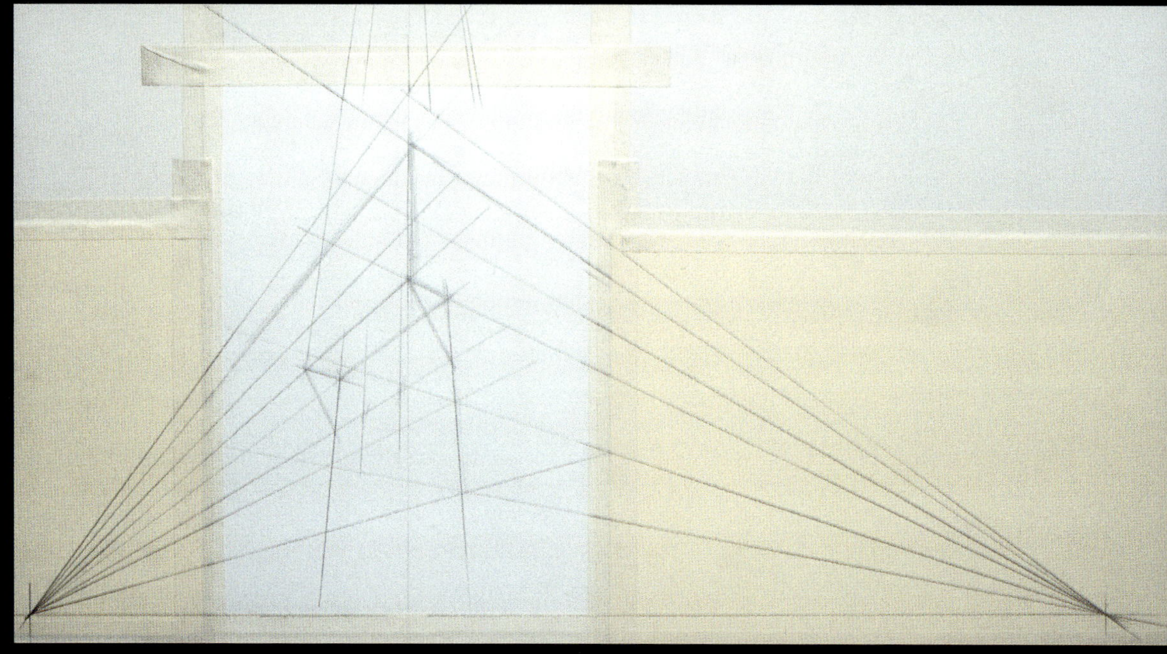

If the vanishing points originate outside the paper, we add a couple of pieces of paper to extend the vanishing lines.

SIDE MEASUREMENTS. Another way of working with vanishing points located outside the drawing is to mark measurements on both sides of the paper and then to project the vanishing lines. This method is very useful for drawing buildings with many windows.

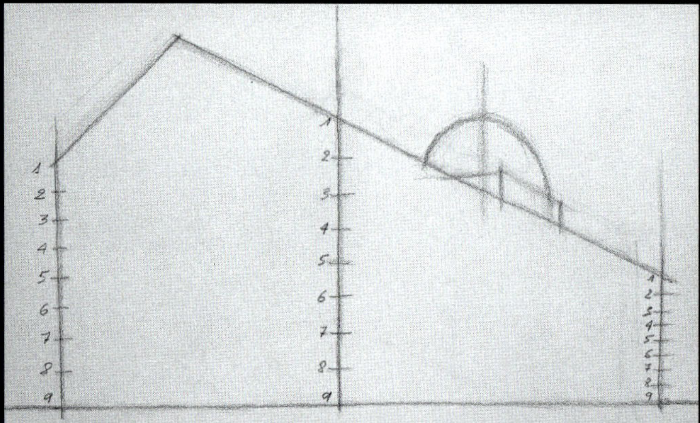

Using a ruler, we divide the perpendicular lines of the sides of the building into nine equal parts.

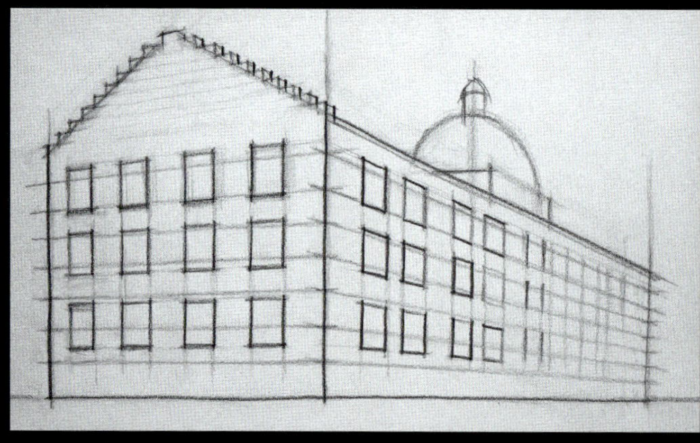

We connect all the parts with straight lines to create the perspective view of the windows on the façade.

VANISHING POINTS OUTSIDE THE DRAWING AND SIDE MEASUREMENTS. In this section we are going to deal with two interesting subjects: how to incorporate the perspective lines of the vanishing points that are outside the drawing, and how to do the same with vertical measurements that complement the vanishing lines of a landscape.

PLUMB THE VERTICAL STRAIGHT LINES BY EYE. The ability to work measuring by eye is very useful. With the drawing board in a vertical position and one eye closed, we move our heads slightly to the left and right until the edge of the board can be used as a plumb line to determine the size of each part of the objects. Then we mark those points on the edge of the board and project them downwards.

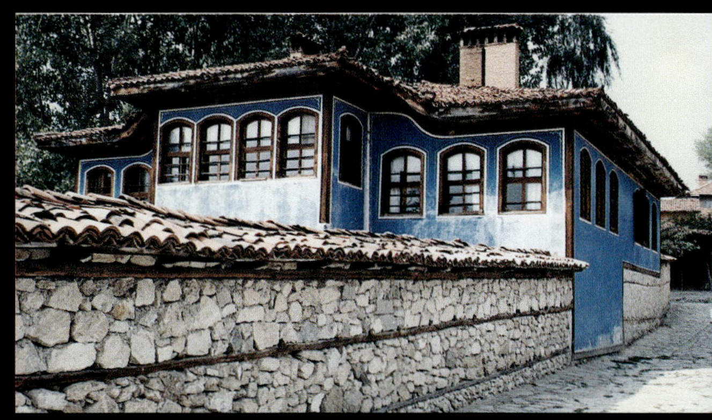

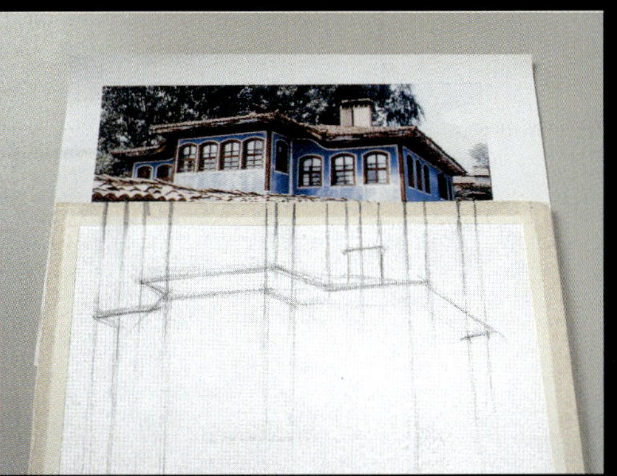

Closing one eye and standing in front of the subject or a photograph of it, we indicate the position of the vertical lines on the upper part of the board.

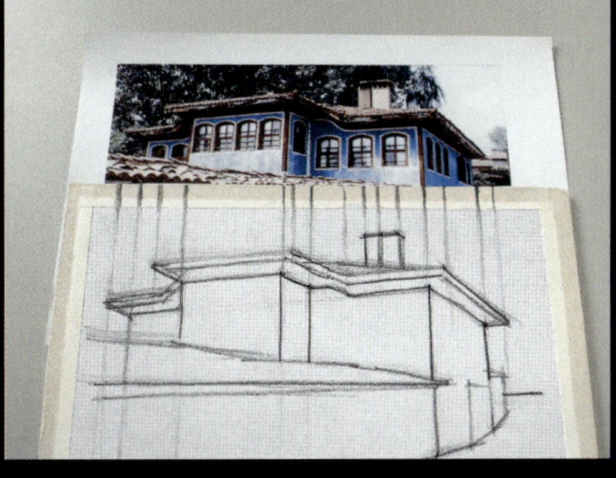

We project the marks of the upper part of the paper with parallel lines.

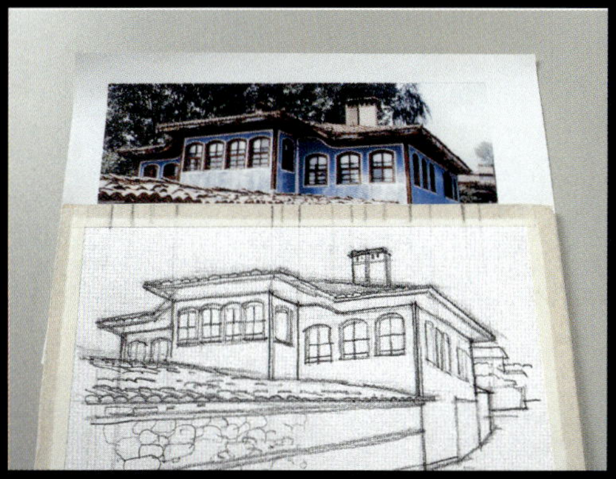

The vertical lines combined with the perspective provide greater control of the measurements of the drawing.

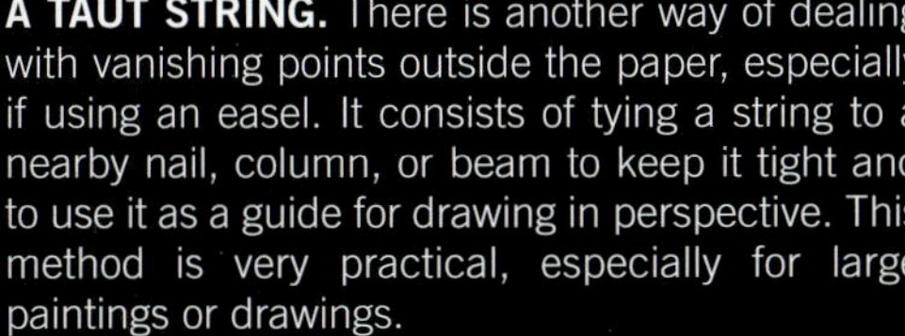

A TAUT STRING. There is another way of dealing with vanishing points outside the paper, especially if using an easel. It consists of tying a string to a nearby nail, column, or beam to keep it tight and to use it as a guide for drawing in perspective. This method is very practical, especially for large paintings or drawings.

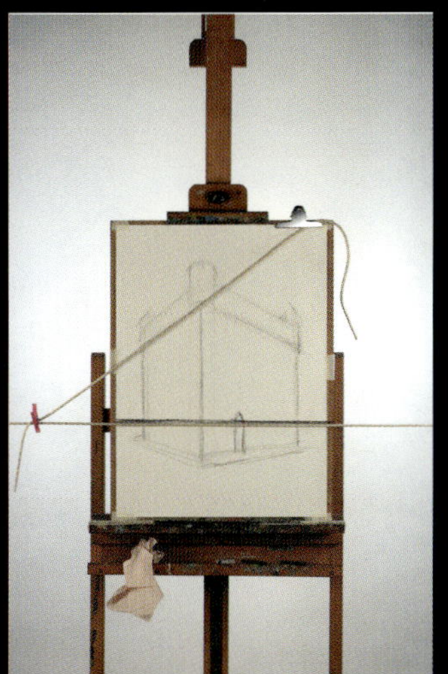

The taut string acts as the horizon line. With a second string held tight with clips, we project the vanishing lines on the paper.

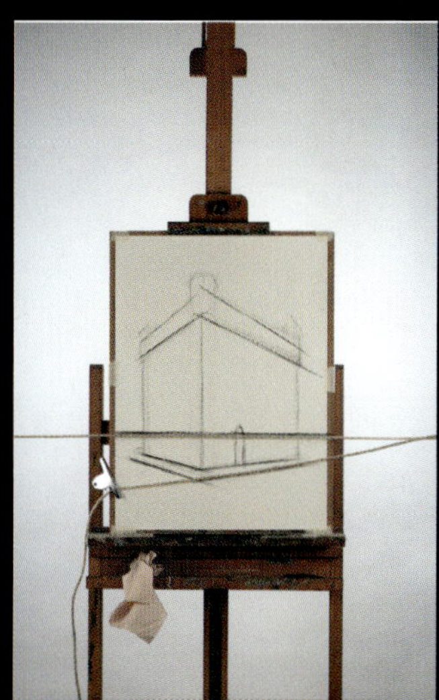

We can move the string as needed. The vanishing points are at either side of the taut string.

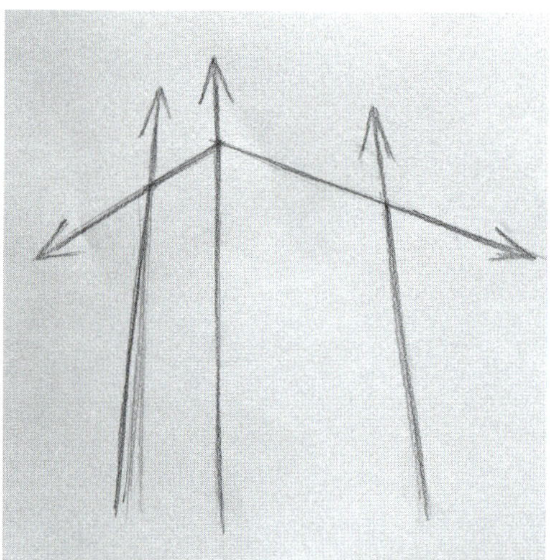

When we draw a building, the upper line for the roof converges at two points on the horizon line. However, the ascending diagonals go toward a single point beyond the model.

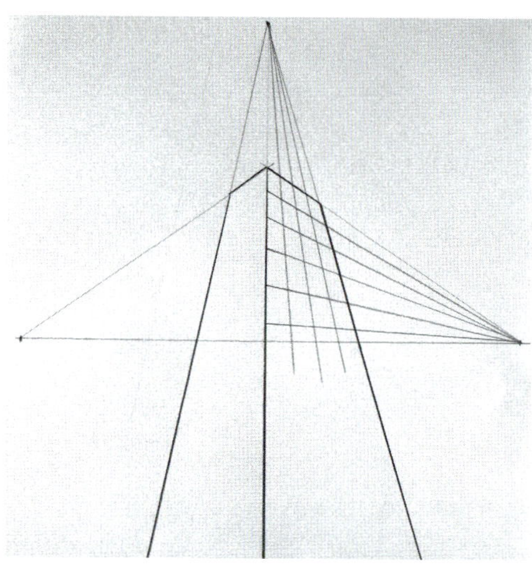

With this exaggerated perspective of a skyscraper, we see how the three vanishing points work to create the feeling of height in the building.

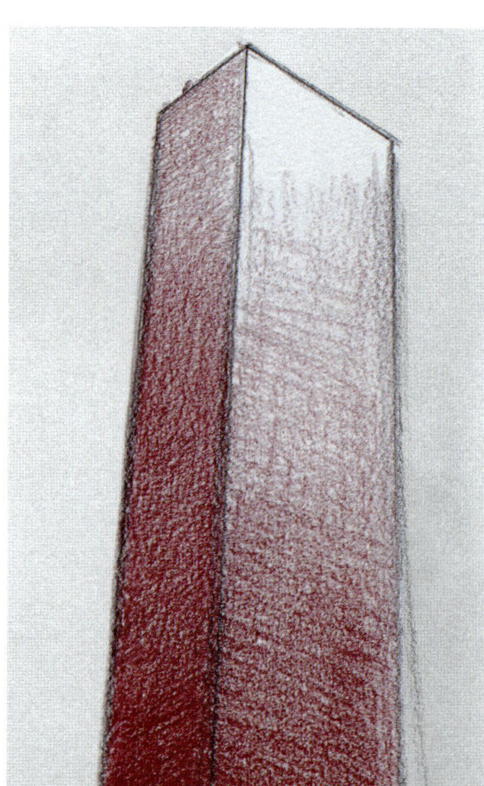

Aerial perspective can be enhanced by shaded gradations that help emphasize the vertical distance of the building.

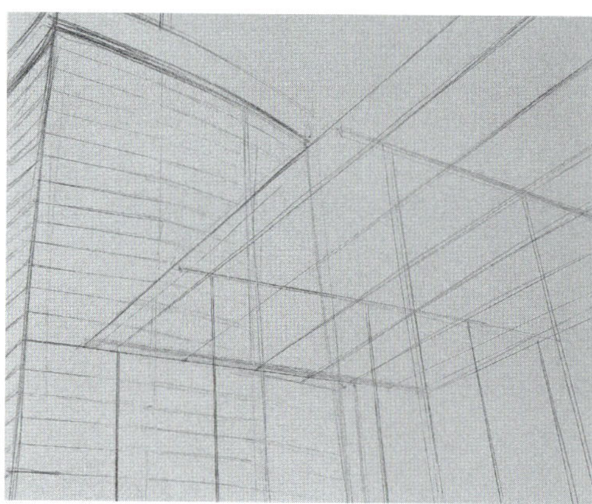

When we draw a very tall building, in addition to the vanishing lines that come from points located at both sides of the subject, we must consider a third one located in the sky, which makes the walls of the building narrower as they go upward.

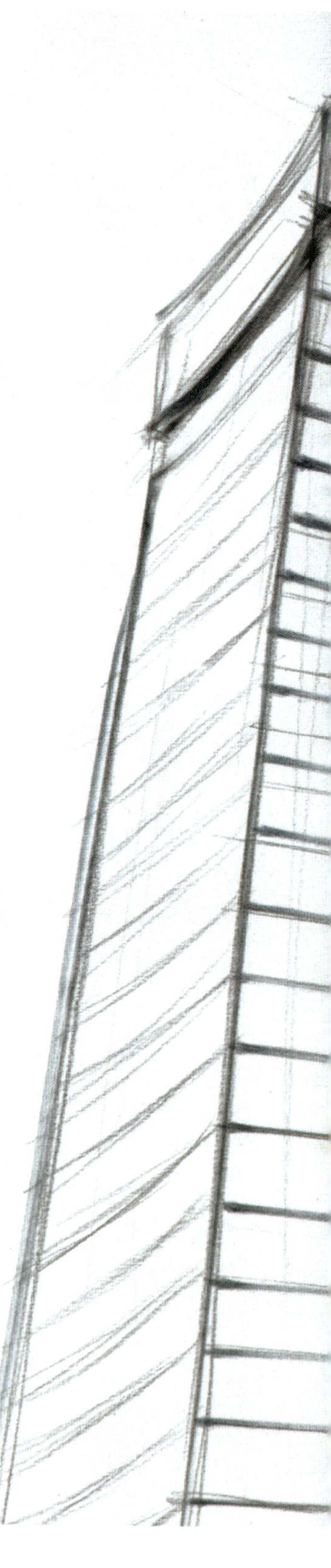

To locate the third vanishing point of the perspective, we simply need to extend the lines of the pillars that support the deck in the foreground. These are not parallel lines; rather, they converge at a very distant point.

AERIAL PERSPECTIVE, LOOKING UPWARD. Until now, all the perpendicular lines have converged in a vanishing point on the horizon line. This is not always the case. In some cases, the vanishing lines converge at a third vanishing point located way above or below this line. This happens when a very tall building is involved.

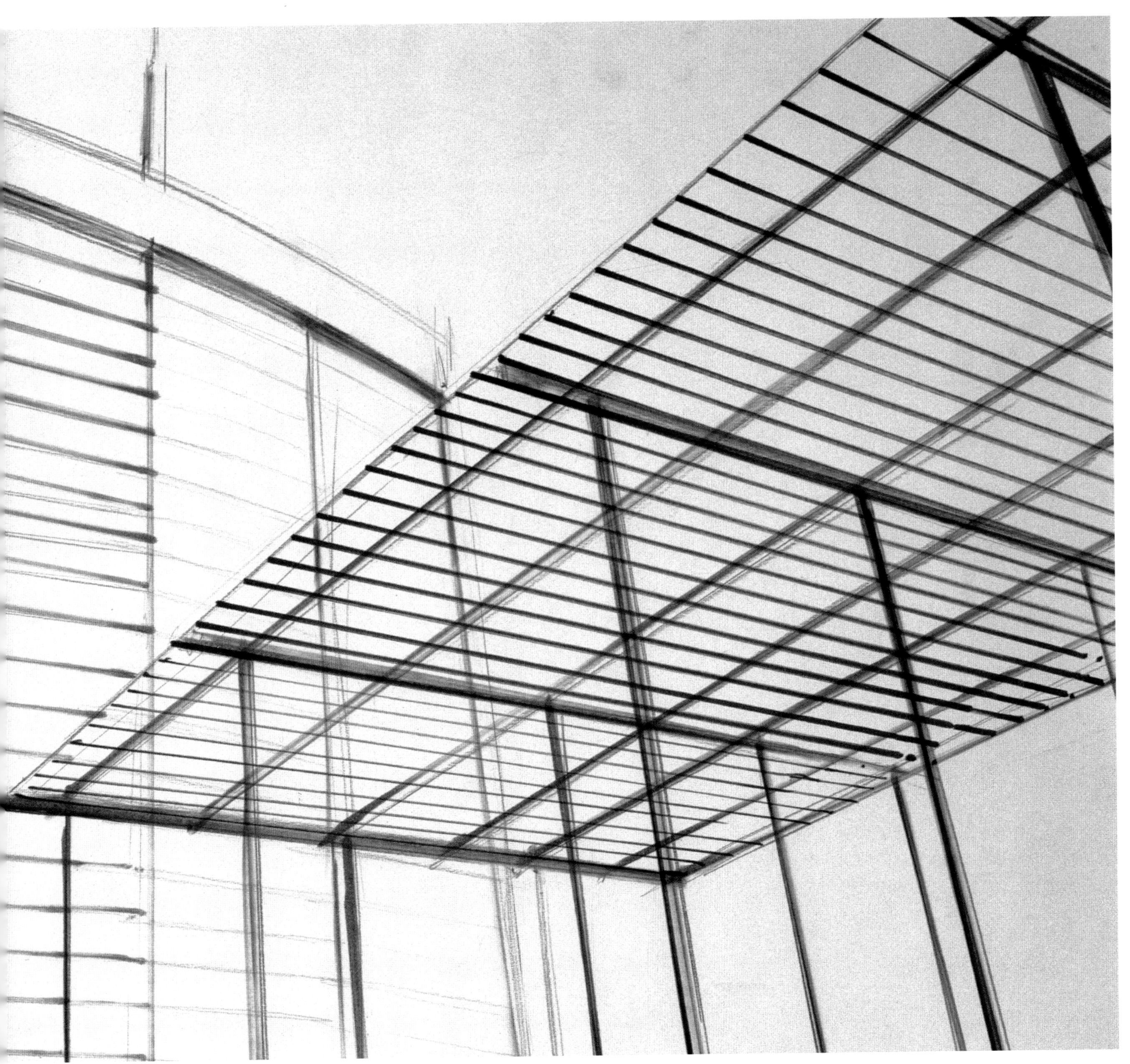

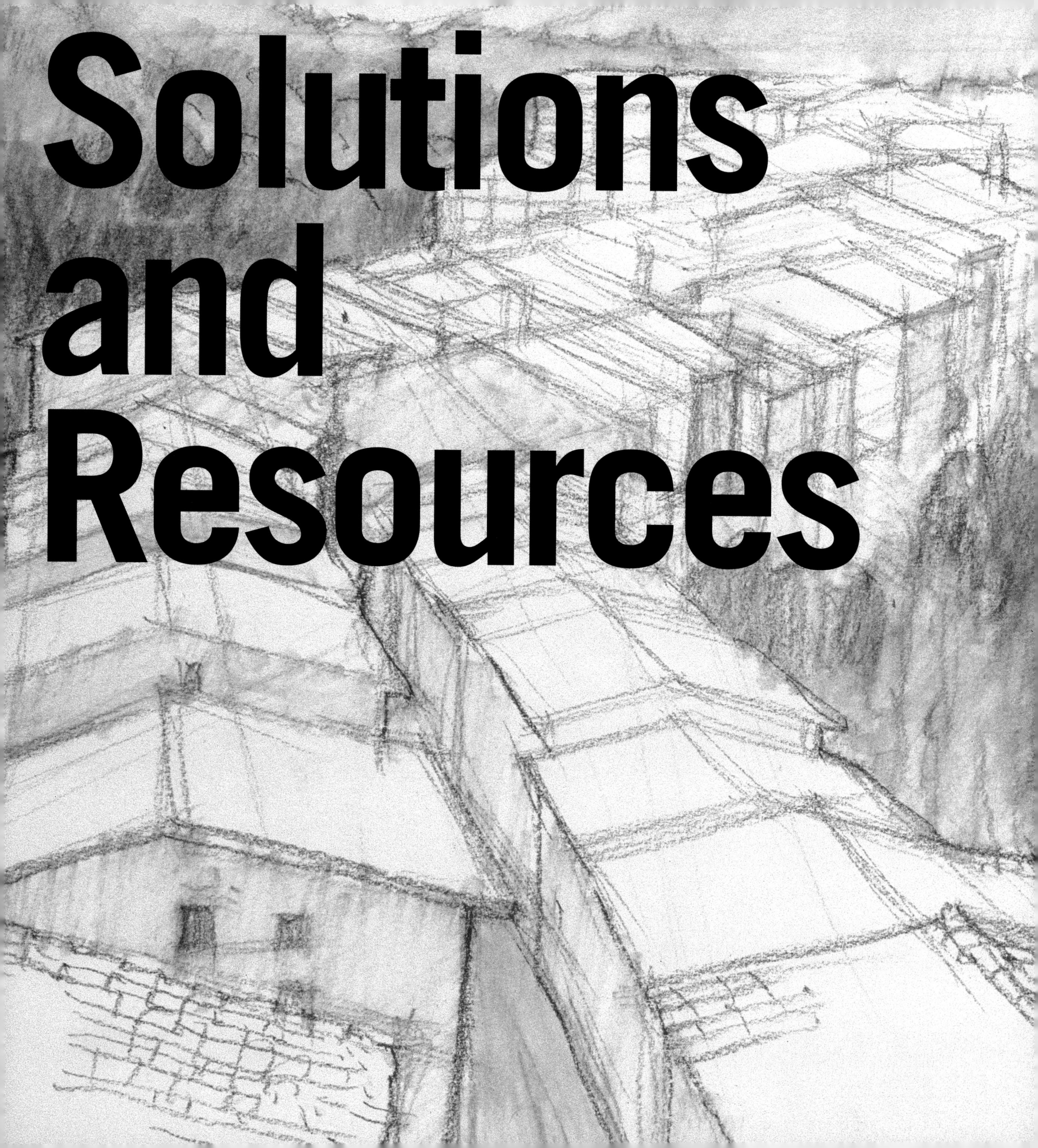

Solutions and Resources

In the first section we have mainly worked with the basics of linear perspective, explaining how to construct regular forms from diagonals that converge at one or several points located on the horizon line. However, from now on, the forms are going to be much more complex: some subjects include inclined planes, stairs, and designs with many vanishing points. In the next chapter, we will look into linear perspective in depth to offer solutions to the problems that may arise, and also to provide resources and ideas that will be very useful in such cases.

LEARNING BY DOING

A STREET IN PERSPECTIVE. After studying the previous exercises, we know enough to create a more complex drawing; in this case it will be a street with rows of houses on both sides, which gets narrower as it moves farther away. This subject is an effective means for understanding perspective projection in an urban setting and for pulling the viewer's eye into the drawing. Exercise by Carlant.

8.1

FAÇADES IN PERSPECTIVE. The first step consists of establishing the horizon line and projecting the main vanishing lines of the buildings. To add some difficulty to the exercise we have chosen a model that includes a small plaza that interrupts the line of façades on the left.

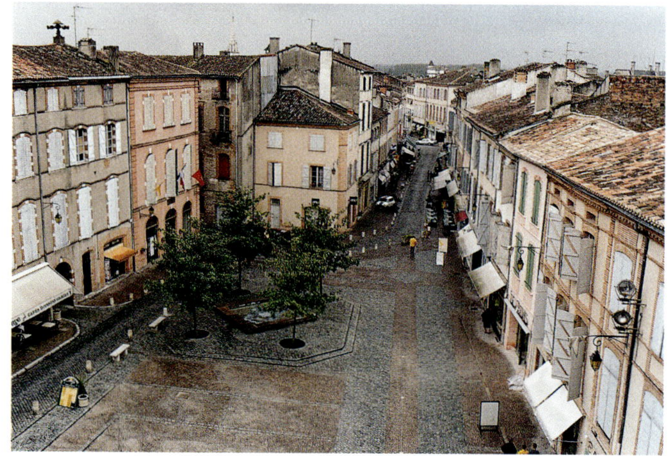

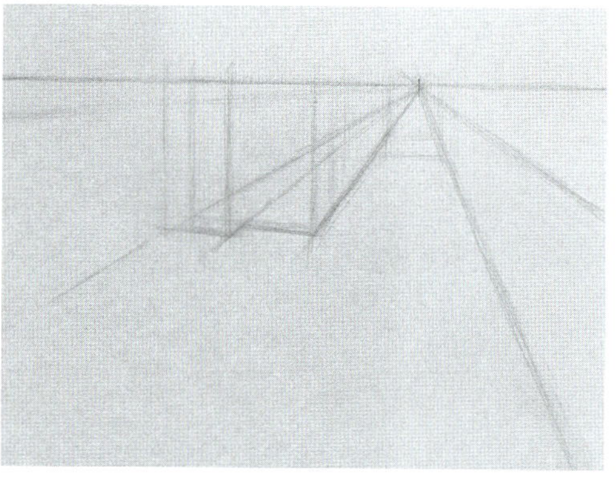

With a 2B graphite pencil we draw a high horizon line. Several diagonals extend out in two directions from a central perspective point to establish the position of the façades. We draw four lines on the left side to indicate the corner of the small plaza.

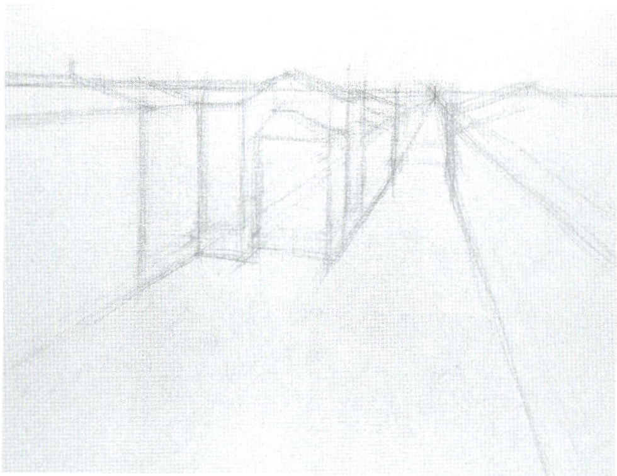

The vanishing lines of the previous step are the references upon which the buildings are constructed. We begin with those that surround the plaza. To make things easier, we approach the buildings as if they were rectangular shapes with volume.

Every time there is a change of direction on a street with buildings at different distances, one must remember that each line of façades has its own vanishing lines.

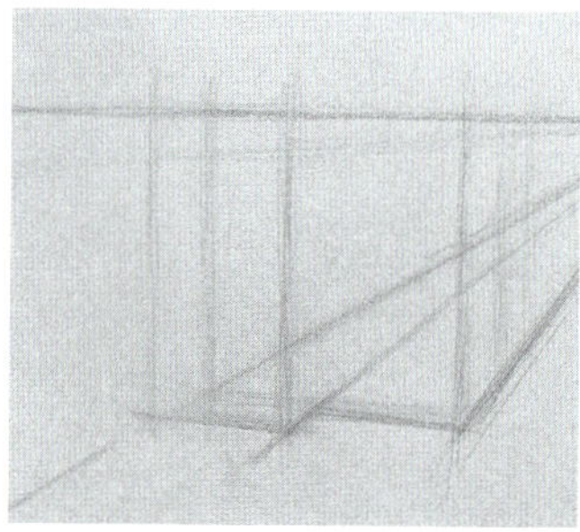

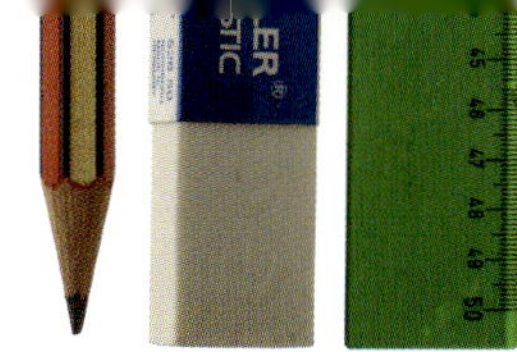

8.2

FROM PROJECTION TO STRUCTURE. After laying out the street's perspective, we focus our attention on the structures of the buildings, which are drawn by combining different geometric shapes, such as rectangles, cubes, and pyramids. In this phase, we continue working with the 2B graphite pencil.

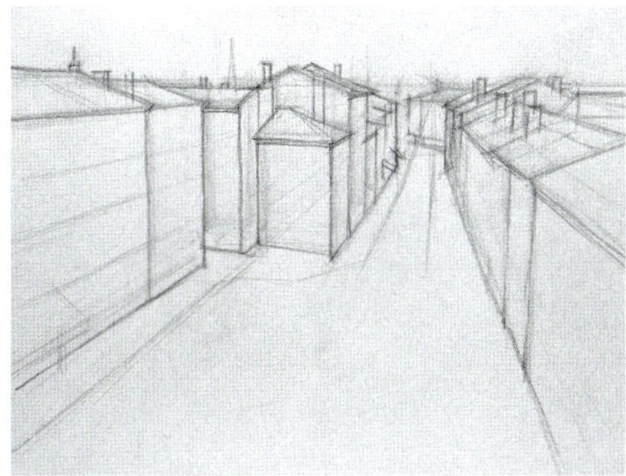

The line that defines the base of the buildings is the same vanishing line used from the beginning; the variation of the roofs is greater due to their different sizes and slopes. At this point we draw the lines for the windows.

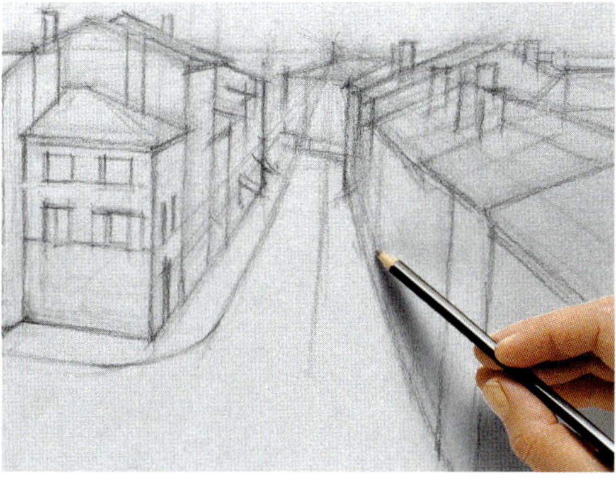

Until now the façades were empty; they had no architectural features. Doors and windows are drawn with very light lines.

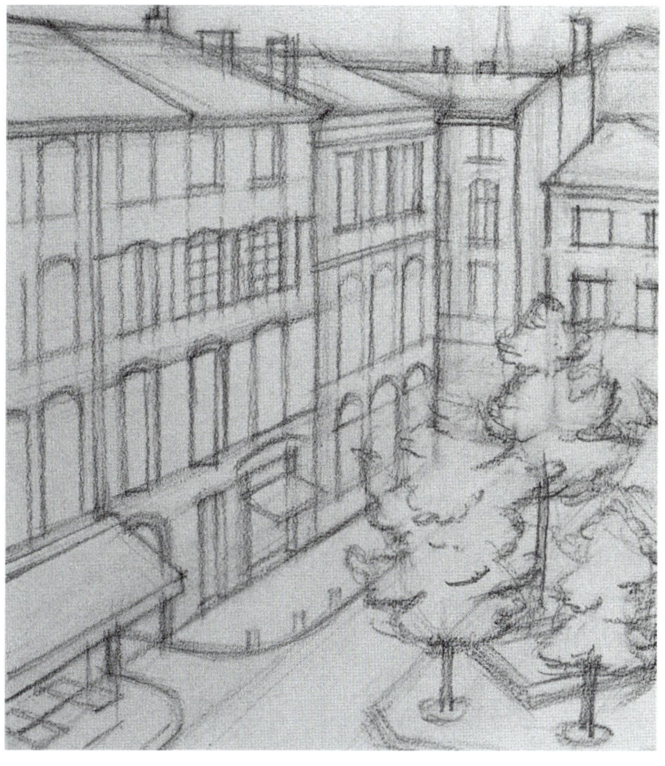

To draw the windows we begin with the opening in perspective, then we add the details, paying close attention to their shapes, the windowpanes, and to the positions of the shutters. We draw very lightly, using a 2B pencil.

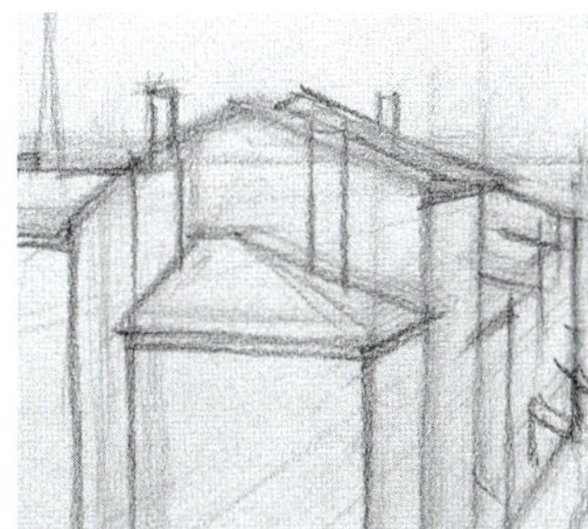

The buildings are constructed with rectangular shapes or boxes and triangles or pyramid-shaped tops for the roofs.

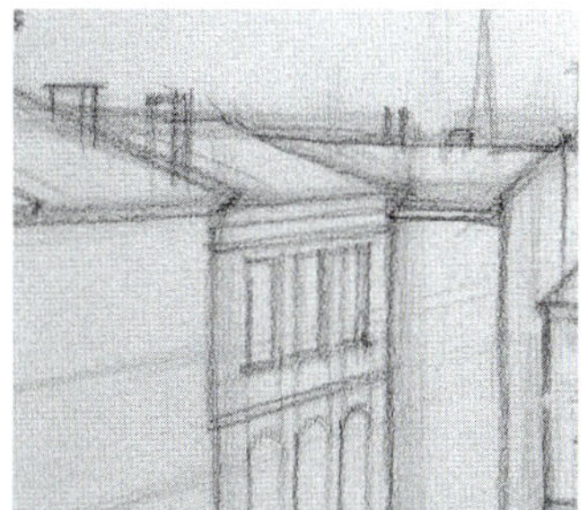

To draw the doors and windows we project new vanishing lines over the façades to align them correctly. The window is carefully drawn freehand.

8.3

ARCHITECTURAL DETAILS AND SHADING. The forms are increasingly more complex; the façades are covered with windows, the plaza with trees, and the sidewalks with posts and cars. We set aside the structural aspects to pay more attention to the architectural details and the urban elements.

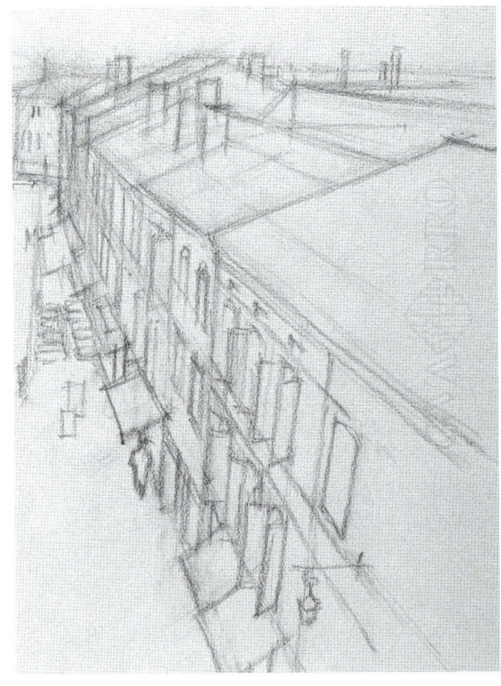

The treatment used on the left side of the street is applied to the façades on the opposite side. The vanishing lines determine the positions of the windows and the store awnings. The foreground should have more detail than the façades located farther away.

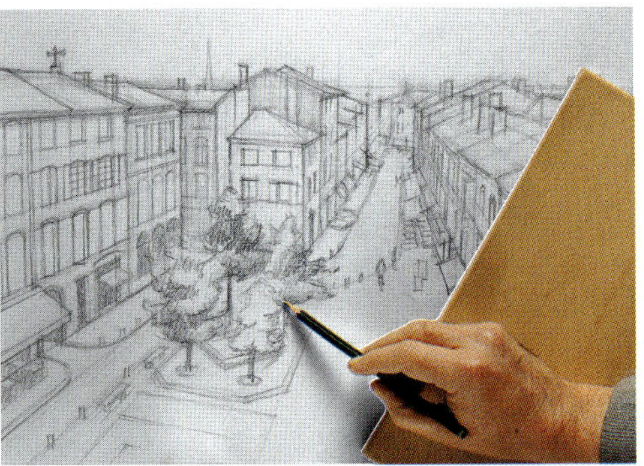

The shading is applied after the line drawing is completed. With a 4B pencil we apply light shading to avoid covering all the lines. We rest our hand on a board to prevent smearing the drawing with the fingers.

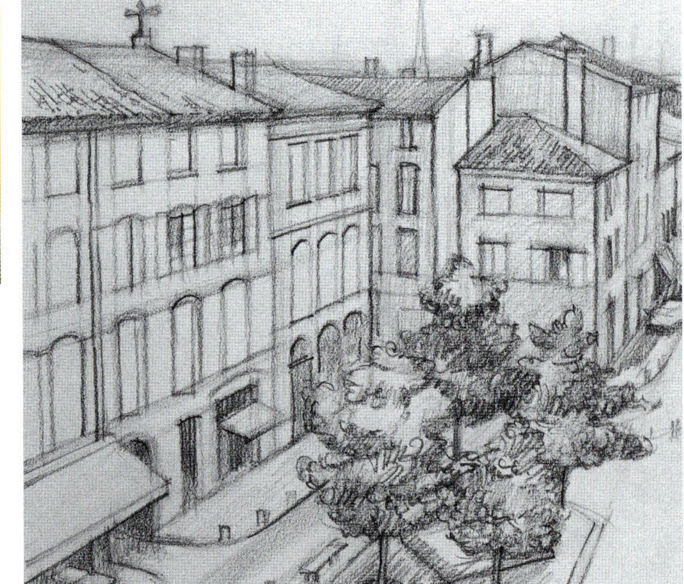

Gentle shading on the roofs of the houses creates greater contrast with the sky in this area and highlights the three-dimensional effect of each block. We go over the straight lines to define the outlines.

People are depicted very loosely. They look like simple marks.

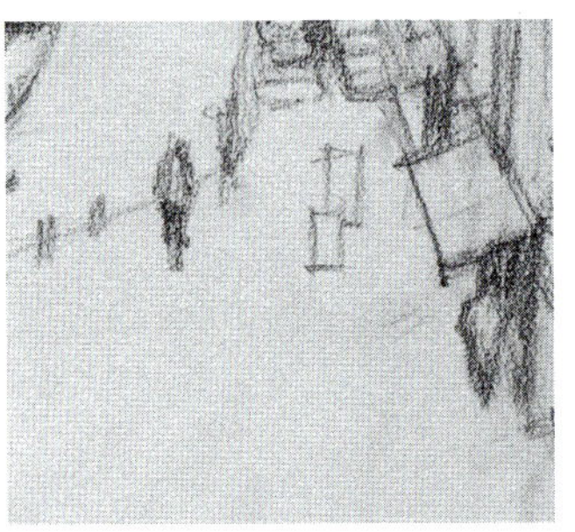

The group of trees is not affected by perspective. The approach is much more intuitive with very spontaneous and organic forms.

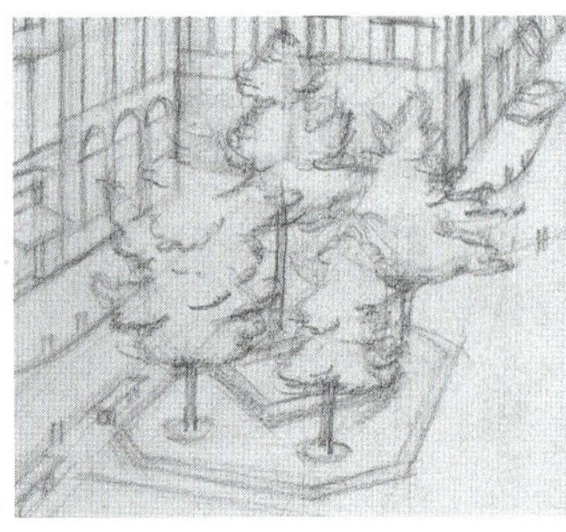

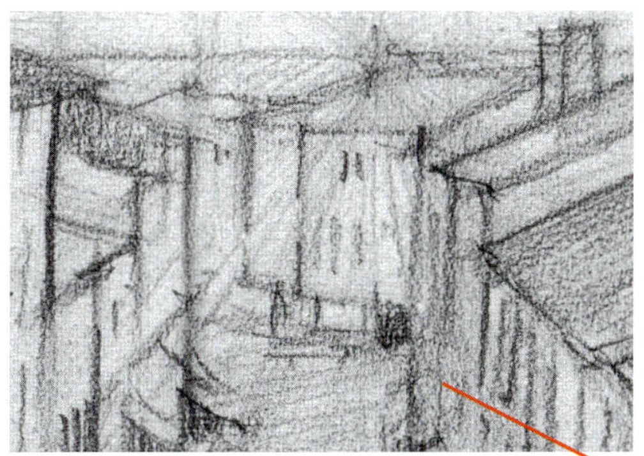

As we look down the street, the urban elements and the architectural features are less detailed and specific. However, the original linear structure drawn by projecting vanishing lines must remain constant.

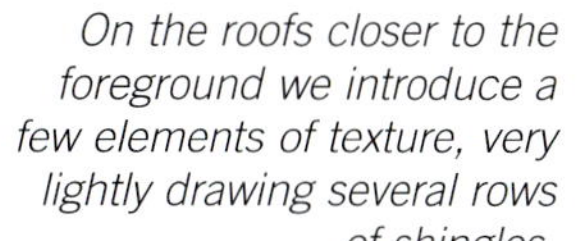

On the roofs closer to the foreground we introduce a few elements of texture, very lightly drawing several rows of shingles.

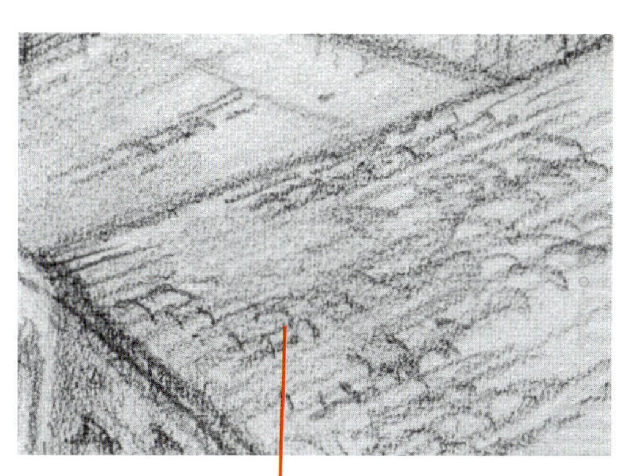

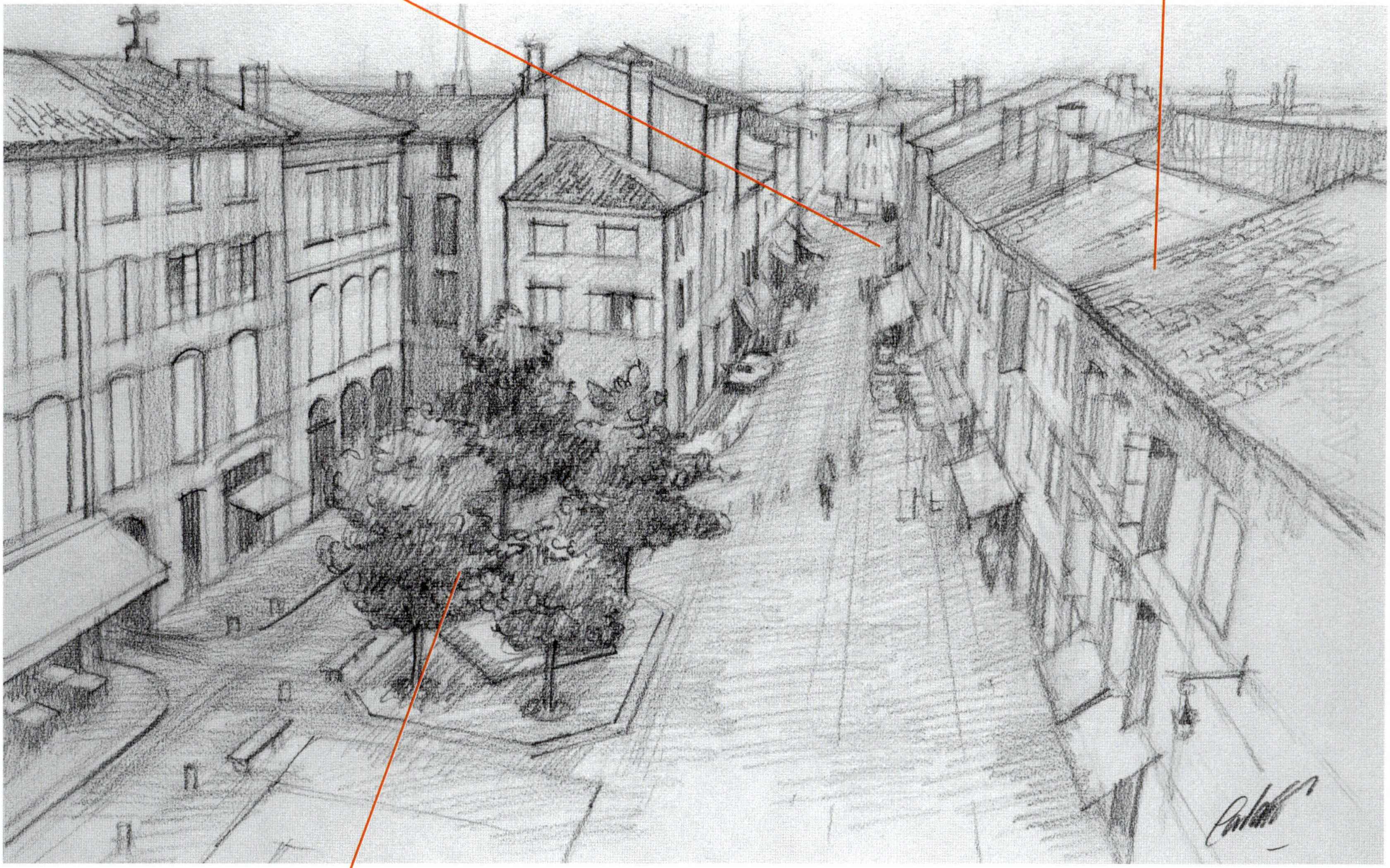

The shading on the pavement of the street is very light and is applied by gently stroking with the tip of the pencil at an angle, forming areas of barely visible diagonal hatching. The intensity of the gray on the trees constitutes the greatest contrast in the drawing.

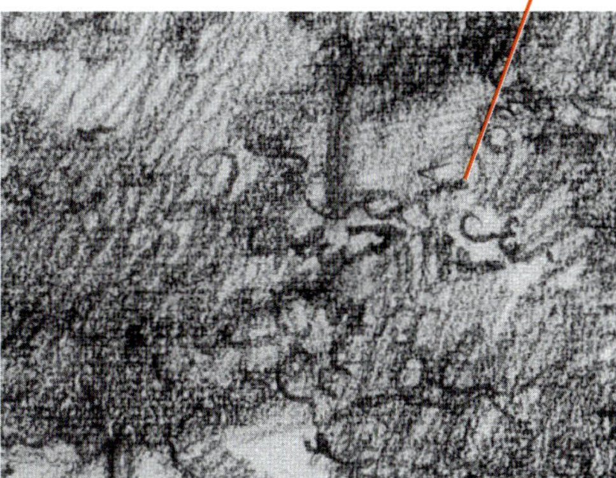

The effect of volume on the trees in the small plaza is created with gradations applied with the 4B graphite pencil held at a slight angle.

PERSPECTIVE OF THE ROOFTOPS. From the top of a lookout point, a tower, or a bell tower, we can see the rooftops of the houses nearby. If these are all lined up, perspective can be useful to organize the elements and to emphasize the effect of depth. Exercise by Carlant.

9.1

CHANGING DIRECTION. When the distribution of the rooftops shows a change of direction, the drawing is constructed with as many vanishing points as there are directions in the line of roofs. The direction is determined by the layout of the streets. In this case, two vanishing points are sufficient to carry out the exercise successfully.

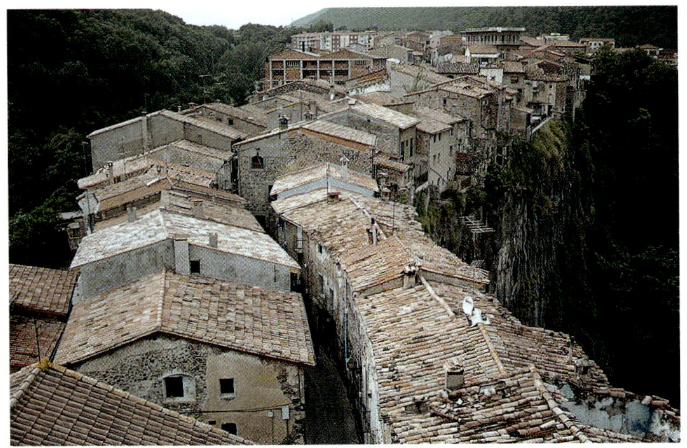

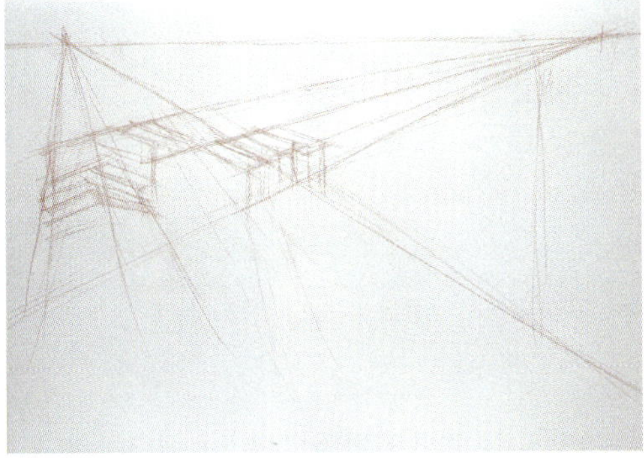

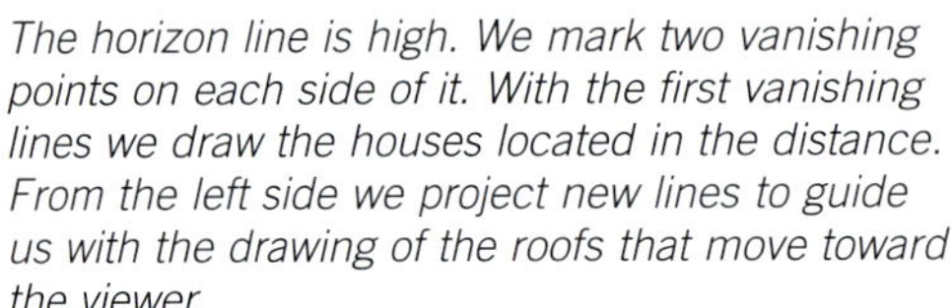

The horizon line is high. We mark two vanishing points on each side of it. With the first vanishing lines we draw the houses located in the distance. From the left side we project new lines to guide us with the drawing of the roofs that move toward the viewer.

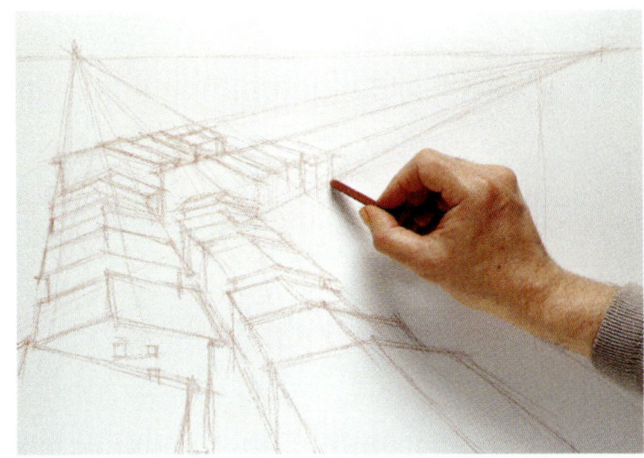

We use the diagonals that extend from the vanishing point on the left side to construct the rooftops of the foreground. Halfway through the painting there is a change of direction in the street; this requires continuing the drawing with the vanishing lines that turn toward the point on the right.

Here, the layering of elements is especially useful to create a staggered sequence of visual objects to suggest a feeling of depth, even though other perspective resources are used to deal with the space.

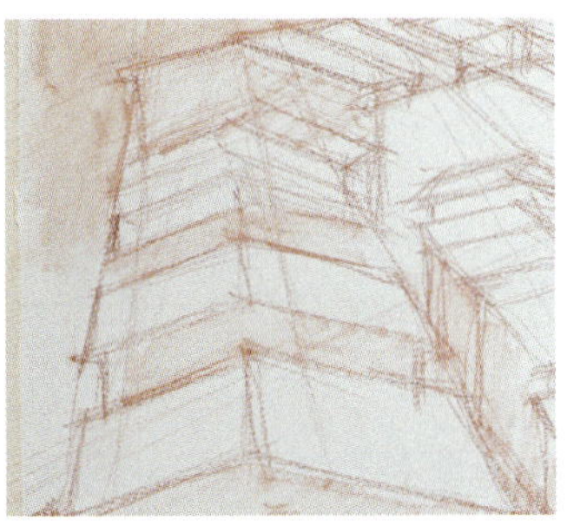

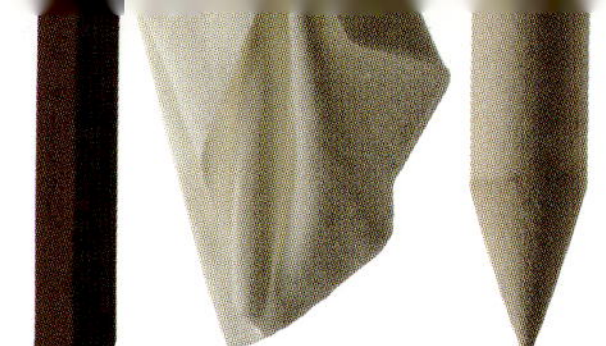

9.2

DRAWING THE SURROUNDINGS. After constructing the houses and the rooftops following the rules of perspective and geometry, it is a good idea to create a context for it—in other words, to create the natural backdrop, the space that contains the architecture. Since we are working with sanguine, we use this to introduce some tonal effects.

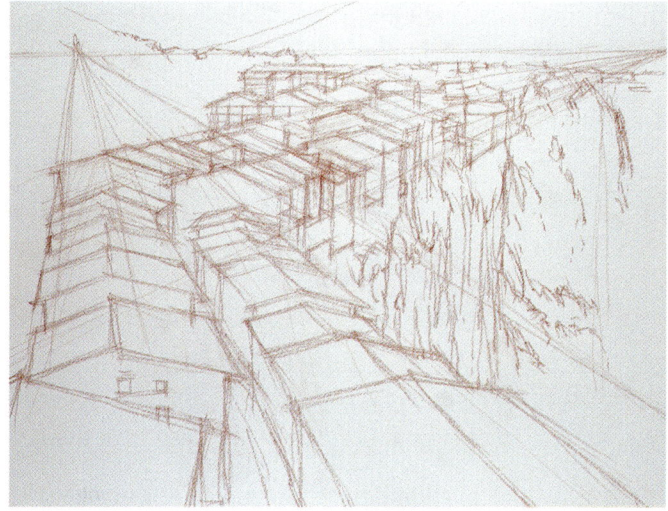

Drawing lightly with the tip of the stick, we introduce the cliff and the group of houses into the landscape. Little by little, the horizon line disappears and the technical and mechanical drawing of the perspective loses its rigidity upon blending with the organic forms.

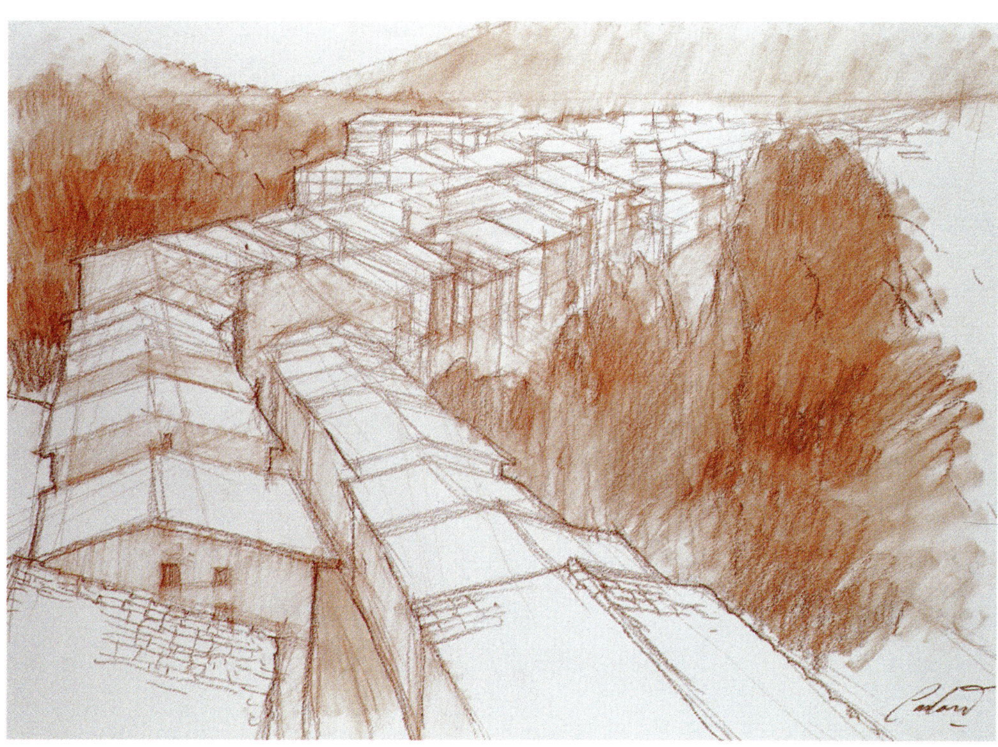

We finish it quickly by shading with the tip of the stick placed at a slight angle and without applying much pressure. The tonal effect is lightened with a blending stick; we rub it gently over the houses and more vigorously over the vegetation. A cotton rag may also be used.

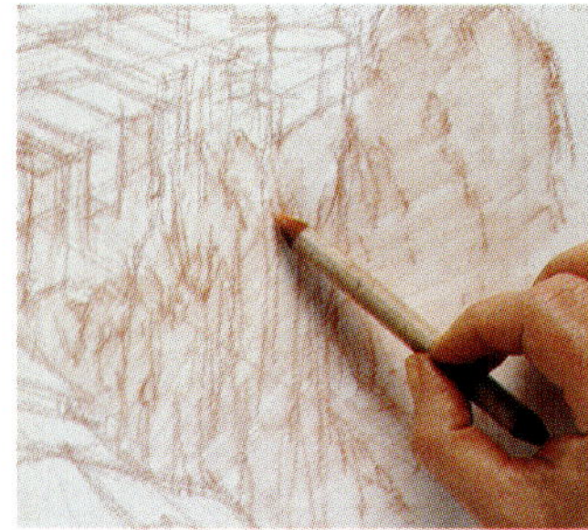

The work carried out with the blending stick is very delicate. Shading must be soft, blending the lines gently but without erasing them.

STREETS THAT GO UP AND DOWN. On a slope, or a street that goes up or down, there are two horizon lines, a true and a false perspective. The principles applied to create steep slopes and inclines are identical to the ones used for a flat horizontal surface, with the exception that the vanishing points stem from a false horizon line that is located a little above or below the horizon line.

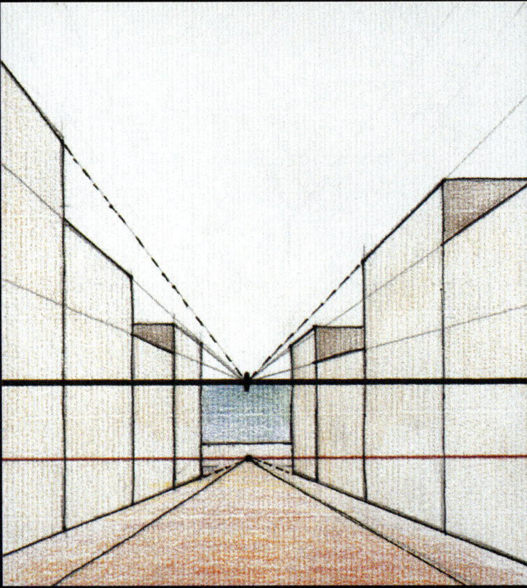

On a slope, the horizon line for the street is located a little below the real horizon, out of which stem the vanishing lines for the buildings.

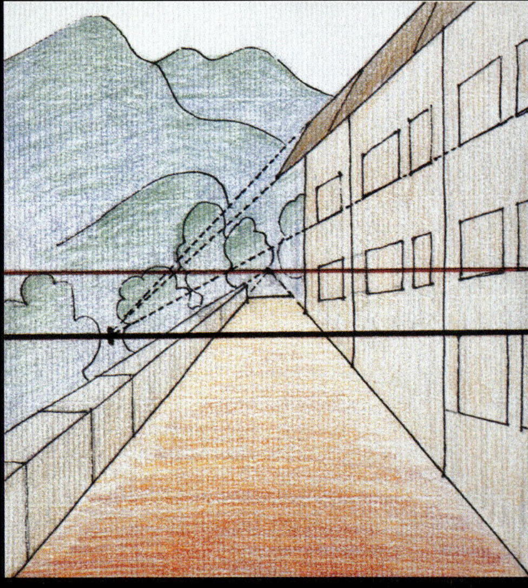

On a slope, the false horizon is located above the real horizon.

COASTAL AND RURAL TOWNS. Many coastal and rural towns have steep streets. While the street has its own vanishing point, the houses are represented as usual, by taking the horizon line as reference.

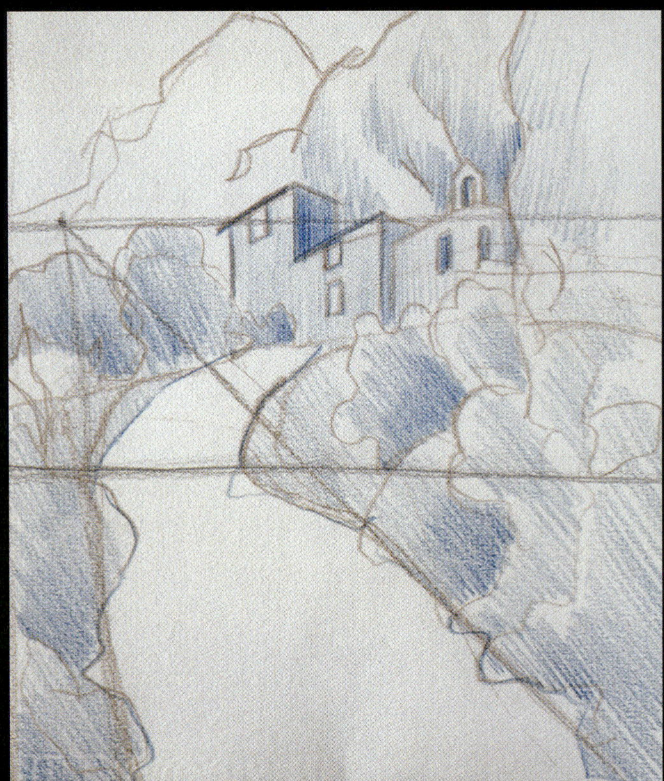

In rural towns, we find many slopes that can be used to practice the false horizon.

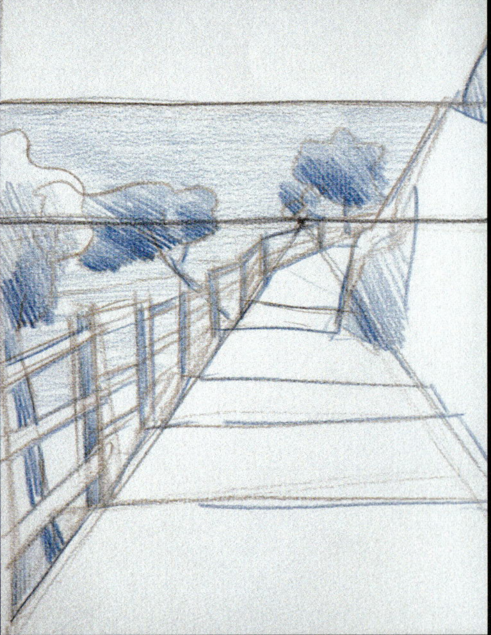

In the steep slopes of coastal towns, the false horizon is located below sea level.

INCLINED SURFACES AND STEPS. Many artists include slopes and inclines or steps in their drawings to create a feeling of rapid movement and rhythm, and to play with the steepness of the planes. At first, the steep surfaces can throw the artist off, but the work is simplified if perspective lines support it.

A FALSE HORIZON. In a rural landscape with steep slopes, one cannot speak of a real horizon, as we know it. Here, we must identify a false horizon located below the real one to draw houses located at different heights on the hill.

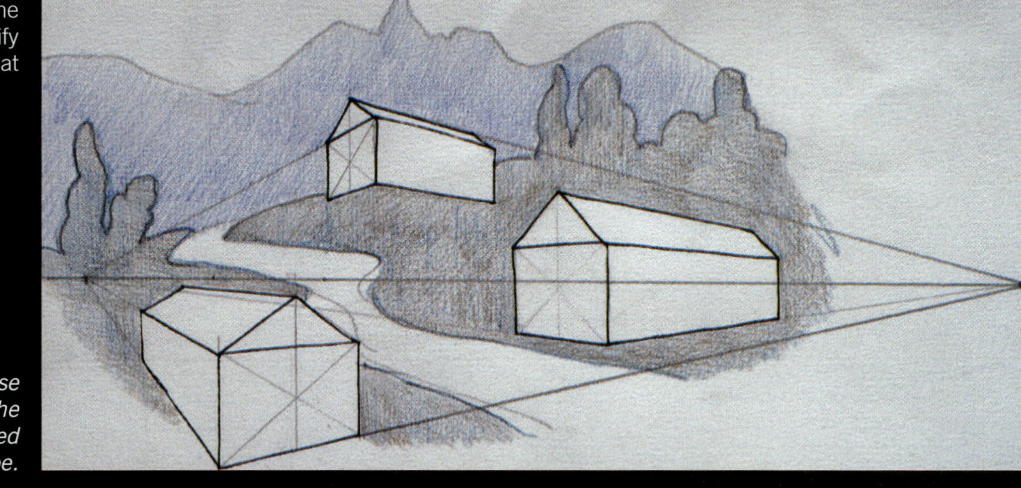

It is necessary to create a false horizon to represent the elements that are distributed throughout the slope.

STEPS. The perspective of the stairs, the same as that of the rooftops, is based on the presence of the ascending and descending planes. As we go up, not only do the steps get narrower, but also the distance between them is reduced.

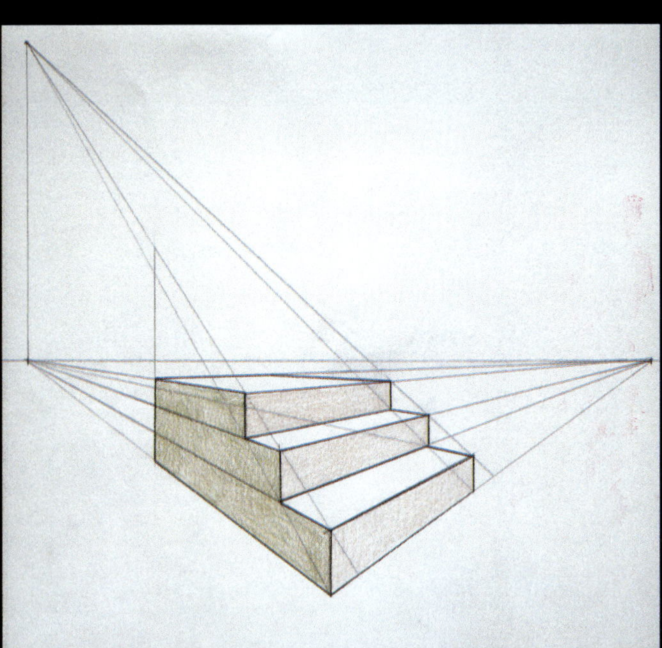

Drawing stairs in perspective requires the use of two vanishing points to draw the steps, and a third one (aerial) to establish the degree of inclination.

GOING UP AND DOWN THE STAIRS. Normally, when we go up and down the stairs we see them in very distinct perspective, because not only do we see them from above or below, but we also have to add the height of our body.

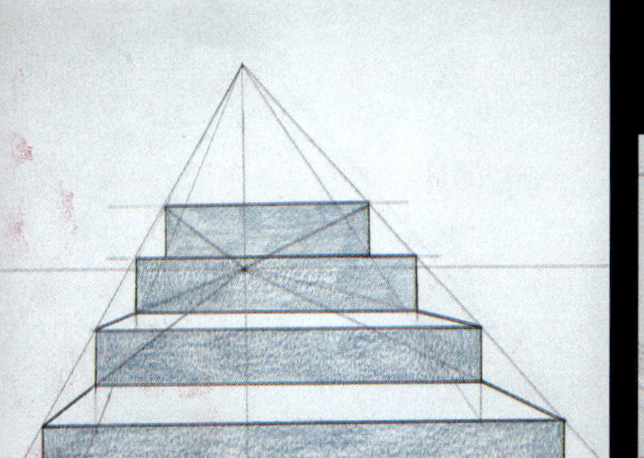

Steps seen from below. The incline is decided with a single vanishing point, while the width of the steps is determined by the central vanishing

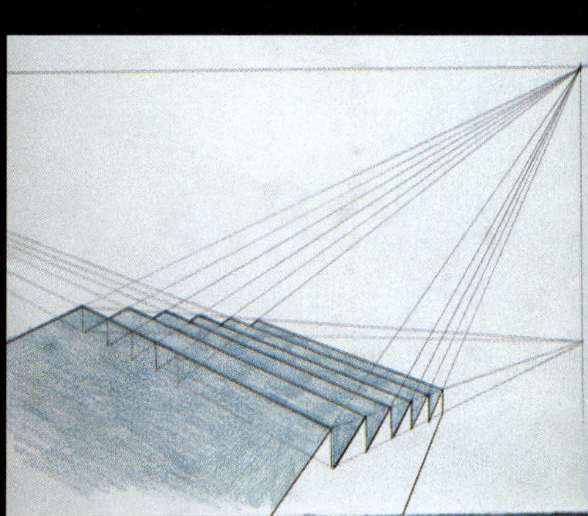

Descending steps are more difficult; they also require three vanishing points that are located far away from each other.

LEARNING BY DOING

DRAWING STAIRS. Drawing stairs like those shown in this picture should be manageable at this point. To make drawing them easier, we reduce the number of stairs and increase their steepness. Drawing by Carlant.

10.1

A VARIATION OF A SLOPE. Drawing stairs may seem difficult. However, it is only a variation of a slope on which we project new lines that divide the space to represent the steps. We begin drawing with an HB graphite pencil.

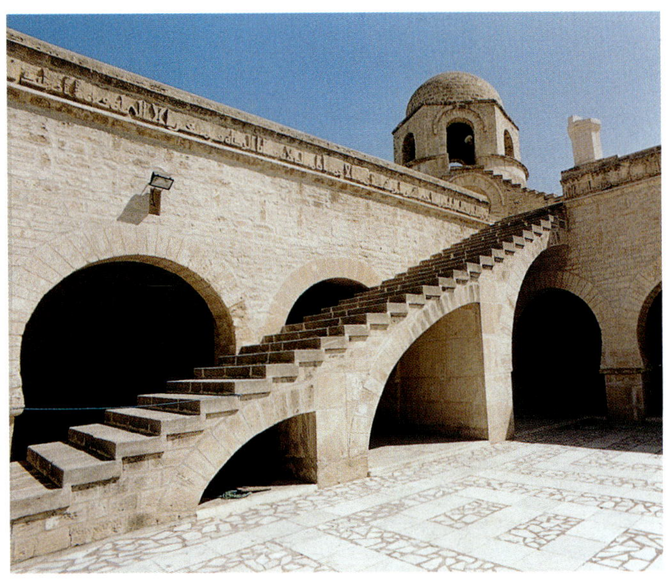

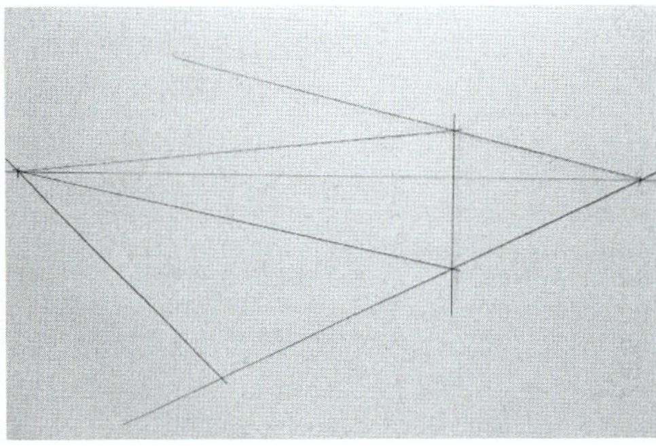

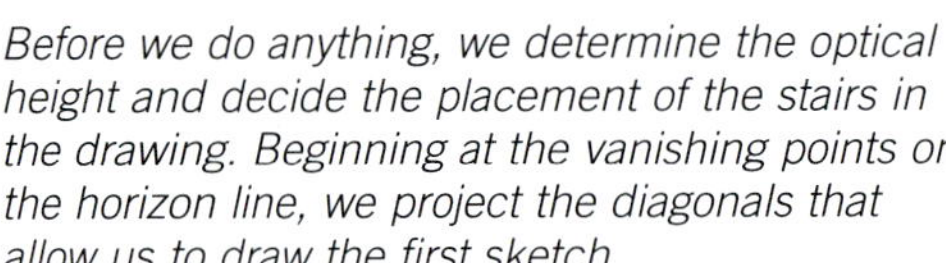

Before we do anything, we determine the optical height and decide the placement of the stairs in the drawing. Beginning at the vanishing points on the horizon line, we project the diagonals that allow us to draw the first sketch.

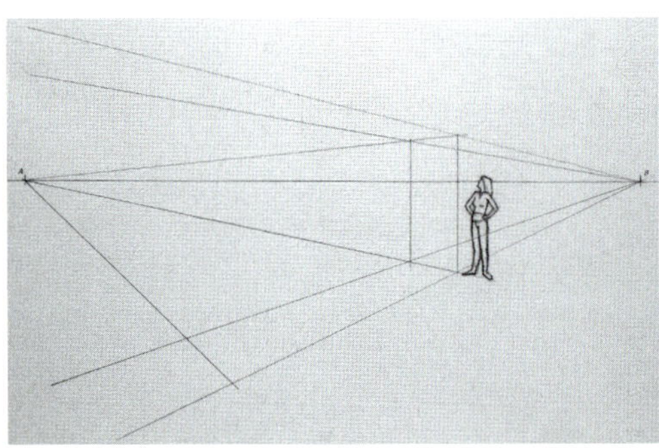

From the intersecting points of the vanishing lines, we project perpendicular lines that determine the width of the stairs. Next to one of these lines we sketch a figure, which will serve as a reference to determine the size of the steps.

The line on the background is used as a reference to determine the height of the steps. We check the accuracy of the segments by comparing the lower segment against the figure to verify that it agrees with the height of a real step.

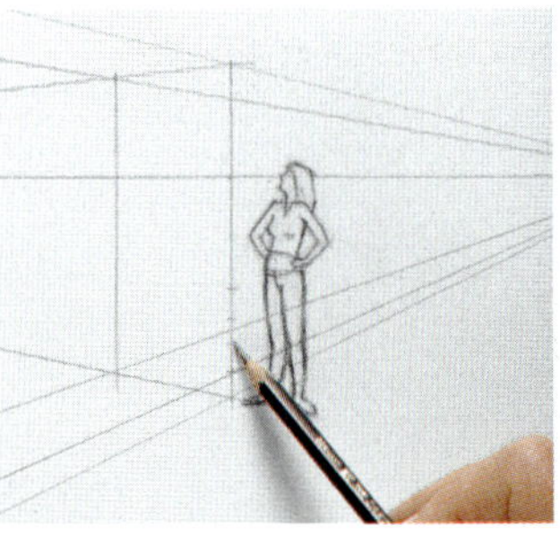

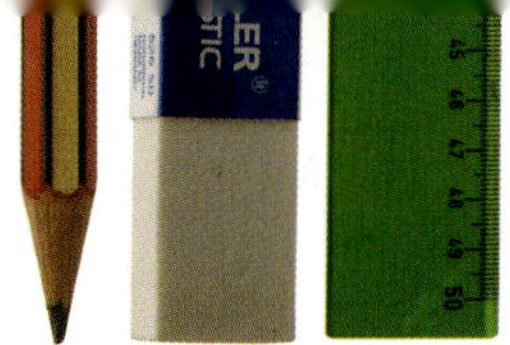

10.2

THE HEIGHT OF THE STEPS. Using a segmented line, we establish the size of the steps. From both vanishing points we project lines that use these measurements as a reference to determine the height and angle of the steps.

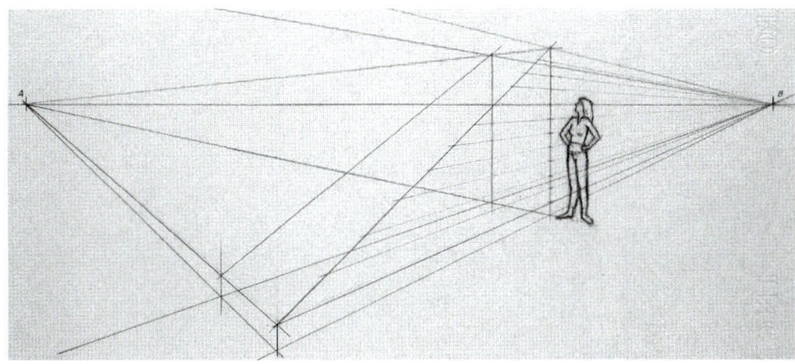

We decide on the height of the steps. To do this, we divide the perpendicular line in equal parts. From the vanishing point on the left side we project lines that cut through each one of these divisions and meet the diagonals that determine the angle of the stairs.

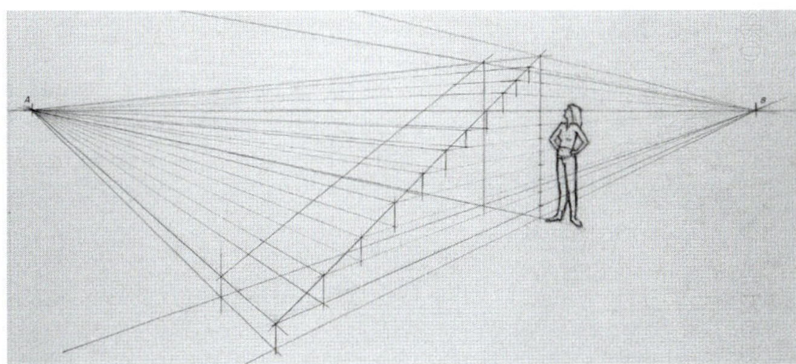

From the vanishing point on the left we draw new diagonals in perspective that merge with the previously established intersections. These lines determine the angle of each step.

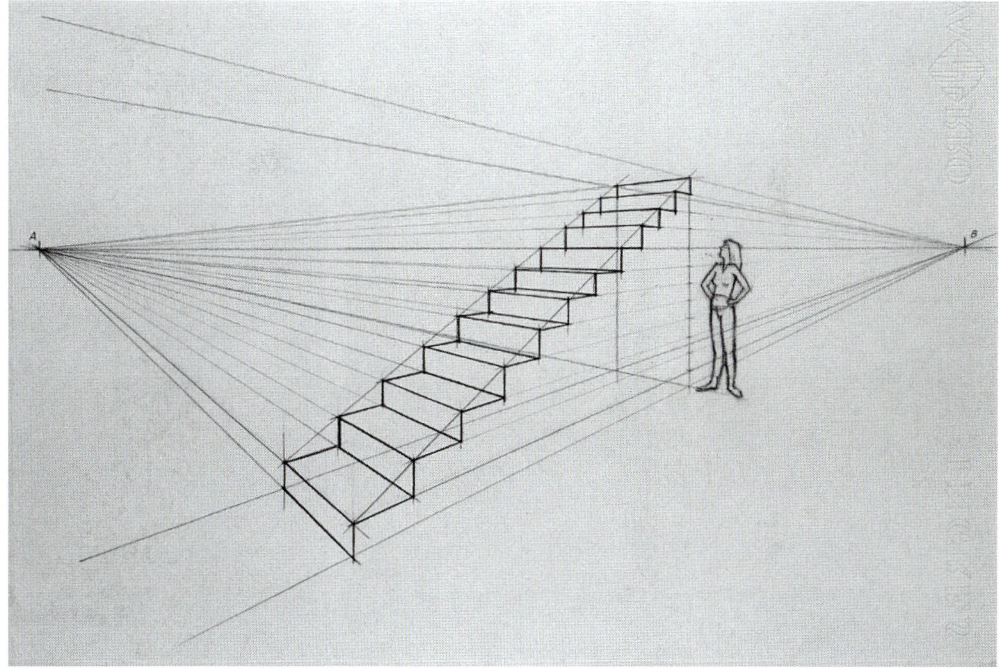

Using the previous lines as reference, we only need to project the perpendicular lines for the stairs; all of them are parallel to each other. With a 2B pencil we darken the drawing and finish the exercise.

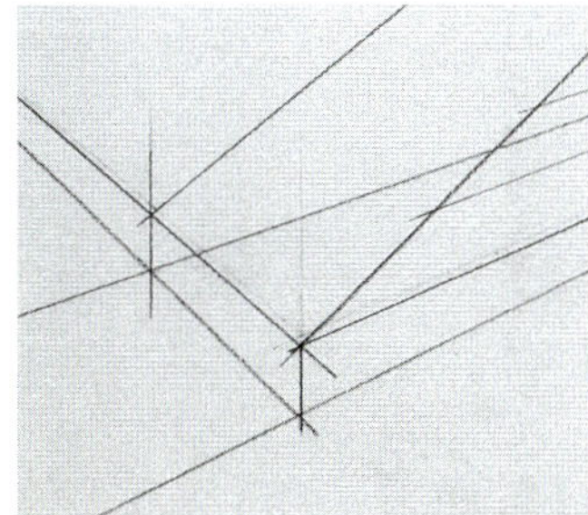

Beginning at the first step, we connect the top and the bottom of the staircase with two lines as if it were a flat sloped surface.

LEARNING BY DOING

A BRIDGE WITH ARCHES. All around us there are many objects that have curves (elliptical, circular, parabolic, among others) that require greater involvement with perspective drawing. In this exercise we face the challenge of drawing the ellipses of the arches on a bridge, which also cast a reflection on the water. Drawing by Carlant.

11.1

DISREGARD THE PHOTOGRAPH. To represent the bridge in perspective correctly, we begin with a real subject, although in this case we have simplified the shapes to make the drawing easier. With this in mind, we will imagine that the top of the bridge is a flat and straight road without any elevation, and that all the arches have the same width.

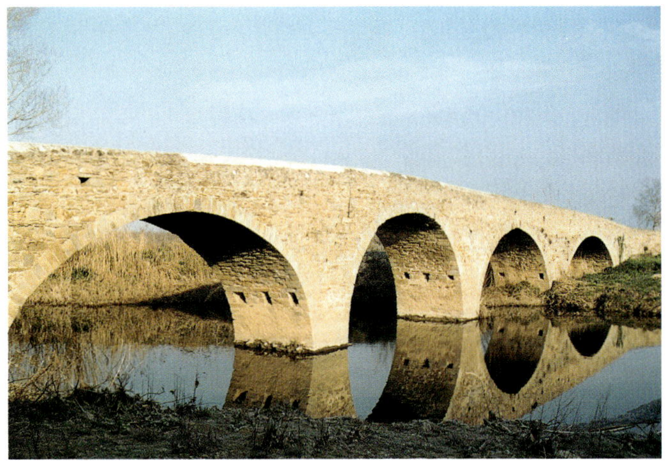

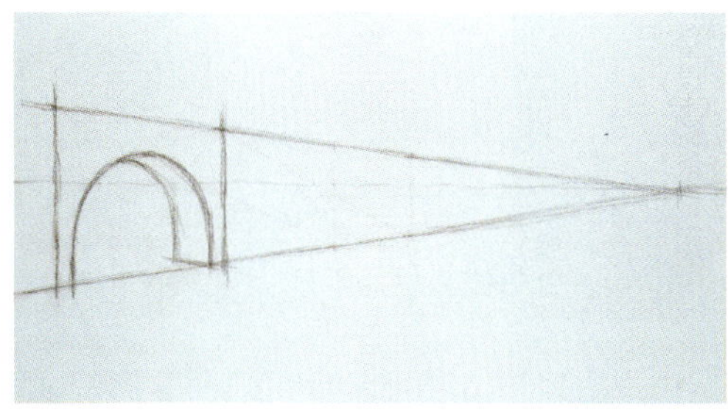

We establish the horizon line a little below the middle of the paper. On its right, we locate a point from which we will project the diagonals for the bridge. We draw a square, which will house the first arch.

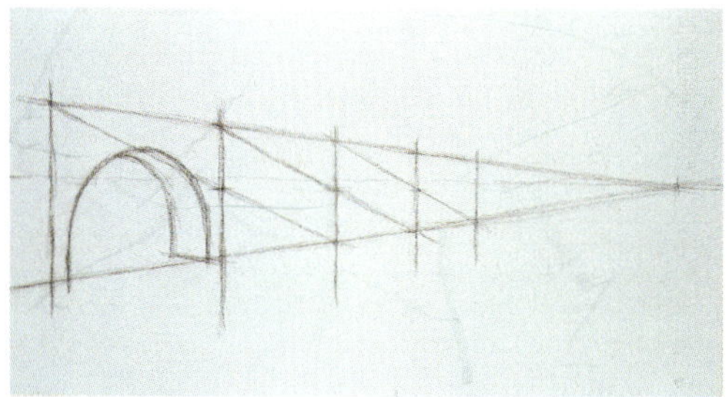

We draw a diagonal from the top corner of the first perpendicular line, which cuts exactly through the second one and then touches the vanishing line. This last point establishes the width of the second arch. This procedure is repeated until all the arches have been drawn.

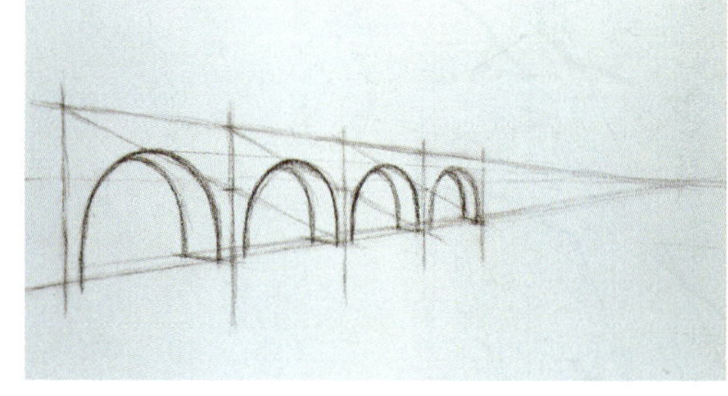

Inside each rectangle we draw the different arches, paying special attention to the elliptical shapes described by them. To draw the ellipses correctly we draw a line through the perspective center of each rectangle.

If we draw two diagonals that connect the edges of this rectangle in perspective, we will find the center of perspective. A vertical line drawn through this point will help us find the center of the arch.

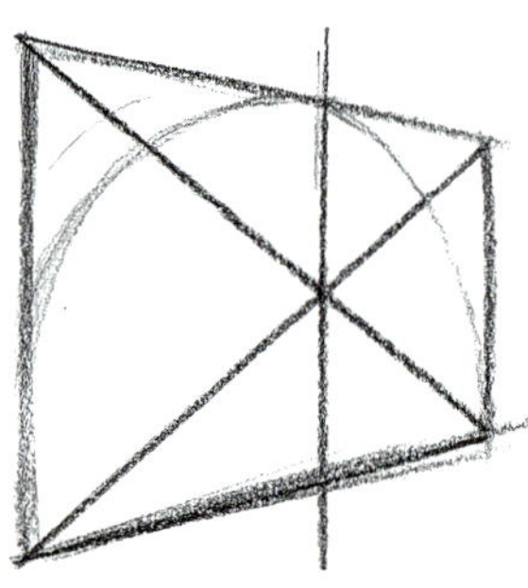

11.2

PROJECTING THE REFLECTION. Let us imagine that the water in the river is a mirror and that we repeat the previous process to represent the arches of the bridge, but this time inverted. Then, we shade the drawing establishing the real image from the reflected one by changing the color.

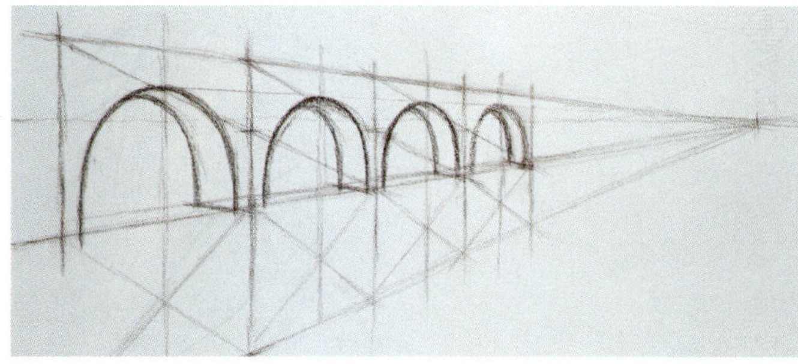

The next step involves drawing the arches reflected on the water by repeating the same procedure but inverted: draw the vanishing line, extend the width of each arch, and find the center of perspective by intersecting the diagonals.

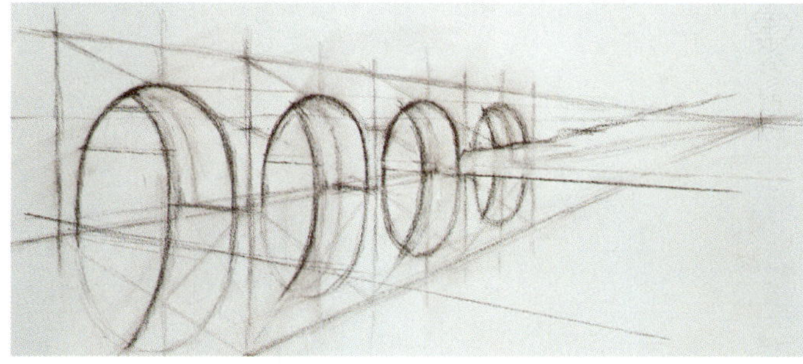

Once the center of perspective and the perpendicular axes have been determined, we draw the inverted arches freehand. They must be symmetrical to the real ones and, together, form a perfect ellipse.

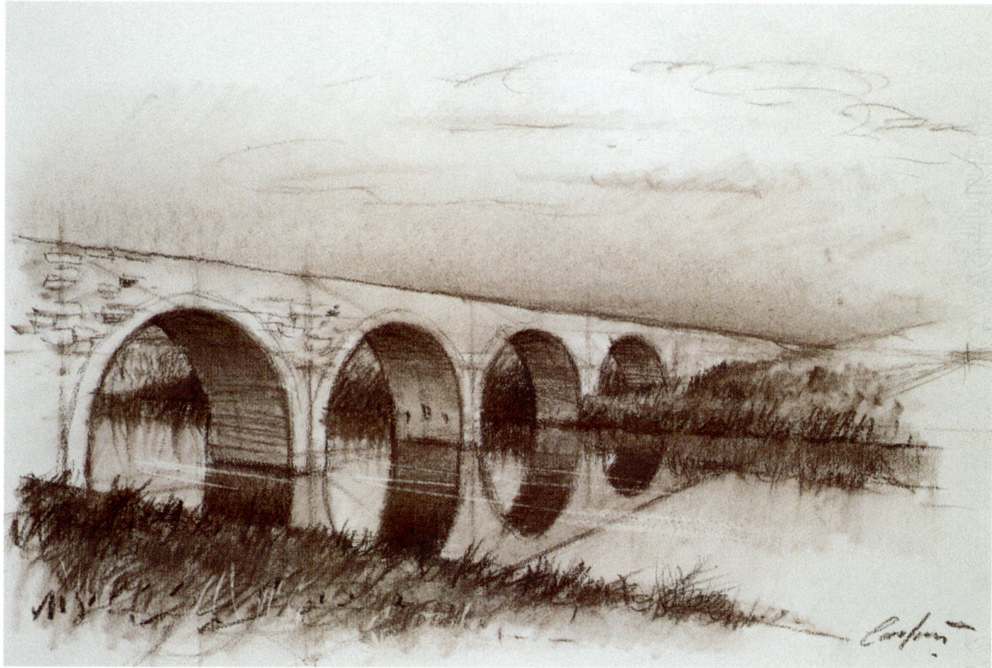

When the line drawing is finished, we need to shade the bridge and the textured effects; the vegetation that grows on each side of the river is loosely drawn.

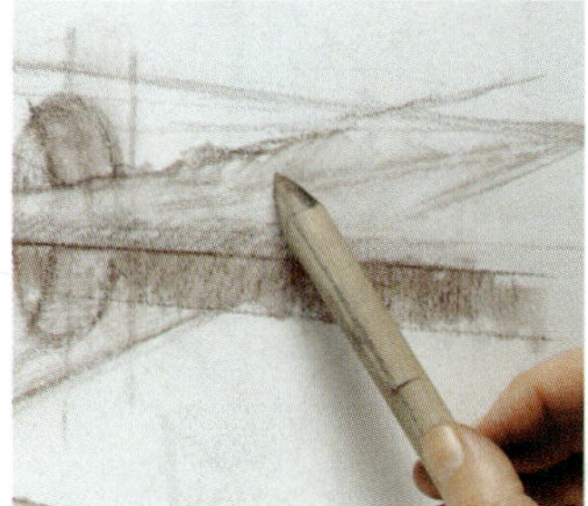

The shading effects with brown chalk are very soft; a blending stick is used to form gradations.

SIZE DECREASES WITH DISTANCE. Texture gradient is one of the first resources used to represent depth. If we look at road fences, we notice how the posts become shorter and the distance between them narrower the farther away they are. We will use a method that can help us achieve this effect.

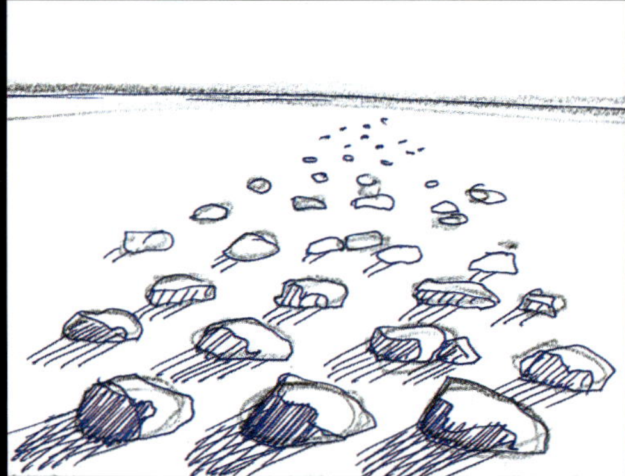

A field full of different size stones can create this partial gradient effect.

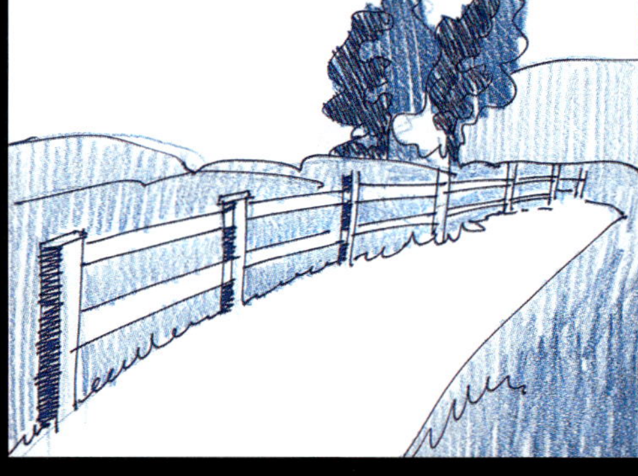

The posts of a fence on the side of the road become shorter and the distance between them narrower as they move away.

DRAWING POSTS. To figure out the decrease in their distance we follow several steps: we draw the first post and we project the lines on a vanishing point. We draw a second one wherever we feel it is most appropriate. We draw a line that begins at the top of the first post, cuts through the center of the second one, and ends on the vanishing line. This last intersection should mark the third post. The method used for the second and third posts is repeated with the rest of the posts.

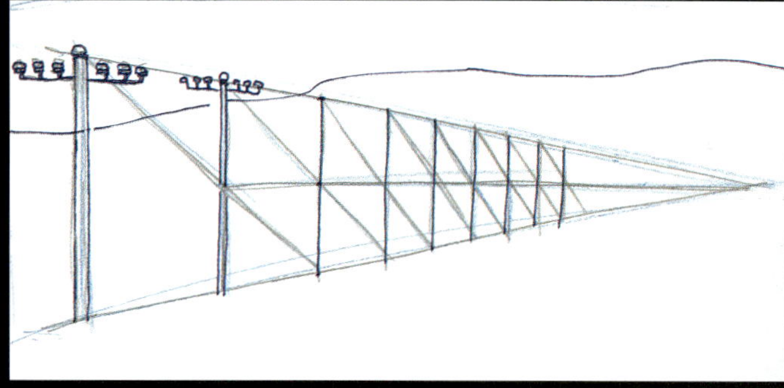

Using this method, not only the height of the objects decreases but also the distance between them.

MOVEMENT GRADIENT. Just as the distance between the objects or the telephone posts decreases, the speed of the object also decreases the farther away it is. A movement gradient increases the effect of depth in a landscape when we see it from a moving vehicle.

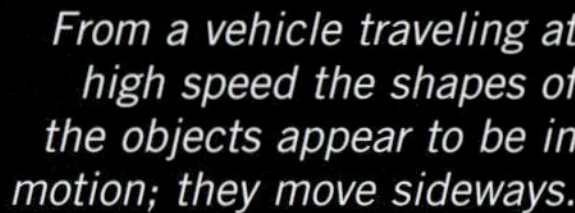

From a vehicle traveling at high speed the shapes of the objects appear to be in motion; they move sideways.

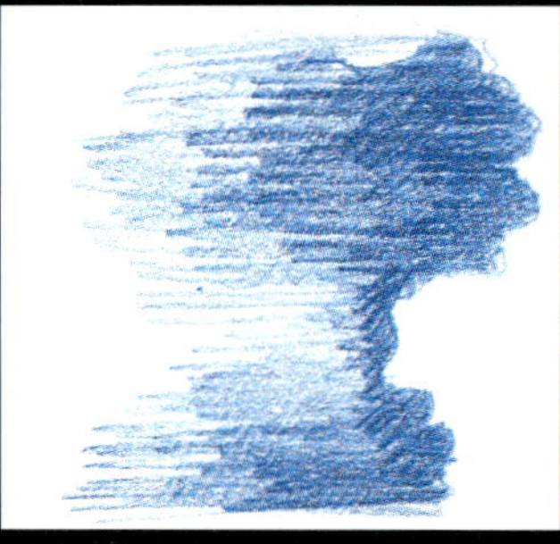

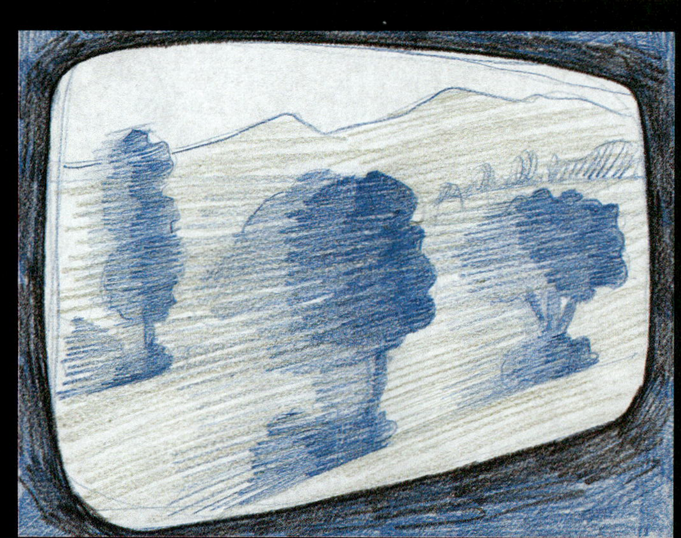

The buildings and the trees in the foreground next to us move faster than the ones in the distance, and the difference in the apparent speed correlates to our distance with respect to what we see.

TEXTURE GRADIENT AND THE CENTER OF PERSPECTIVE. Texture gradients are the main reason that we see the rows of telephone posts, trees, or columns decrease in depth. In addition to the size reduction experienced by those vertical points of reference, the space between them also decreases.

CENTER OF PERSPECTIVE. Often, it is necessary to mark the center of an object to draw it properly, to complement it, or to add new geometric shapes that represent it in perspective correctly. To find the perspective center or middle point of an object, we draw two diagonal lines from its corners. The perspective point is located where these two lines intersect. This approach does not change at all if the square is in perspective.

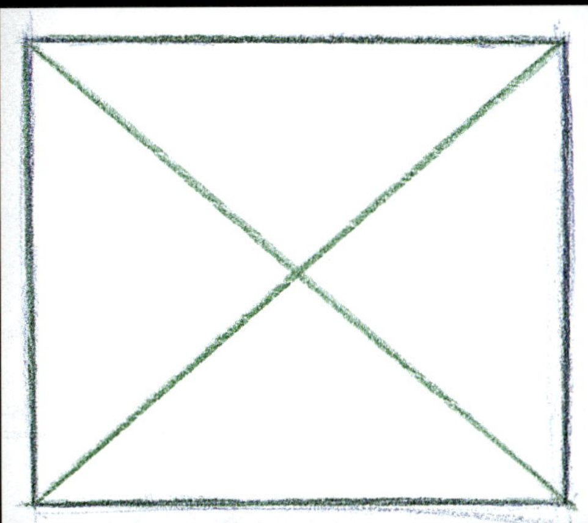

If we connect the corners of a rectangle with diagonals, the perspective center is at the point where they intersect.

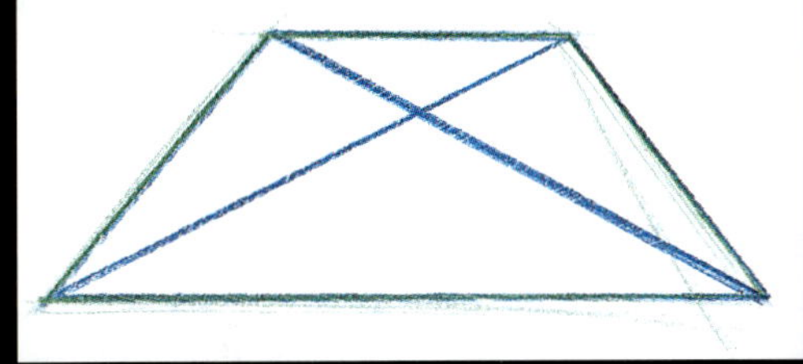

The same method is applied for a rectangle drawn in perspective

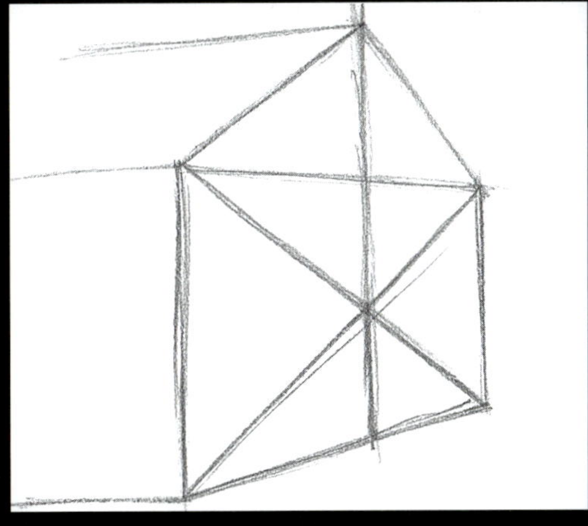

Being able to establish the perspective center is very useful for drawing the triangular shape of a roof in perspective.

From the perspective center, a perpendicular line is drawn to help us draw an arch in perspective.

DRAWING A RUG. We determine the center of perspective of the rug, which is a rectangle in perspective. This is very useful for drawing the designs on it, provided that the rug is subdivided symmetrically.

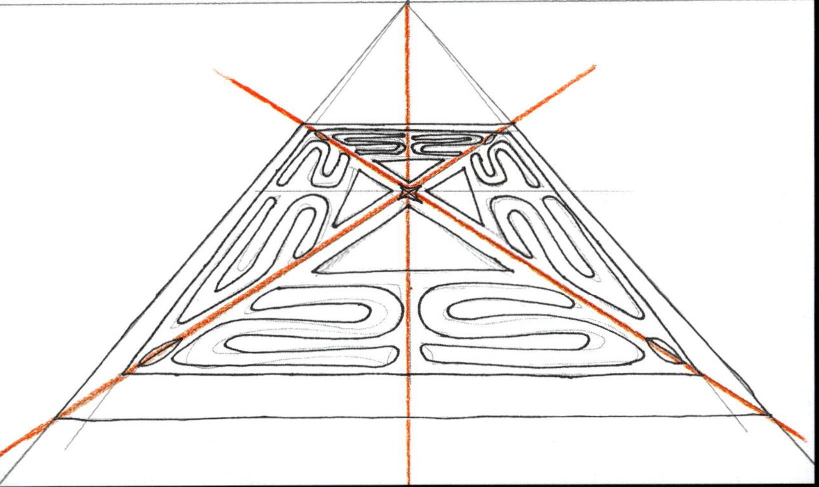

We approach the rug as if it were a rectangle falling away from us. The diagonal axes determine the center and contribute to the proper distribution of the decorative designs.

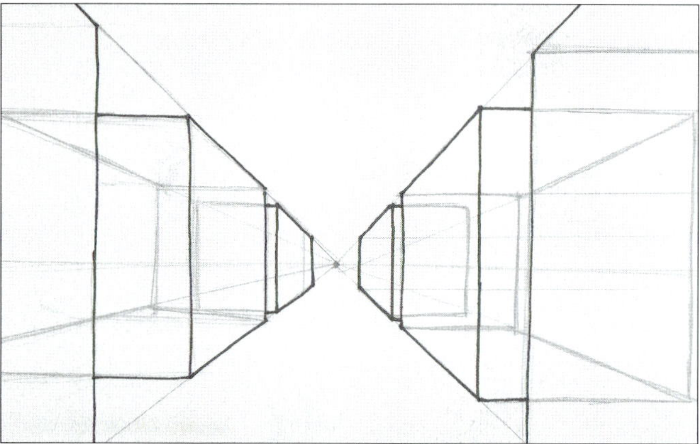

To better understand the structure of the drawing, it is a good idea to reduce the forms to simple transparent cubes that are projected from a single central vanishing point.

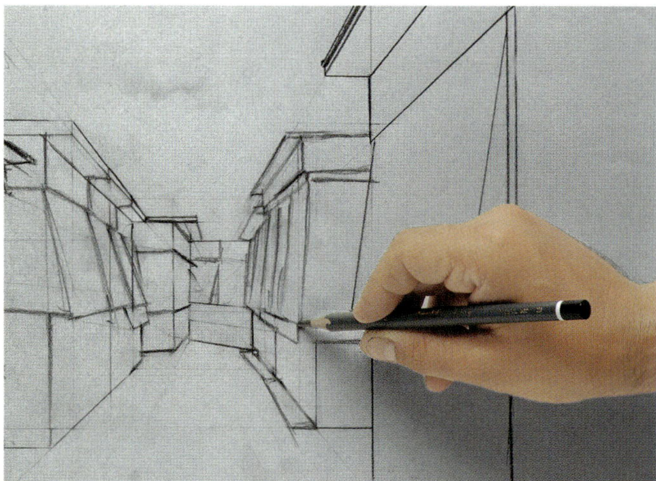

Then, the artist has conformed the initial cubes to their final form as market stands, focusing on the canopies and the slopes of the shutters.

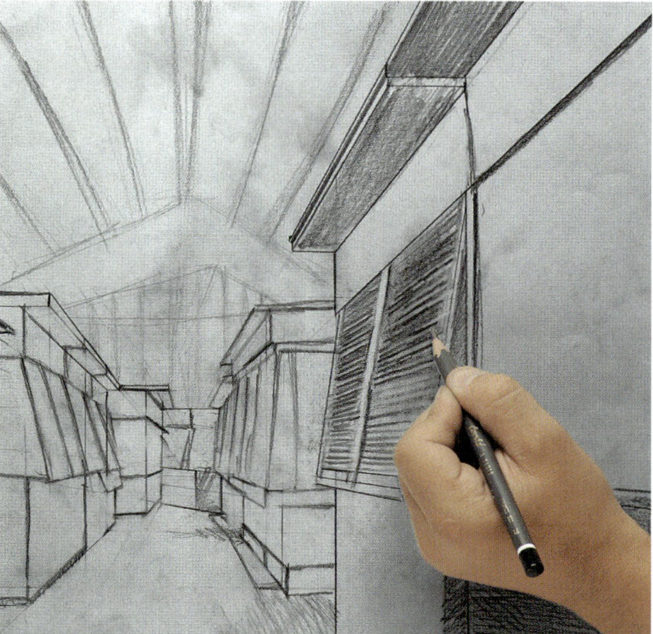

The many lines of the shutters have been drawn freehand, taking their slope into consideration. The lines are not parallel; they are arranged in a fan shape.

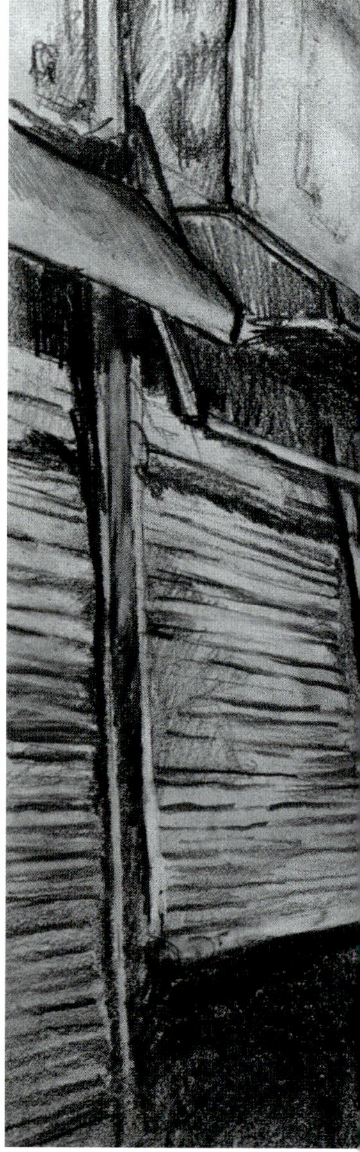

This drawing can intimidate a beginner who is not very proficient at perspective. However, behind those façades full of lines and shadows lies a simple structure that is easy to draw.

INTERIOR OF A MARKET. Drawing interiors requires the use of some of the rules of perspective. With them we will create the correct distribution of the space and, in this particular case, the correct representation of each market stand. We recommend using a single vanishing point and approaching the forms as if they were transparent cubes.

In the drawing the artist has not depicted the letters over the canopies; they are very blurry. If they were to be included, a good way to do it is by writing them inside rectangles drawn in perspective.

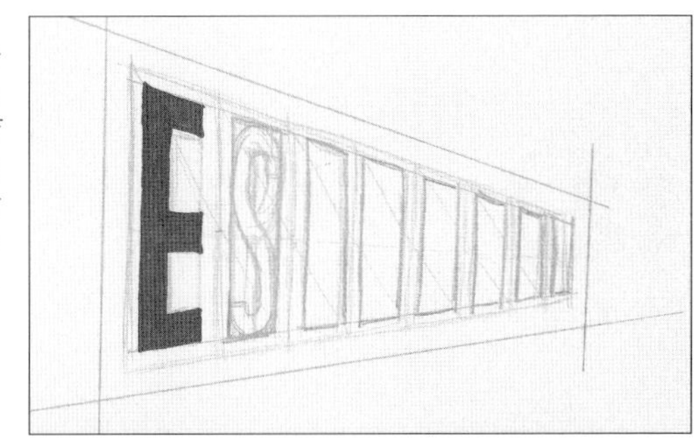

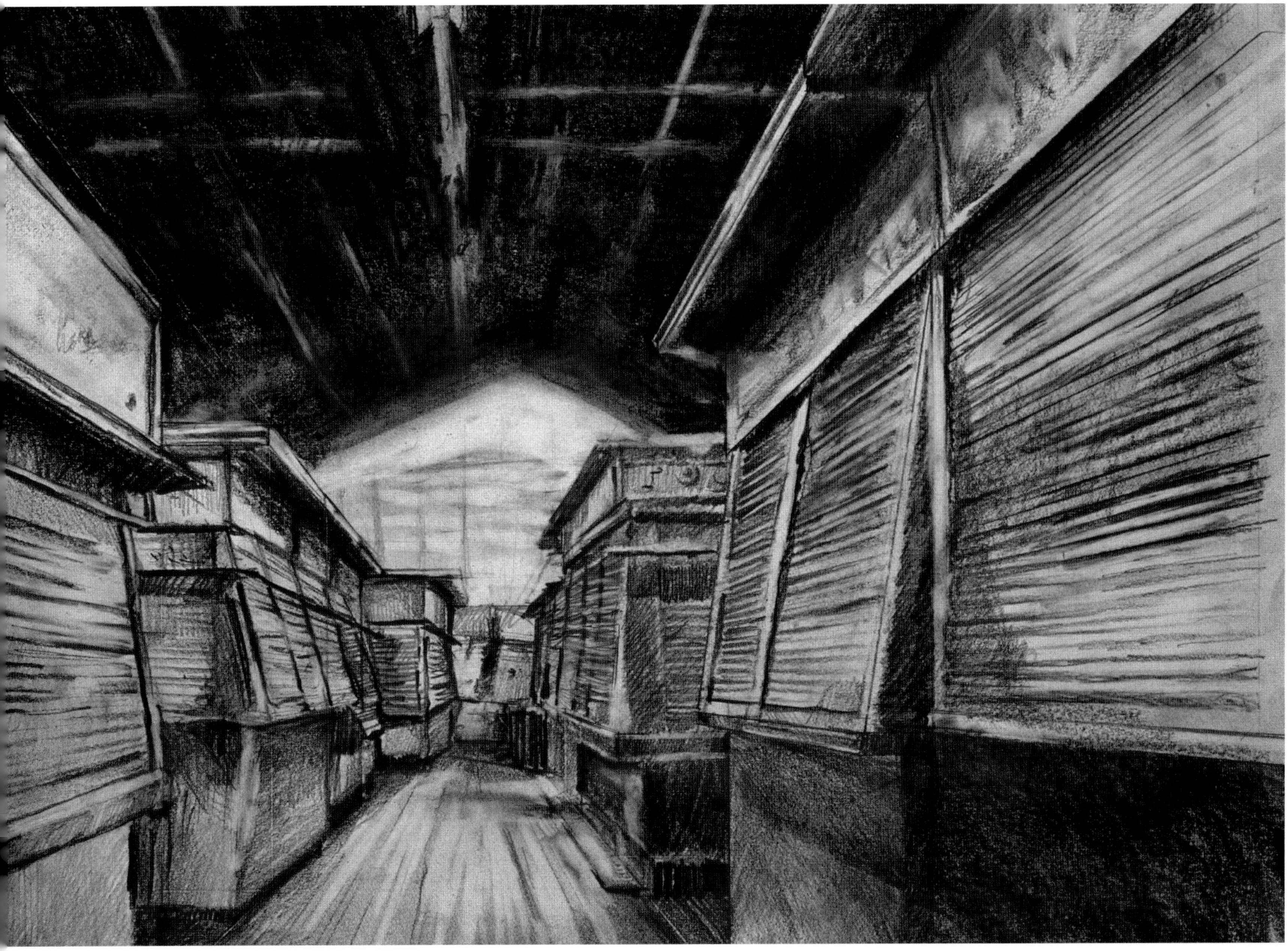

ANGULAR PERSPECTIVE. To draw a small space, like the interior of a vehicle or a small room, the best approach is to use angular perspective. This method, however, produces a strongly distorted effect, which needs to be examined. Drawing by Gabriel Martín.

12.1

THE INTERIOR OF A VEHICLE. The idea of angular perspective is to include in the drawing's plane the space that is not within the viewer's field of vision; to take it all into consideration we would have to move the head sideways and up and down. This is a problem because the elements outside this visual field begin to get distorted and rounded.

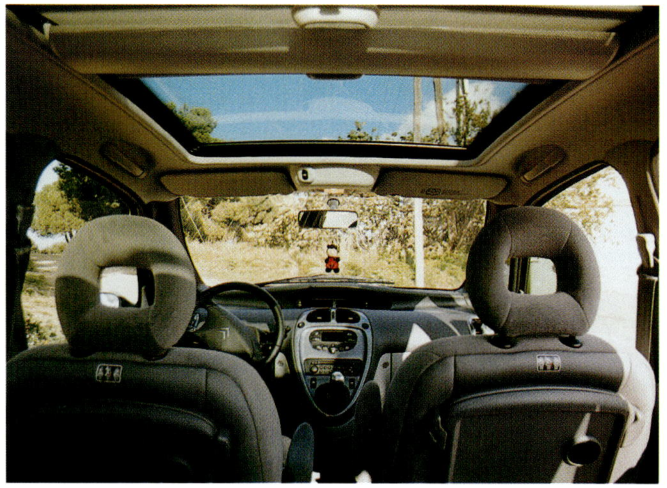

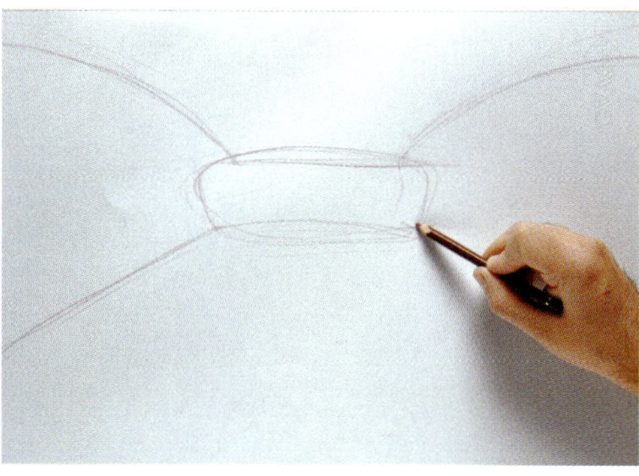

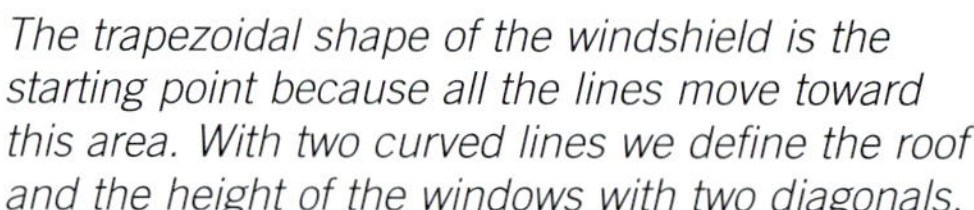

The trapezoidal shape of the windshield is the starting point because all the lines move toward this area. With two curved lines we define the roof and the height of the windows with two diagonals.

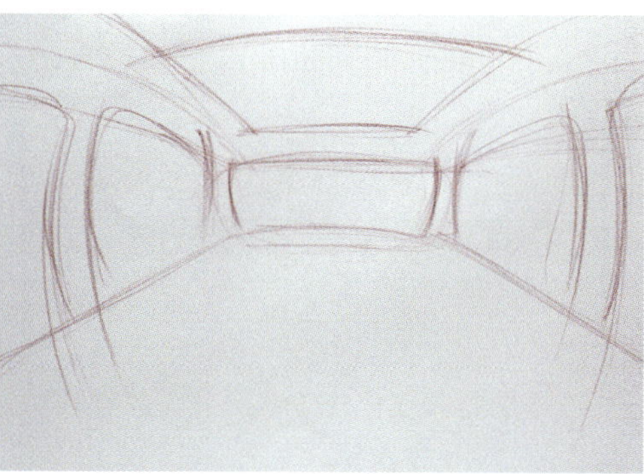

The perpendicular lines for the windows show a more pronounced curvature as they move farther away from the windshield. The same is true for the crossbar in the sunroof.

Angular perspective drawing distorts the lines as they move away from the hypothetical central vanishing point. The closer they get to the viewer, the more curved they look.

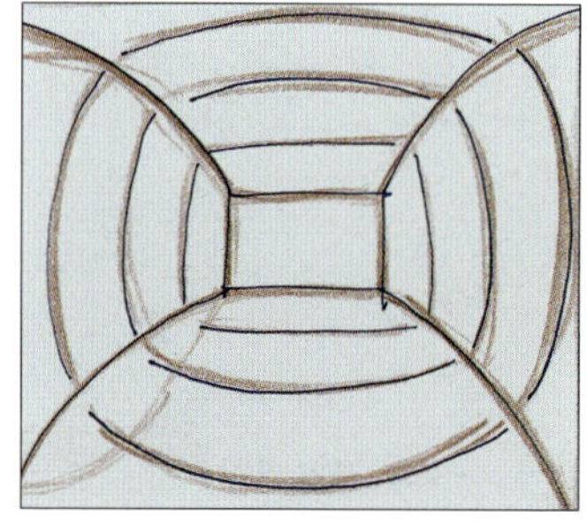

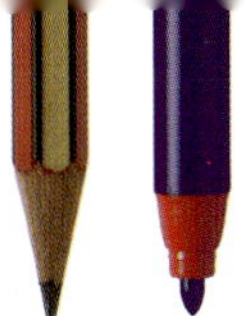

12.2

A SPACE DISTORTED BY CURVES. This way of approaching a space tends to distort the sizes, to make all the straight lines, forms, and distances rounded to indicate depth. Therefore, distortion is the main resource for representing depth within the plane.

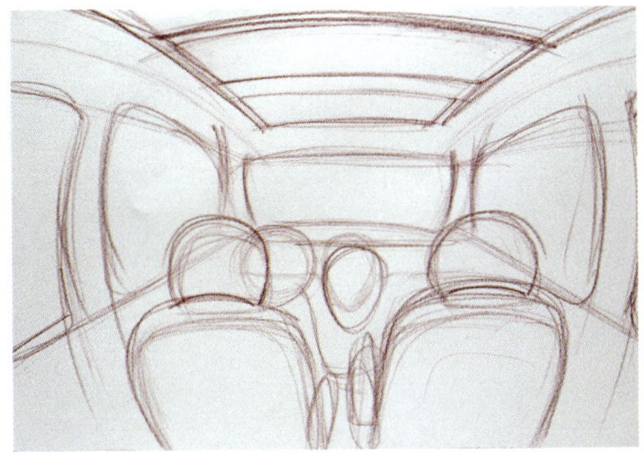

From this point on, the work is very simple. This does not prevent us from drawing the steering wheel, the seats, and the dashboard by combining several circles.

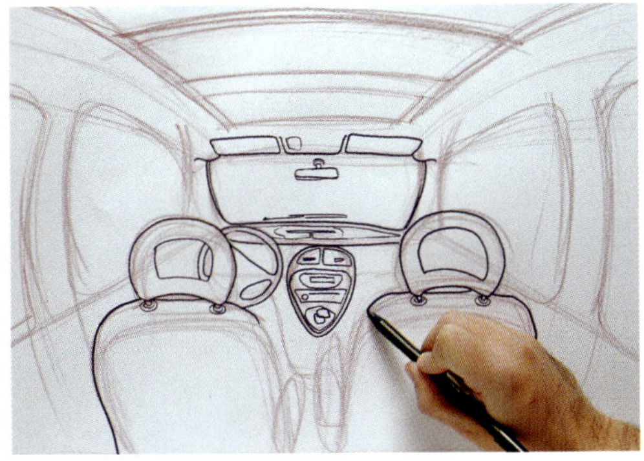

Each element of the vehicle's interior is drawn in more detail over the preliminary lines. We use a marker to make the lines more visible.

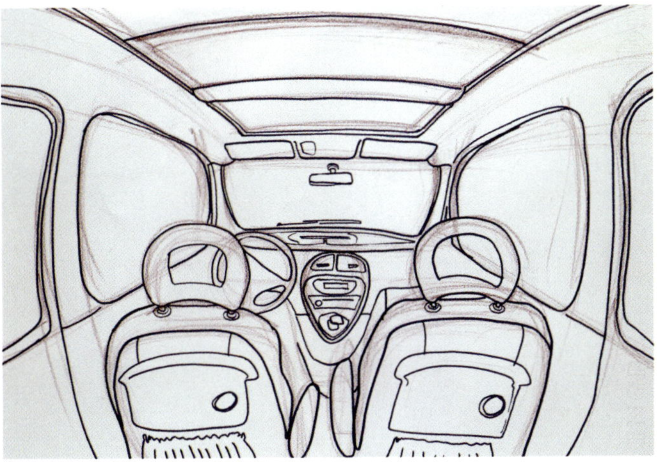

The line made with the marker is very simple, drawn with a steady hand in a single stroke. Using the marker, we refine the components of the car, even adding some details. The work is done quickly to avoid making it look like a photograph.

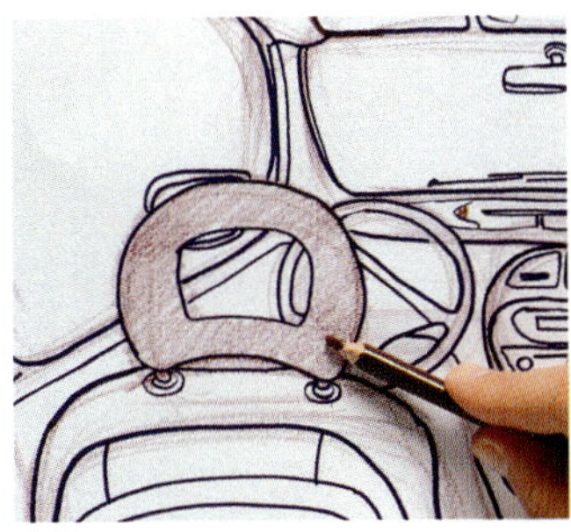

Once the line drawing is finished, we begin shading to emphasize the volume of the seats and to enhance the feeling of depth with gradations.

LEARNING BY DOING

FORCED AND EXAGGERATED PERSPECTIVE. Distortion is the key factor in the perception of depth, because it decreases the simplicity and increases the tension present in the visual field. This encourages us to manipulate, force, and conform the vanishing lines of a drawing to our creative requirements. Drawing by Esther Olivé de Puig.

13.1

PULLING THE OBJECT. Distortion always gives the impression that the object has been elongated as if it had been pulled. This is exactly what we are going to do—to project several foundation lines as if they had been pulled or forced out of shape to create the effect of depth.

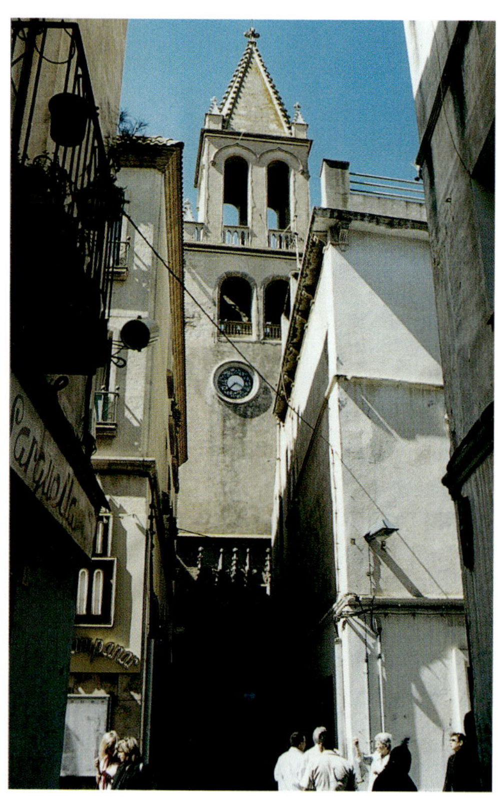

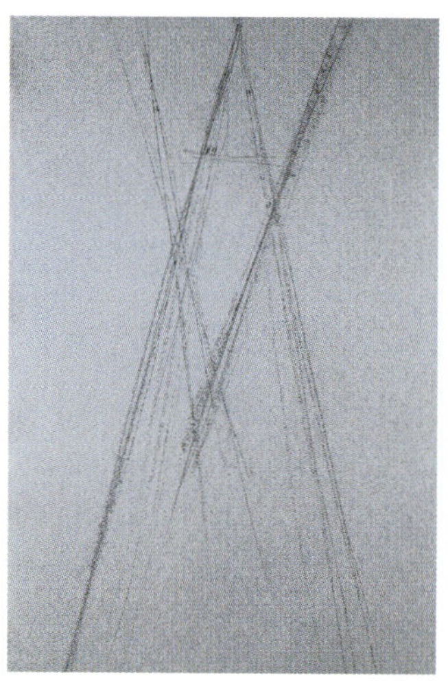

We begin the exercise by establishing two vanishing points: one in the center, from which we will project two diagonals; and the other on the upper part of the paper, which will help us draw the bell tower in perspective.

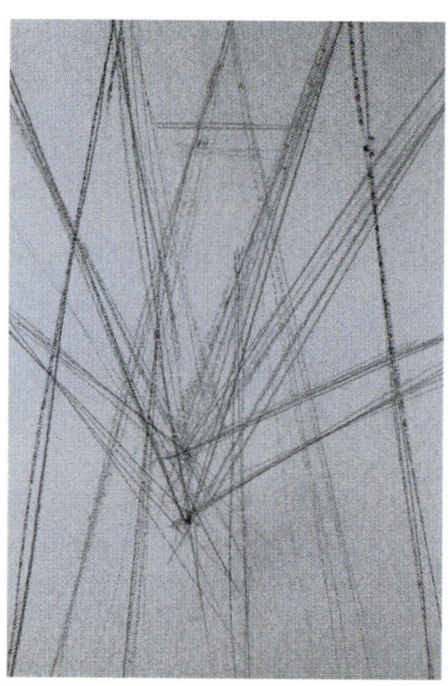

Many lines extend out of the central vanishing point to define the tops of the façades and the angle of the windows and balconies. We mark a second vanishing point over this one to help us distort and force depth.

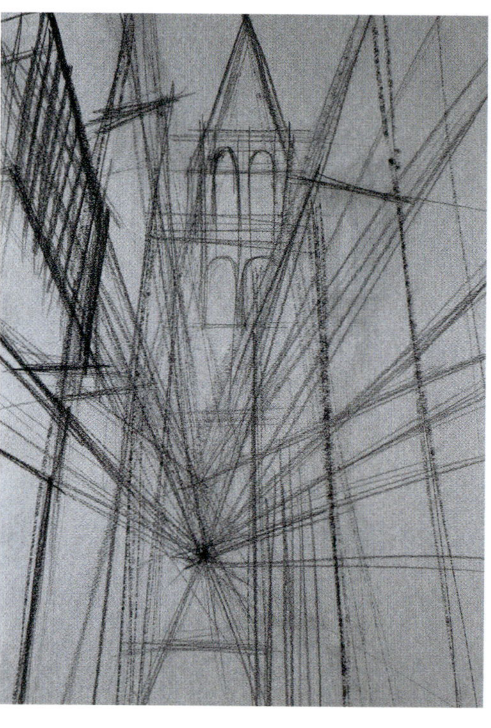

Instead of converging all the vanishing lines into a single central vanishing point, we make them converge at two. This approach is not highly recommended from a technical standpoint, but it offers good expressive results.

If we drag the stick of charcoal lengthwise across the surface of the paper, it will be easier to control the steadiness of the lines.

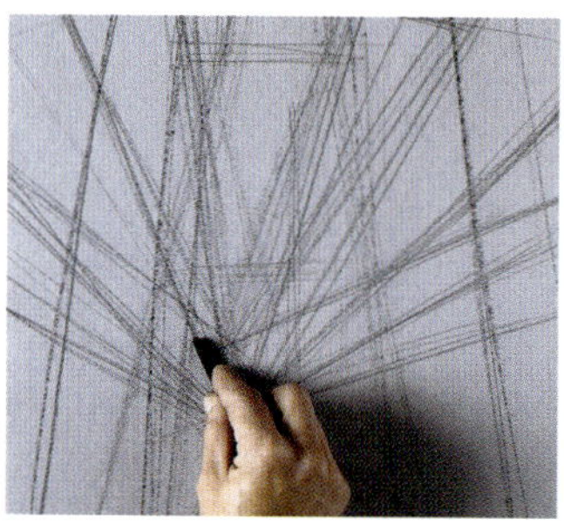

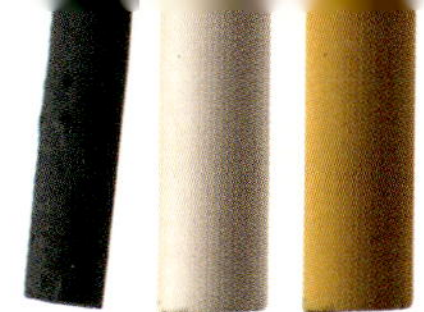

13.2

DEFINITION AND COLOR. From the perspective lines, we draw the architecture of the bell tower and the definite lines for the façades. Since we are working with a medium-tone paper, we add a few elements with sticks of pastel to enhance the volume.

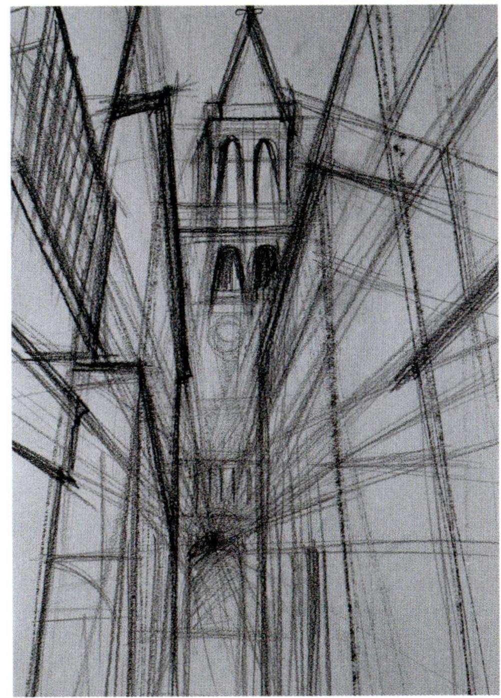

With the tip of the stick of charcoal we draw the structure for the bell tower and we reinforce, with darker lines, the profile of the façades. Notice that the lines for the façades are not perpendicular; instead, they open in a fan shape.

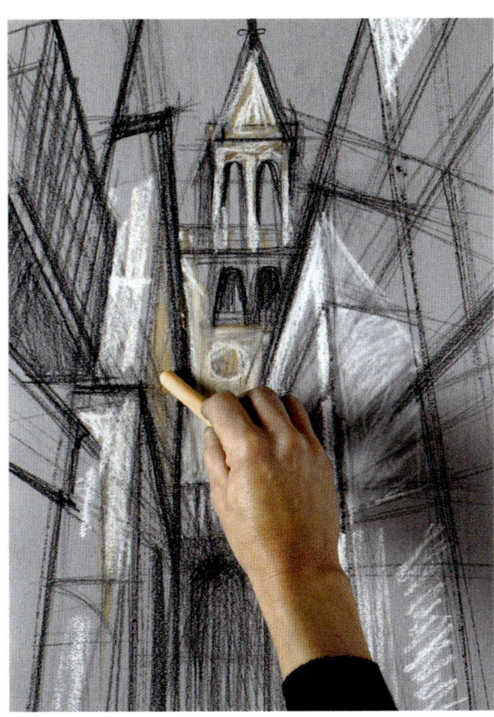

Once the line drawing is finished, we highlight the effect of volume by applying color over the illuminated areas with sticks of white and yellow ocher pastel. The shaded areas are left gray, like the color of the paper.

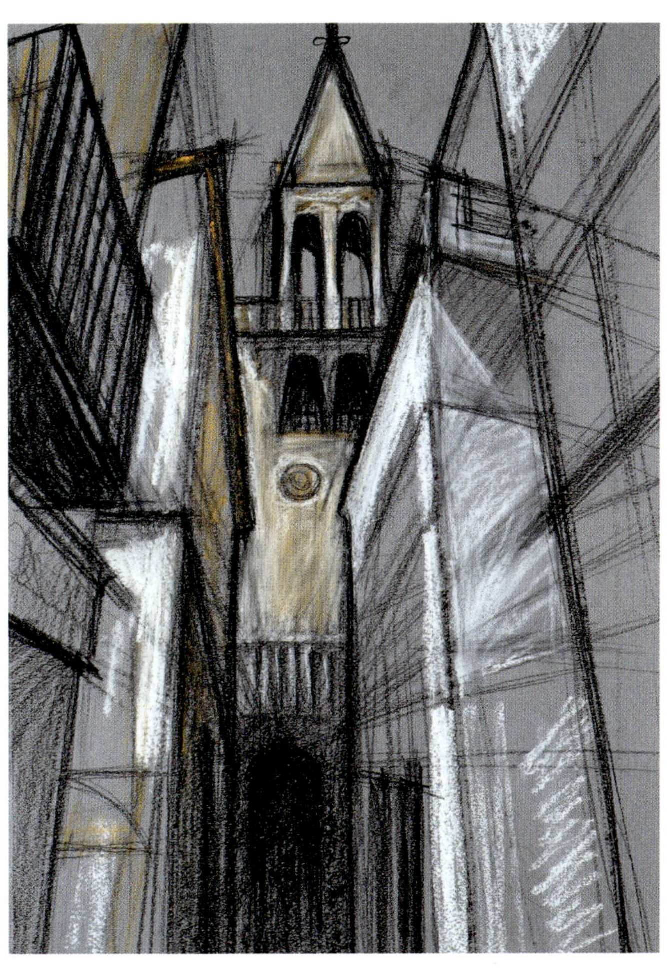

The forced angle of the vanishing lines exaggerates the distance. The planes enhance the three-dimensionality, exhibiting greater depth than normal and acquiring volume, thanks to the effect of the color.

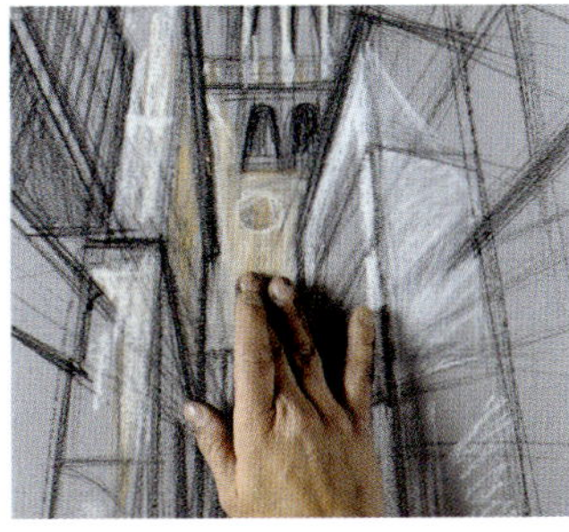

The dark lines should be combined with subtle blended effects that, depending on the dimensions of the paper we use, can be done with the hand.

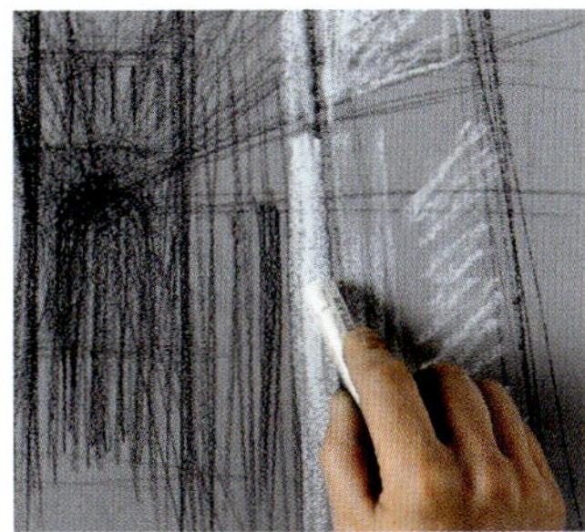

The white highlights over a medium-tone background, in this case on gray paper, show the contrasts and further define the volume of the façades.

LEARNING BY DOING

AN OCTAGONAL FOUNTAIN. The construction method that we use in this exercise will help us draw prisms, such as pentagons, hexagons, octagons, and other similar shapes, in perspective. These figures are usually present in urban settings like kiosks, canopies, lampposts, and fountains. Drawing by Carlant.

14.1

DRAWING WITH ELLIPSES. The objects that present an octagonal structure can be inscribed into a circle, so it is possible to use the method for drawing ellipses to depict the shape.

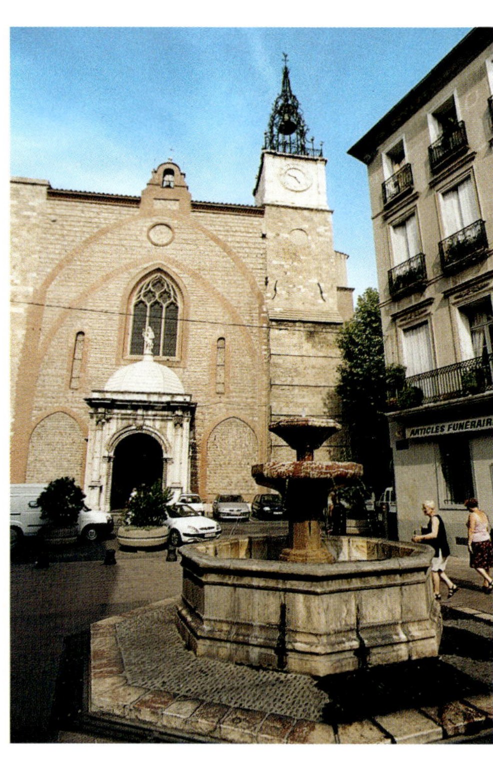

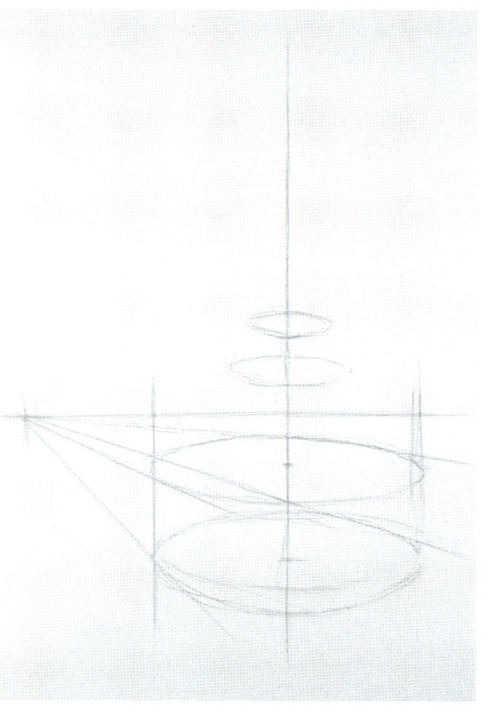

Beginning with some vanishing lines and a vertical axis, we try to define the shape of the fountain by projecting four ellipses. To do this, first we study the section devoted to the projection of ellipses.

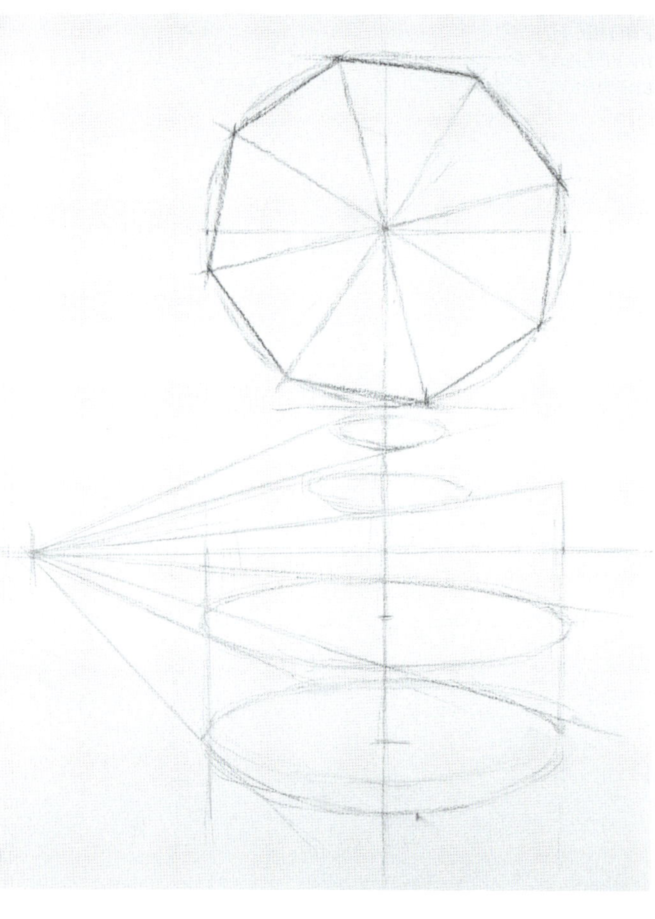

The main problem consists of turning these ellipses into an octagon. To do this, and using the vertical axis, we draw a circle over the ellipses. With a ruler, we divide it into eight sections.

We must avoid drawing any radius of the circle over the perpendicular axis, in order to prevent having too many lines on the same point. To solve the problem we just need to rotate the circle slightly.

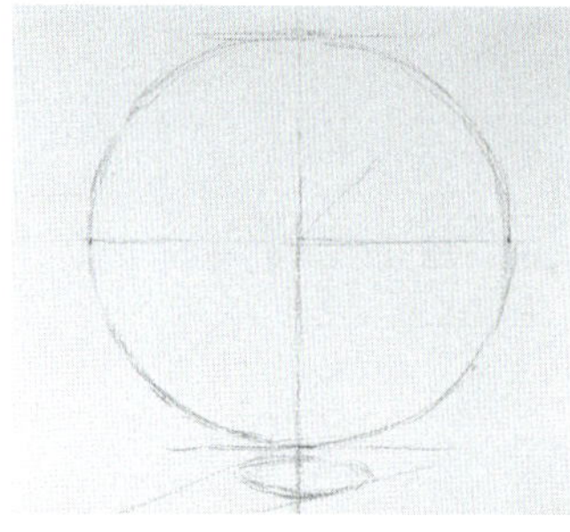

14.2

PROJECTING THE OCTAGON. From the top circle, divided into eight parts, we project the lines that will make it possible to transform the ellipses in octagonal forms in perspective. This simple method assures absolute accuracy.

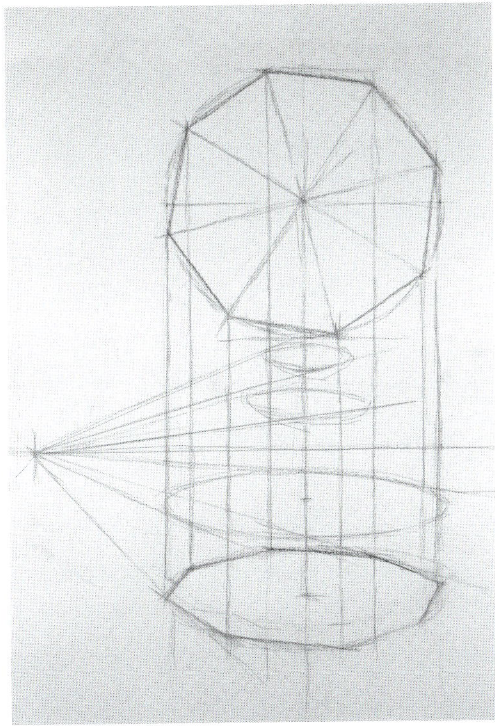

The top circle becomes an octagon. From each of the octagon's corners, we project several perpendicular lines to the lower ellipses. Each one of these intersecting points becomes a corner of the octagon in perspective.

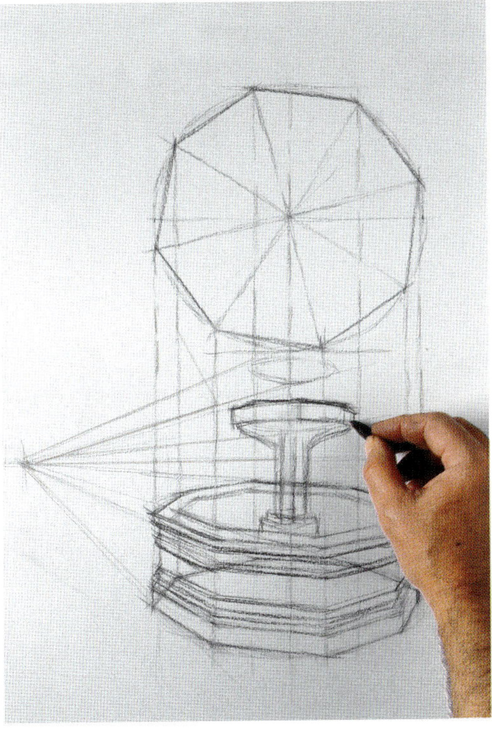

After each ellipse has been converted into an octagon, and using the perpendicular lines as a guide, we erect the body of the fountain, paying attention to the slope of the moldings on each of its sides.

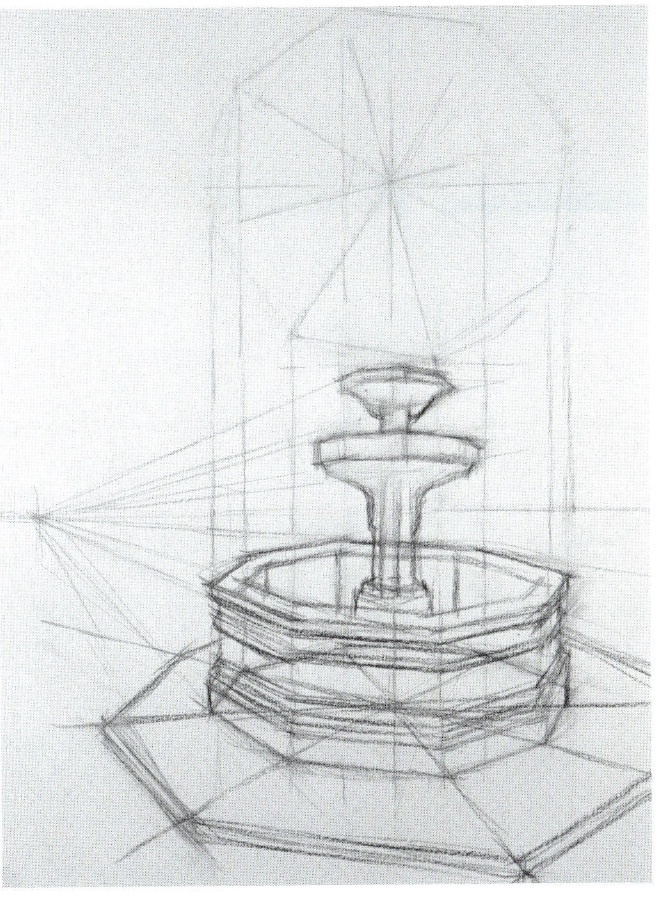

The upper figure is erased since it no longer has any use. From the center of the lower ellipse we draw several lines that pass through each ellipse. We use this projection to represent the step, also octagonal, which surrounds the fountain.

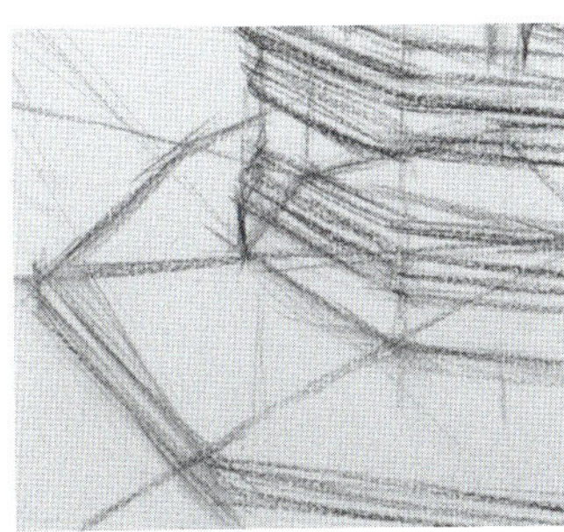

To avoid problems with the slope of the moldings, we must remember that they should always be parallel to the lines that form each side of the octagon.

14.3

DRAWING THE BACKGROUND. Having finished the most complicated part of the exercise, we need to complete the fountain with new details and to draw the architectural background that surrounds it. This must be shown as a simple background, without too many details or contrasts.

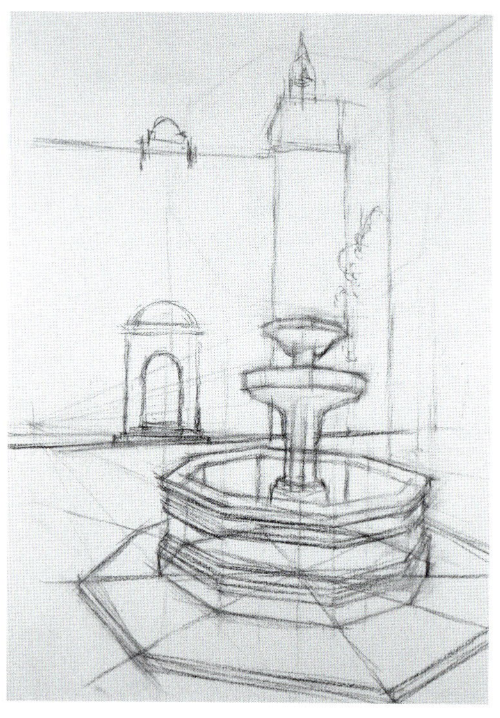

The focus of the drawing now turns to the water jet and to the architectural features of the building in the background. Even though until now we have worked with a medium charcoal stick, we change to a thinner one.

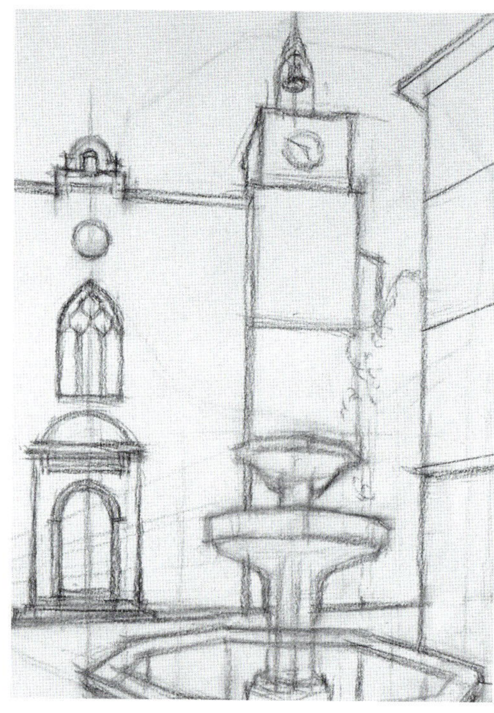

We project vanishing lines to mark the windows on the right side of the façade. Drawing the architectural elements of the church is easy, a simple exercise of symmetry.

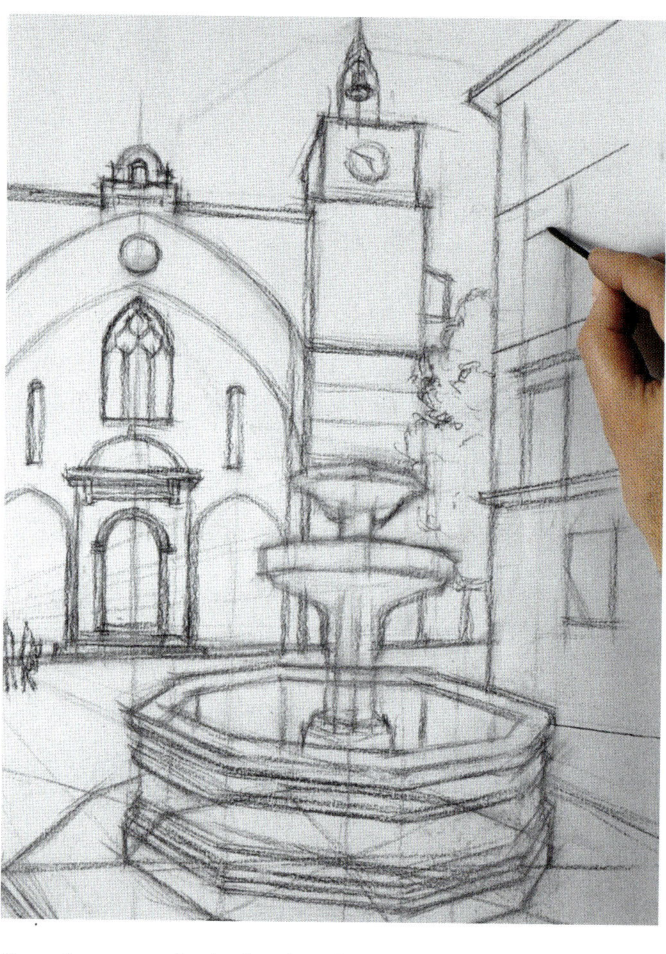

From the perpendicular line that divides the façade of the church into two parts, we draw the arches. We finish the bell tower by reinforcing some of the outlines. The windows on the façade that sit on the vanishing lines we laid out before are drawn one by one.

Right after the line drawing is finished, the fountain's main lines are reinforced with the medium charcoal stick. We use this also to apply light shading.

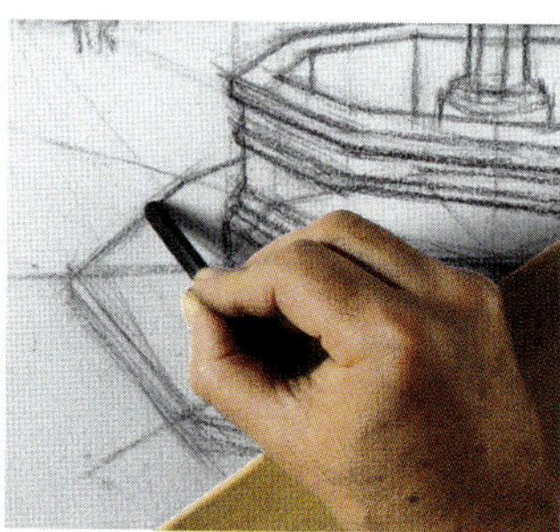

The shading applied with charcoal is very light. In this area, the blending stick, which blends and evens out the tones, has a more important role.

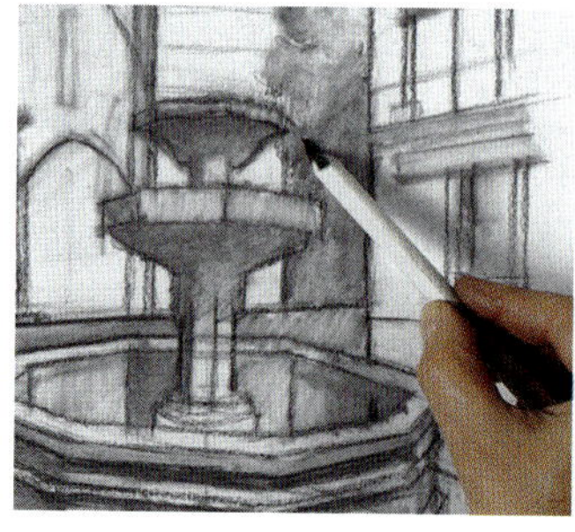

All the precision shown in the drawing of the fountain is lost in the background, which appears lightly drawn with few details. This is ideal to create contrast.

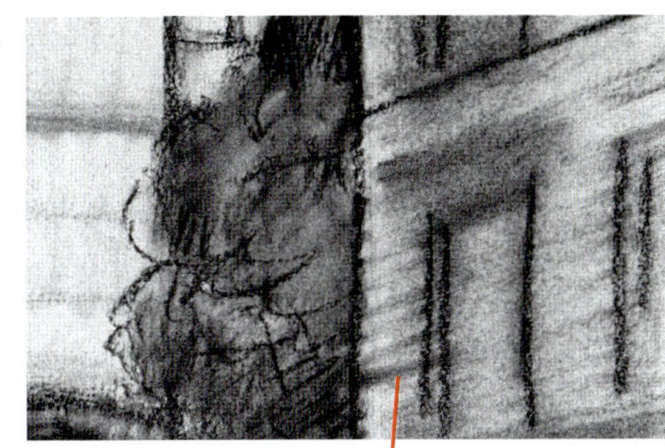

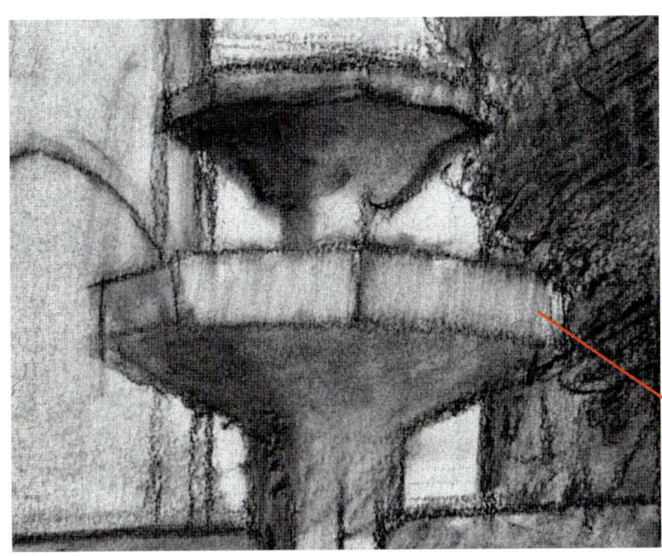

Even though the octagonal elements of the lower part of the fountain have been drawn very meticulously, the upper ones have been done by eye, to avoid prolonging the exercise.

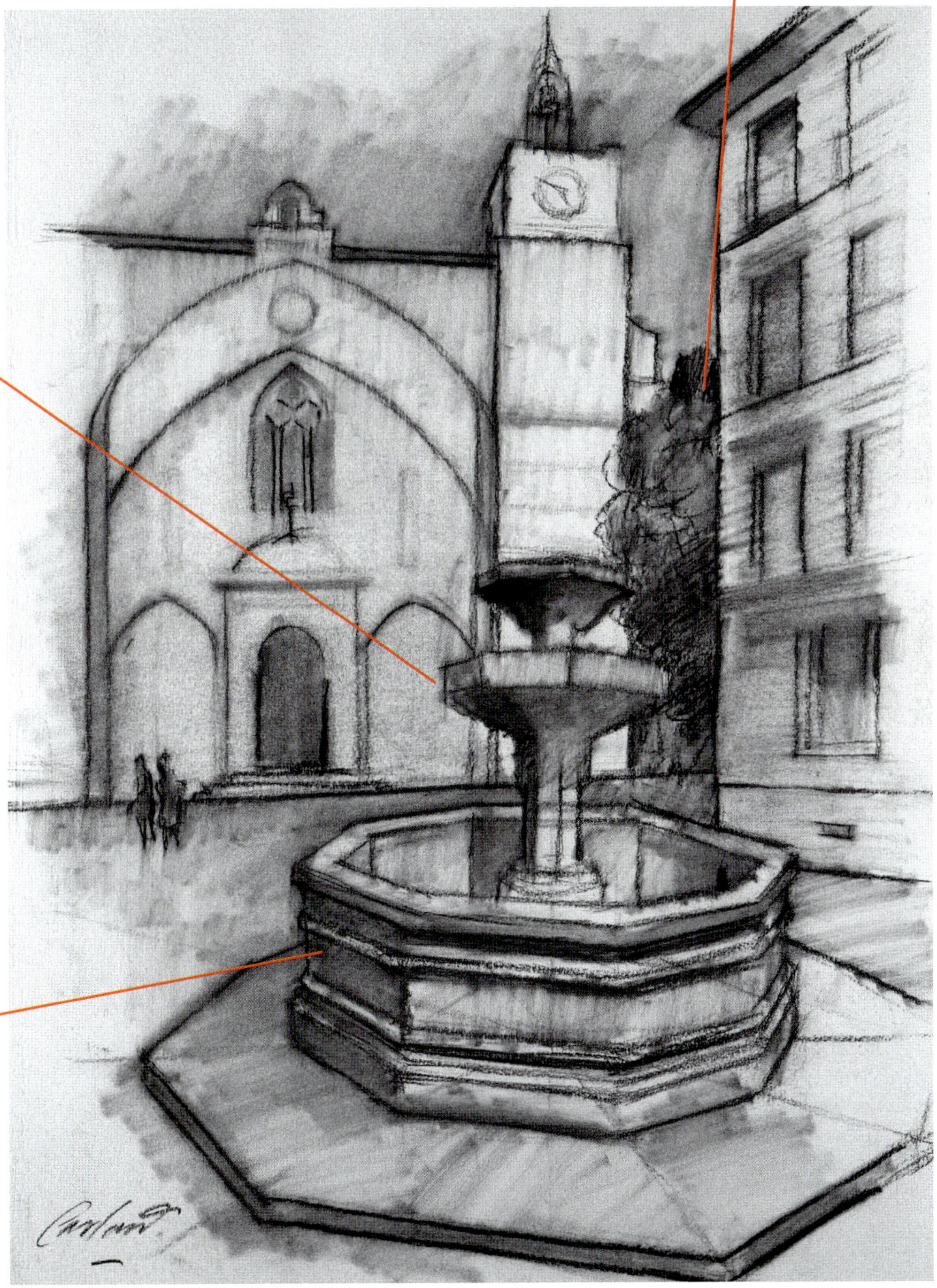

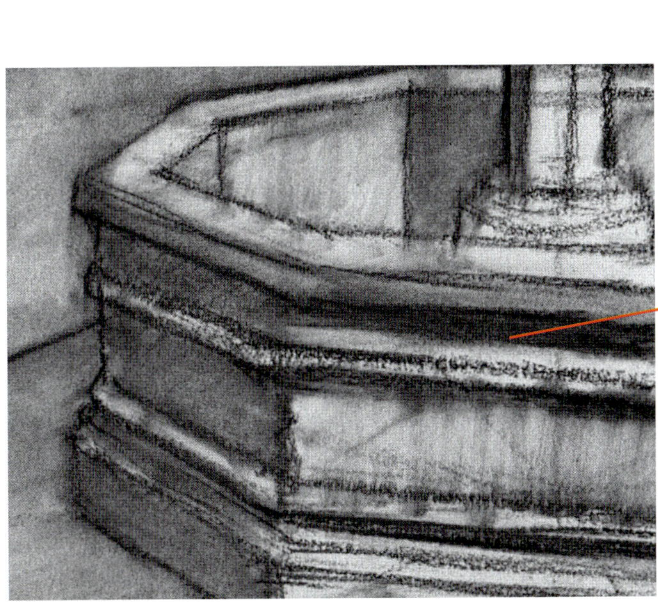

The octahedron, the octagonal form in volume, is done as if it were transparent. This will be very useful for drawing the interior parts of the fountain that are visible.

If you love technical drawings, you can leave this one as a line drawing. If the desired look is more elaborate, we recommend applying some shading and to continue working on the forms with a blending stick until the drawing looks like the one shown here.

PERSPECTIVE OF REFLECTIONS. Until now we have looked at perspectives of objects on land. However, the effect created by them on the water also deserves a brief examination. These reflections conform to a specific construction scheme. Drawings by Almudena Carreño.

15.

PROJECTING PERPENDICULARS. The reflection of a natural subject is created by drawing perpendiculars that extend from the object in the direction of the water's surface. It is important to understand this basic premise before attempting to draw reflections on water.

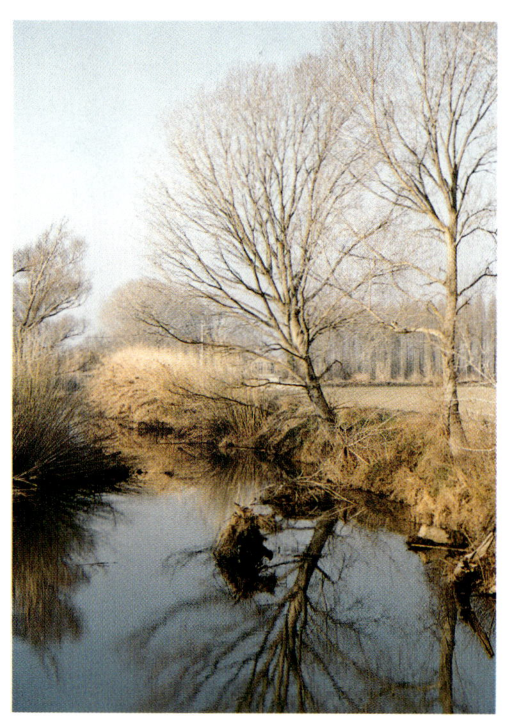

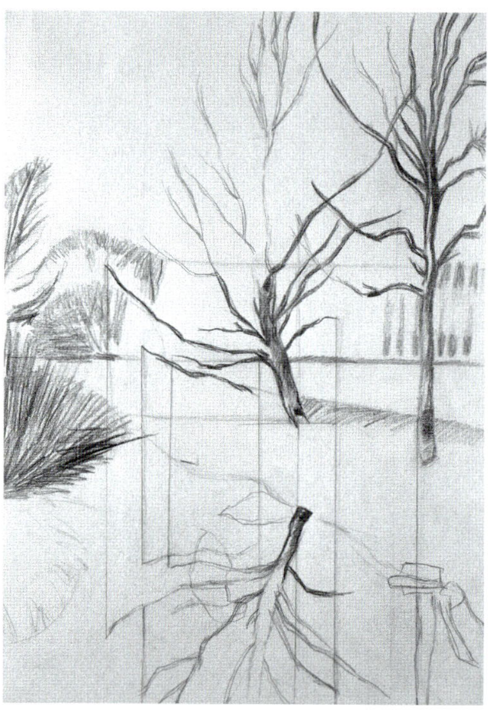

We draw a few trees next to the calm waters of a river. From the ends of the most outstanding branches and from the trunk, we draw several perpendicular lines that are projected over the surface of the water.

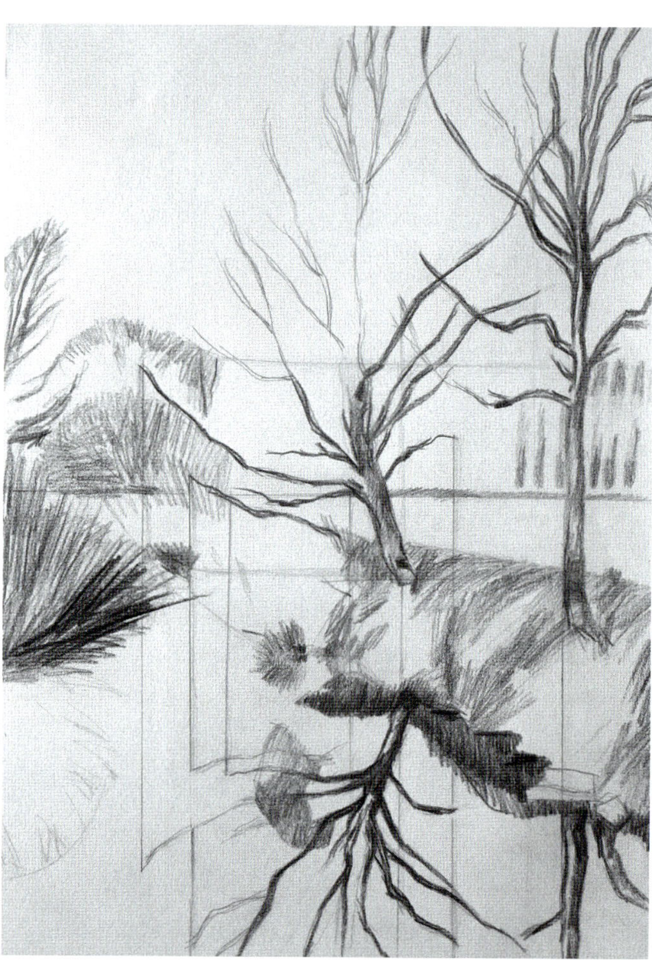

From these perpendicular lines we construct the reflection. When shading, it is important to keep in mind that the reflection is always a bit darker than the real object.

MATERIALS EXERCISE 15 AND 16: gray colored pencil, eraser, and plastic ruler

16.1

BUILDINGS AND CANALS. Now we will address the problem of reflections in perspective. The photograph includes a group of historic buildings that are reflected on the pristine waters of the canals. First, we deal with the architecture.

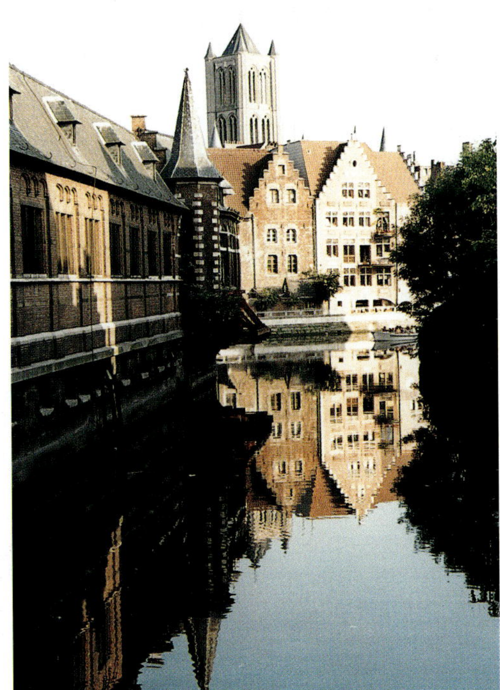

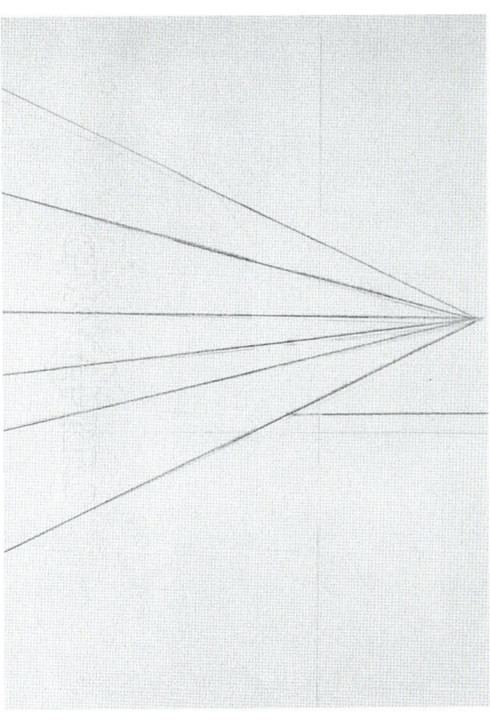

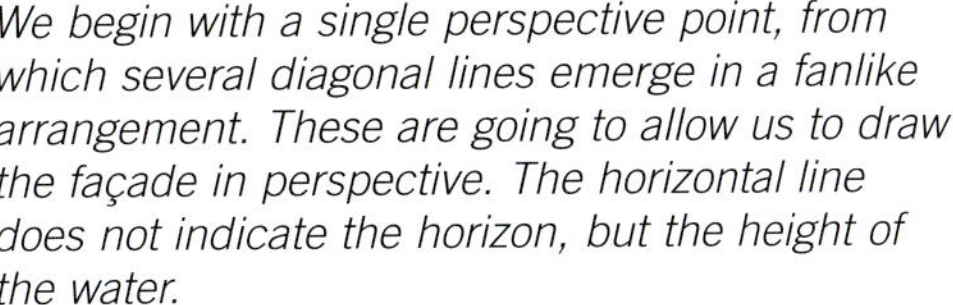

We begin with a single perspective point, from which several diagonal lines emerge in a fanlike arrangement. These are going to allow us to draw the façade in perspective. The horizontal line does not indicate the horizon, but the height of the water.

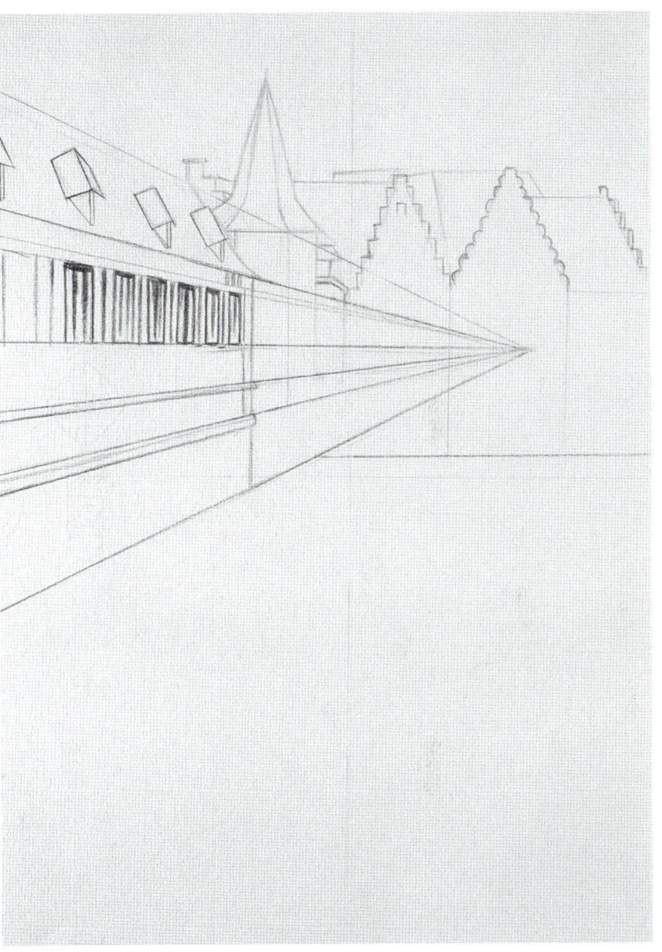

The vanishing lines establish the top of the roof, the window alignment, and the water level. The façades in the background are shown parallel to the plane of the painting; for this reason they look flat, without perspective effects.

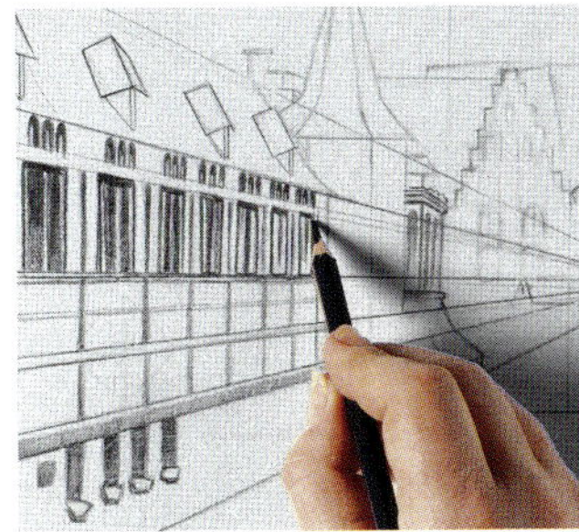

We must be meticulous when drawing the structural elements of the façade; any error could show up duplicated on the water.

16.2

DRAWING THE REFLECTION. Now we are ready to project the mirror image of the buildings on the water of the canal. We draw perpendicular lines that act as points of reference for the measurements and new perspective lines that allow us to draw the vanishing lines for the reflection.

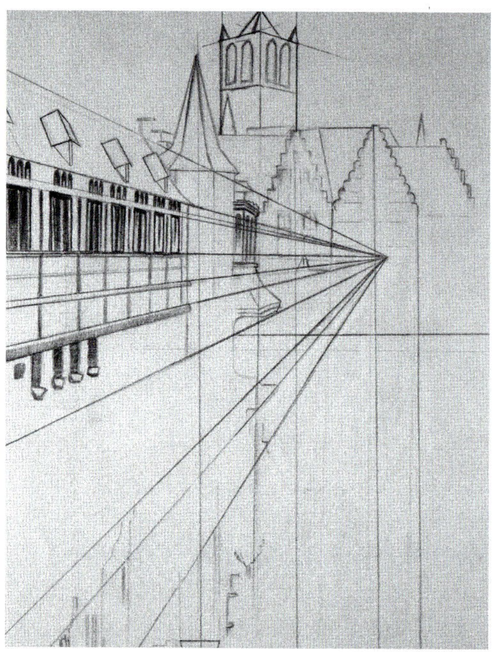

We select a few key points from the buildings: corners, edges, towers or similar features, and from these we project perpendicular lines on the water.

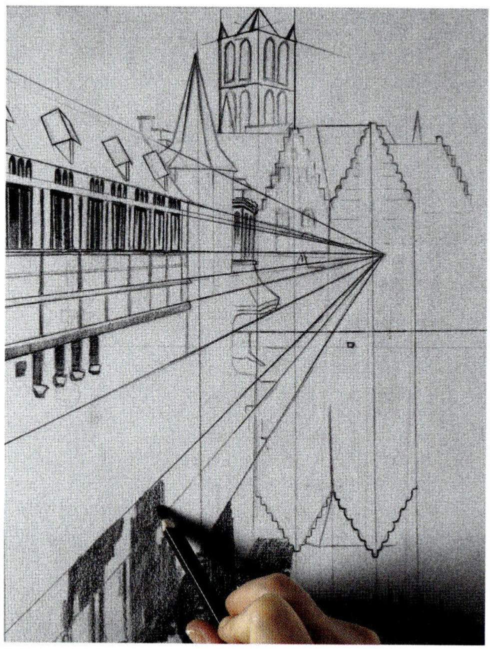

From the vanishing points we project new lines that establish the angle of the façade's reflection. There should be enough perpendicular and diagonal lines in perspective to construct the inverted image of the building.

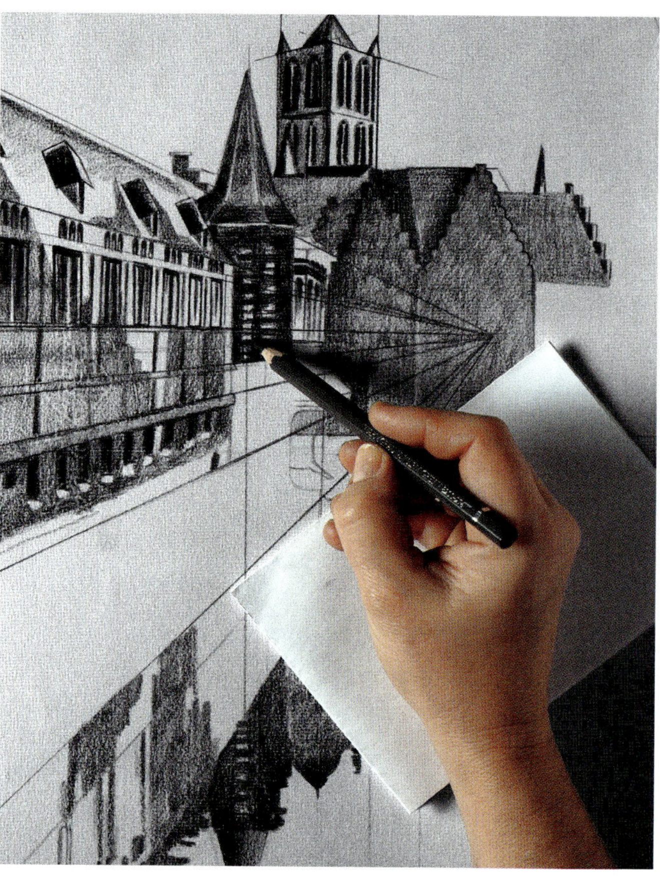

Keep in mind these two important aspects when shading: any small detail will fade in the reflection, and the reflected image will be somewhat somber and darker looking than the actual subject.

The architectural features of the buildings in the foreground show greater detail and contrast, while the façades in the distance look monochromatic and lack architectural detail.

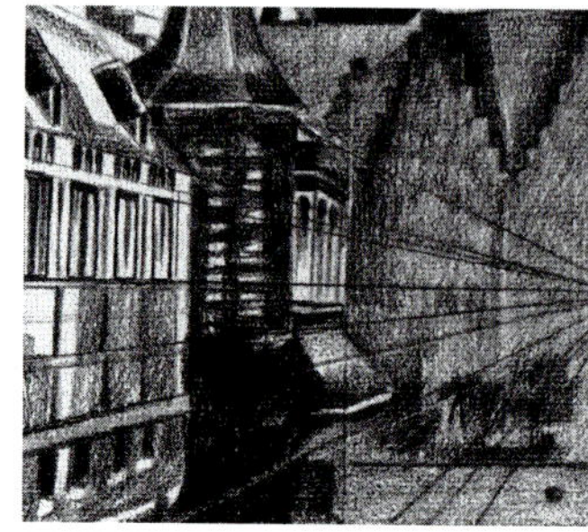

We cannot use the existing vanishing point to draw the church tower that is shown at an angle. We must establish two new vanishing points located at either side of this piece.

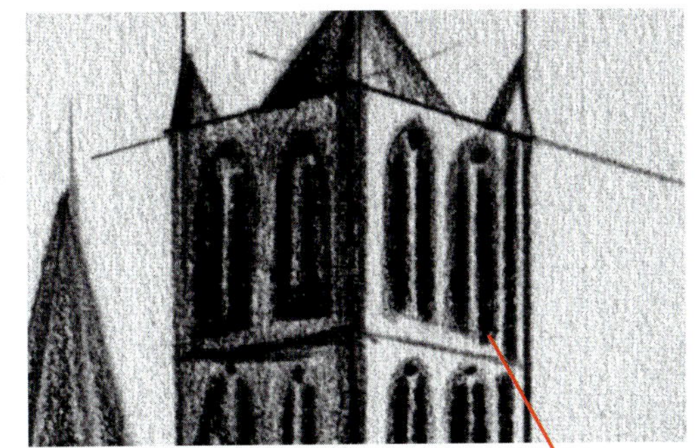

A color image reflected on the water is always less vibrant than the original. Here, the artist has taken artistic license in a few instances by drawing the windows only in the reflection, lightening their overall tone, and reducing the reflection of the architectural details.

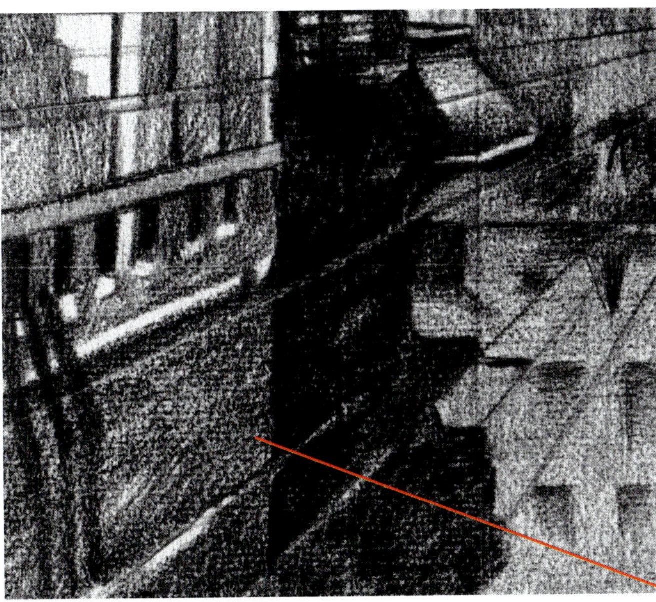

The tonal effects that appear on the façade are repeated on the reflected image, with the exception of irrelevant details, which are blurred out or diffused.

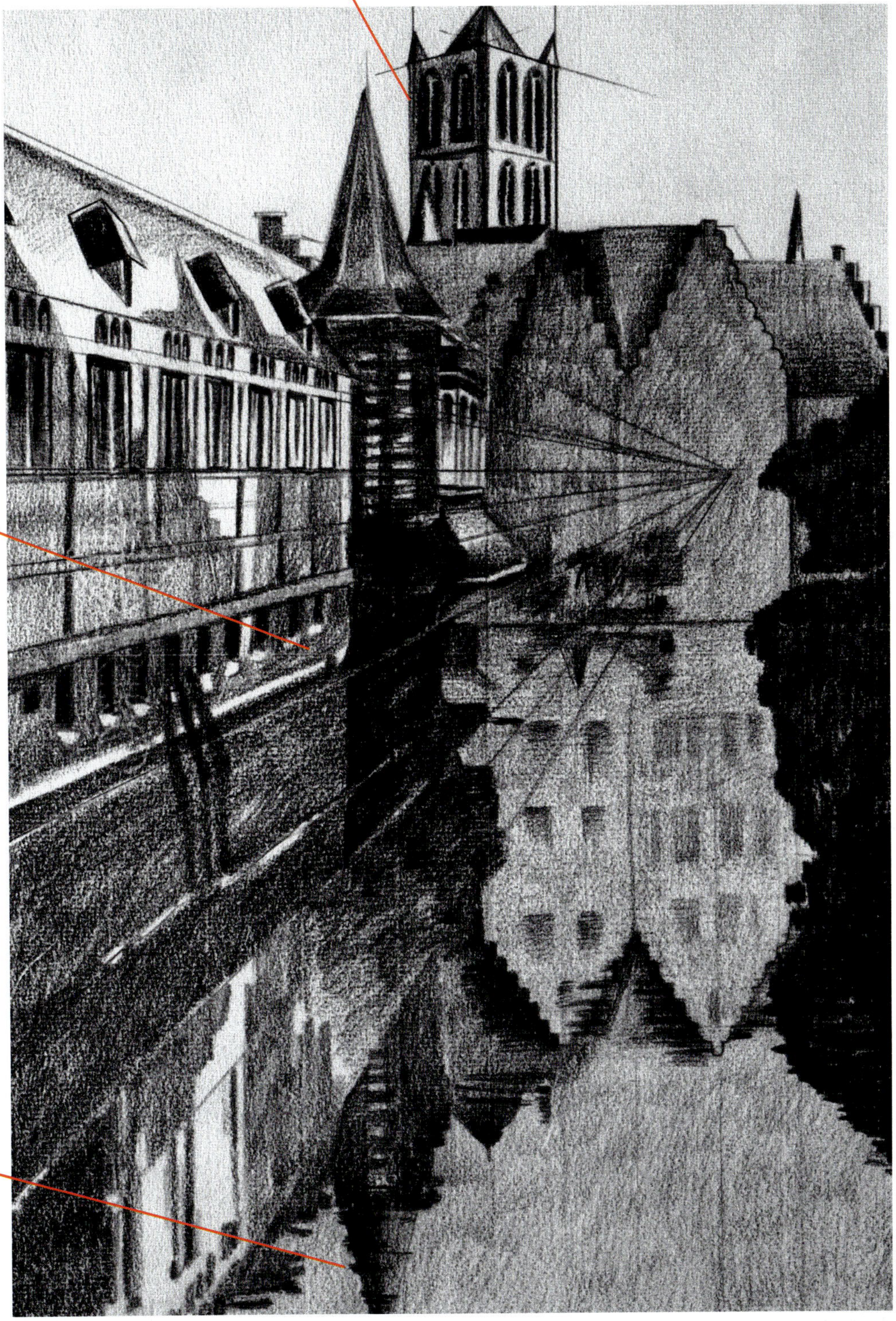

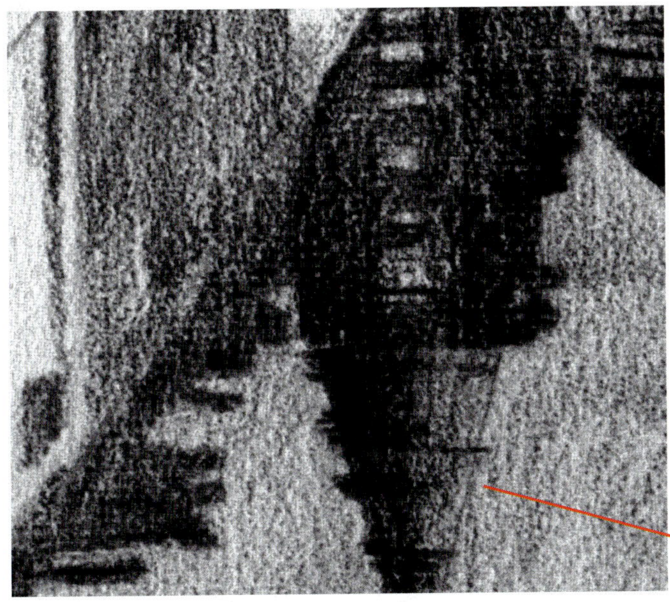

As the reflection goes farther away from the original source, from the edge of the canal, the contour lines look uneven due to the effect of the ripples in the water.

DIFFERENT TIMES OF DAY. The size and dimension of the shadows cast by the sunlight depend on the position of the sun in relation to the artist, the angle of the painting, the time of day, and the shapes of the illuminated objects. With respect to the shadows cast by the sunlight, it is important to consider that these are in constant motion.

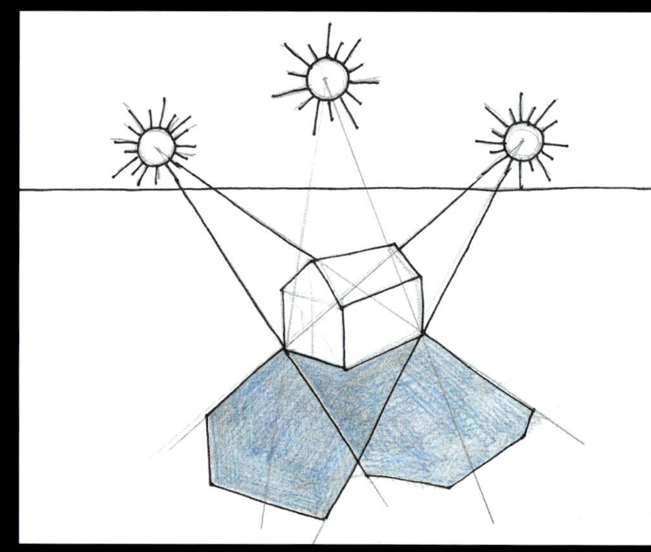

The sun, as it rotates, modifies the direction and shape of the shadows.

PARALLEL AND OBLIQUE SHADOWS. The shadows cast by the sunlight that illuminates an object represented in parallel perspective are also parallel. Their length depends on the angle of their vanishing lines.
In a figure projected at an oblique perspective, the sun rays are parallel to each other and determine the length and shape of the shadow by intersecting with the vanishing lines of the ground.

The shadows cast on an object that is represented in parallel perspective are also parallel, and their length depends on the height of the light source.

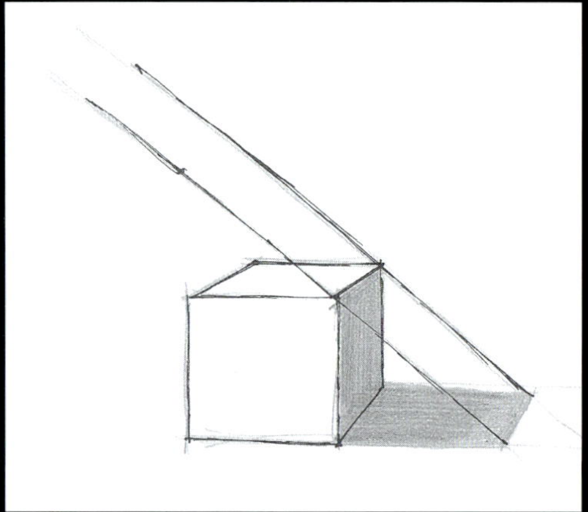

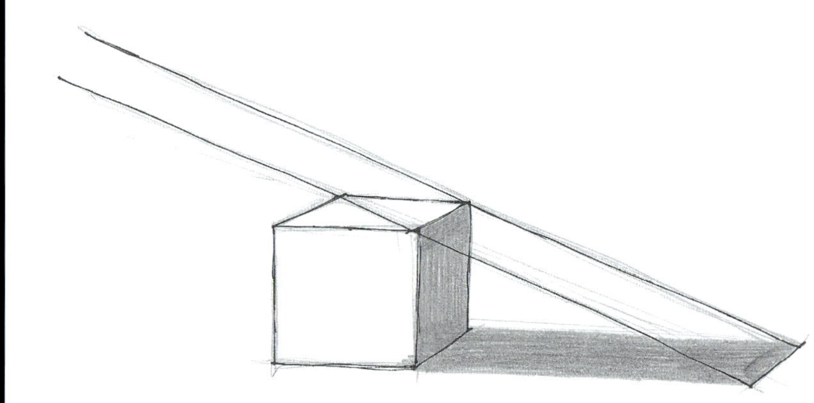

In oblique perspective, the shadows are the result of the sun rays intersecting with the vanishing lines.

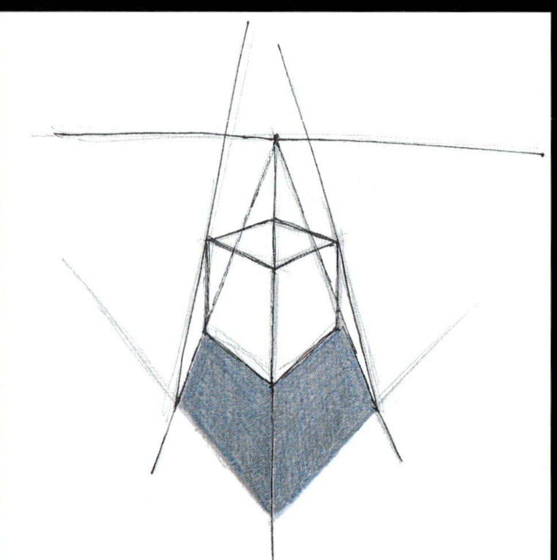

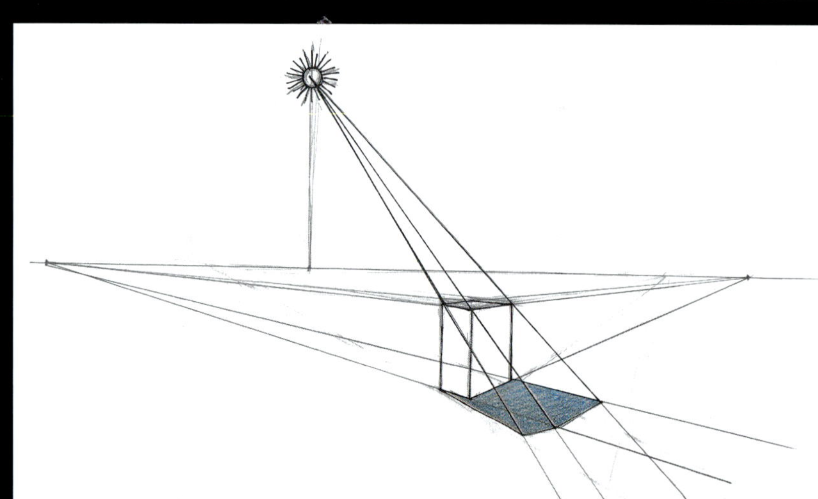

SHADOWS IN PERSPECTIVE. In a drawing, it is often impossible to ignore the shadows. The forms created by these are as interesting and as important to the composition as the objects themselves. These should be drawn carefully because they are also subject to their own rules of perspective.

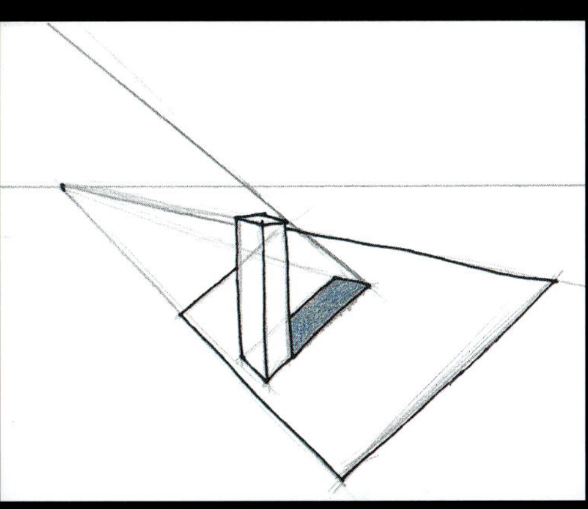

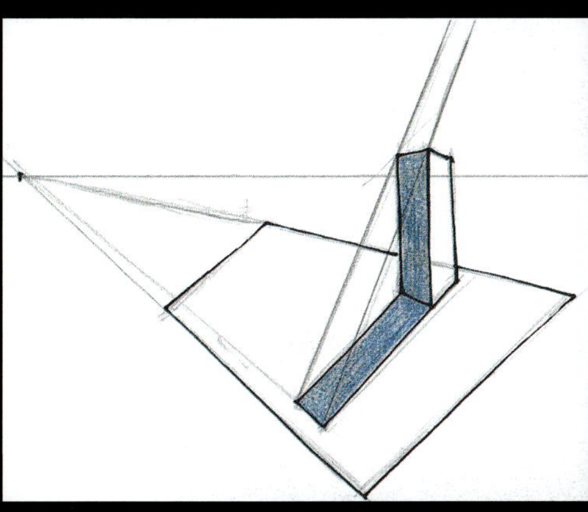

SHADOWS IN ASCENDING PLANES. The shadows cast over an ascending plane are shortened, while those that are cast on a descending plane are lengthened. To calculate the length of a slope's shadow (an angled roof), we extend the sides of the chimney until they touch the horizontal plane.

When the angle plane is ascending, the shadow shortens; the opposite occurs when the shadow is at the descending side.

SHADOWS OVER VOLUMETRIC BODIES. The lines and the extension of the shadows are determined by the intersection of the sun rays with the vanishing points, but their definite form depends on the surface over which they are projected.

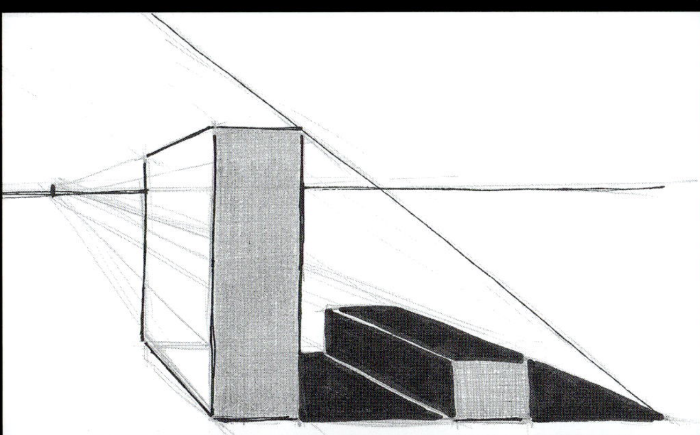

A shadow cast over a three-dimensional object ends up adapting itself to the volume of the form.

ARTIFICIAL LIGHT. The shadows cast by artificial light extend from a point located immediately below the light. These shadows are well defined near the light source, as well as in its main direction, but they are fainter the farther away they get.

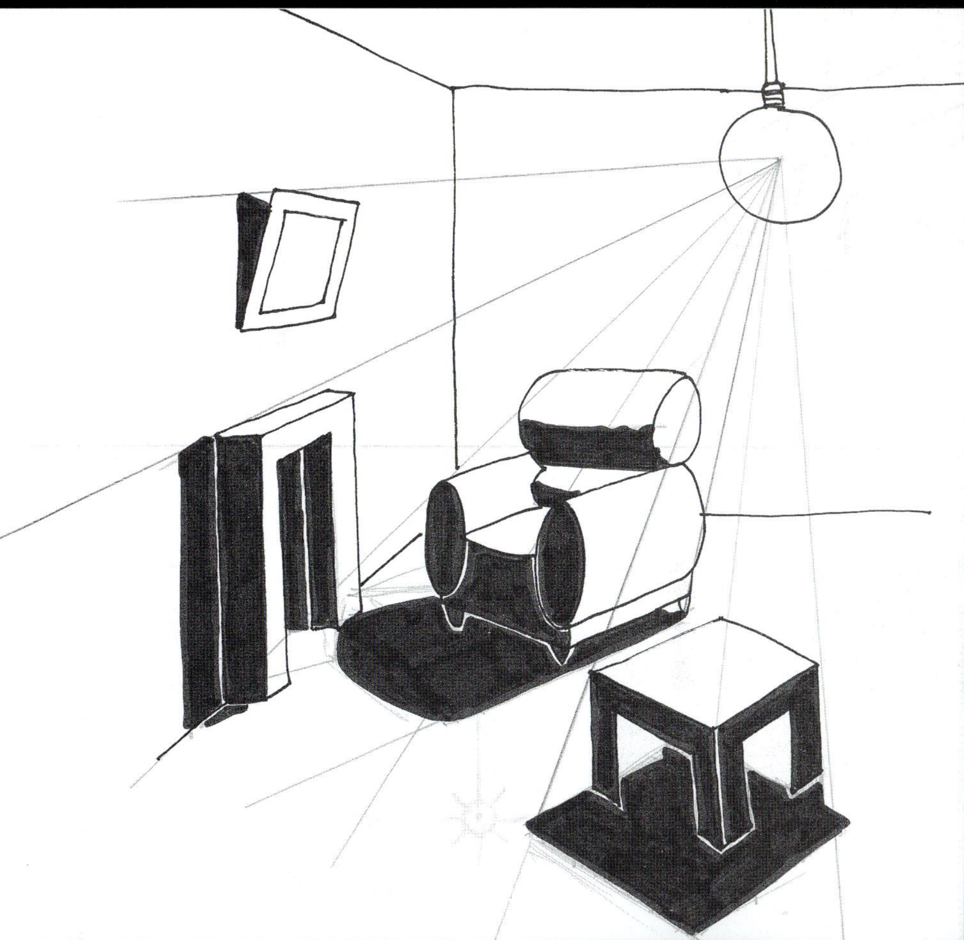

When the lamp inside a room is located close to the ceiling, the light beams extend in a radial fashion. The light beams cast shadows in every direction.

Depth without Lines

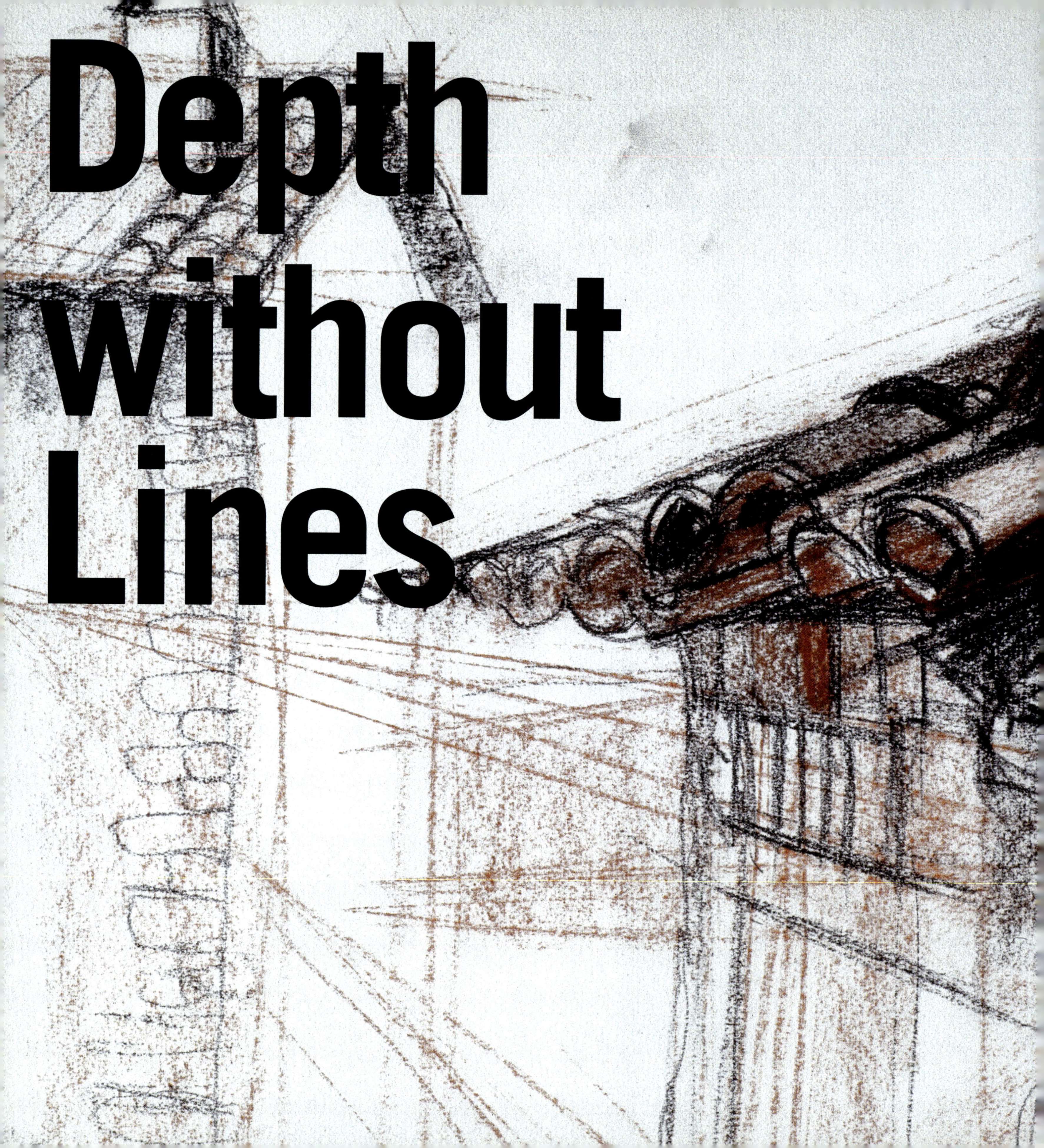

In landscapes, architectural elements are less important; therefore, linear perspective does not work. There is another type of perspective in which distance is conveyed through the use of color and gradation, which play a crucial role in the perception of distance. Therefore, in atmospheric perspective, the foreground is clearer and has more contrast, and the colors are more saturated. The middle planes have less color saturation and forms are less defined, while the ones farthest away lose contrast completely, and the color becomes gray. This approach is less analytical and rigid and gives the drawing a more expressive and artistic finish.

DEPTH EFFECTS WITH COLOR. In open spaces tonal values look very different when we compare the foreground with the background. The color of the closest elements always shows greater contrast within a scale of values than do the views in the distance, which appear less vibrant, with less tonal intensity. Drawing by Gabriel Martín.

17.1

SKETCHING THE LANDSCAPE. Before we begin shading, it is important to block in the main elements of the landscape with lines, paying special attention to the foreground and to the different planes that define depth.

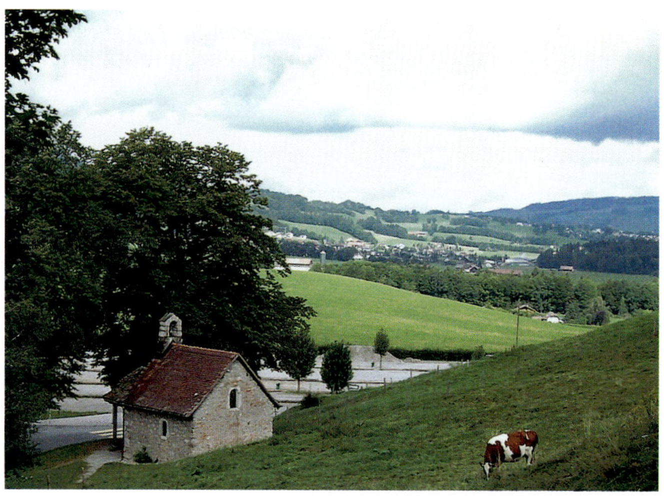

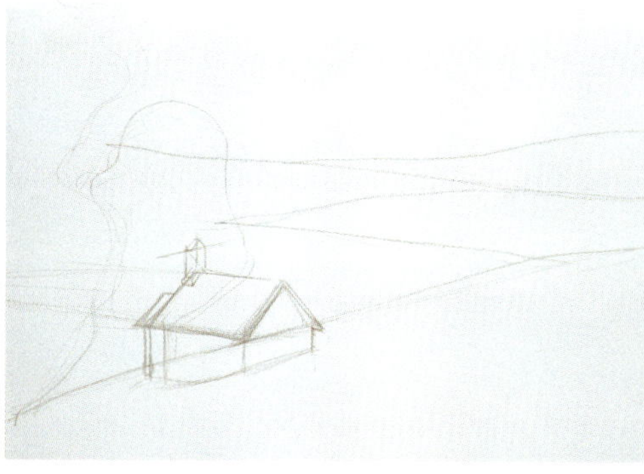

We use rounded lines to define each plane of the landscape. These mimic the superimposing fields, forests, and distant hills. Over this sketch we draw the chapel freehand.

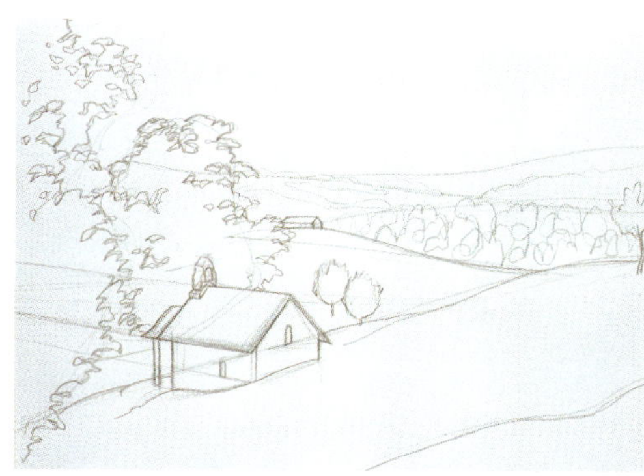

Over the lines that define each area we draw the contours of the most important rock masses. Then, we go over it again with a brown pencil, as we did with the chapel.

The building should be drawn in perspective with a single vanishing point. We can think of it as a cube to which the roof is added later.

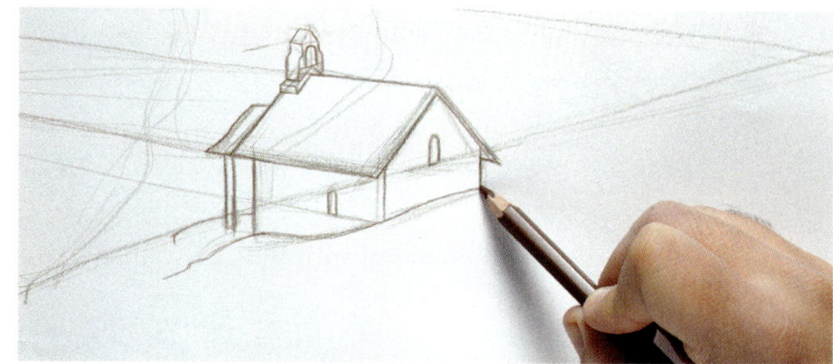

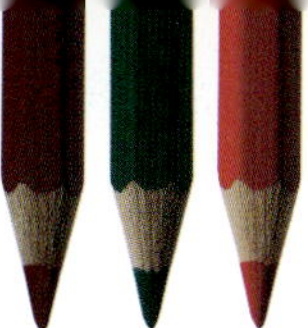

17.2

SHADING AS IF IT WERE A STAGE SET. The tonal value should be applied as if it were a scale of values that turn lighter the farther away they go. Each plane is seen as if it were part of a stage set with consistent shading throughout.

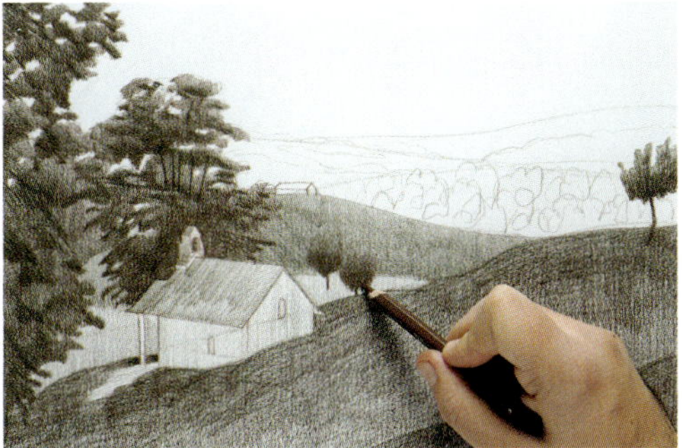

We darken the foliage of the trees with layers of color drawn with a brown pencil. To represent their volume we apply small gradations that show the light oscillation created by the leaves.

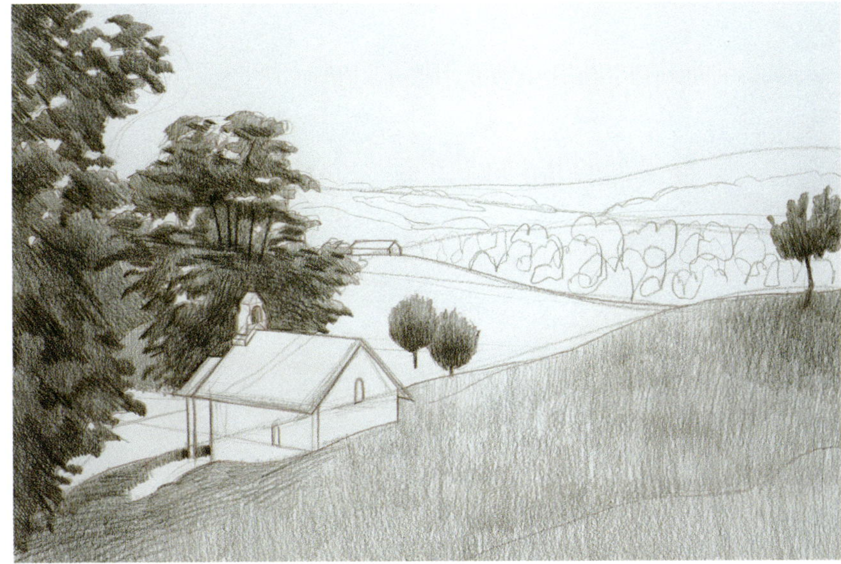

We cover the field and the trees in the foreground with bright green. However, the colors fade away the farther we go, so the field in the middle ground looks lighter than the one in the foreground.

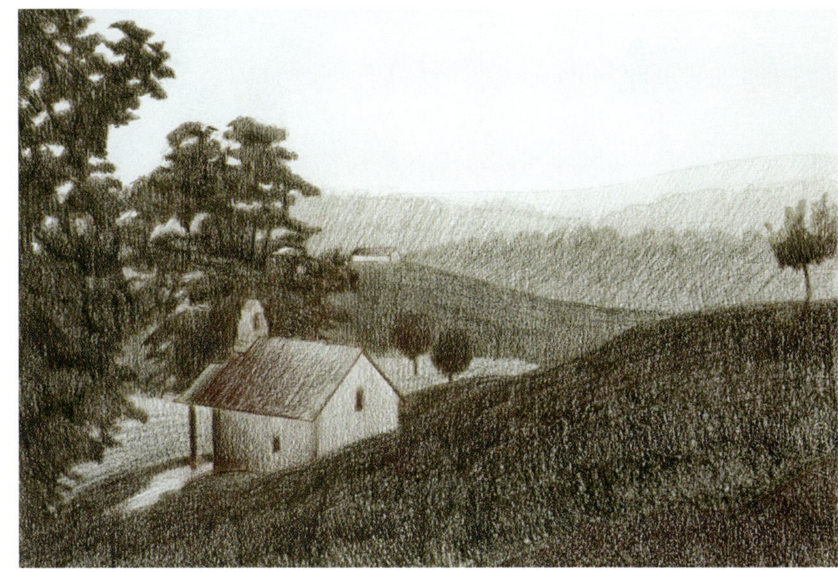

We color the hills in the background by stroking the paper gently with the pencil. We try to draw the contours of the closest elements more vigorously to make them contrast sharply with the areas in the distance, which appear more faded. To achieve this, we intensify the values in the foreground.

The progressive change in value is a good way of defining depth. This transformation has no relationship to great distances or atmospheric effects.

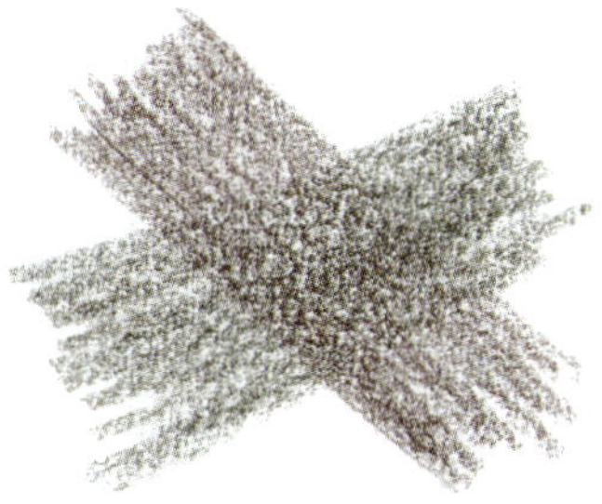

Shading with colored pencils is done through overlaying colors. Overlaying produces more intense and homogeneous colors.

RESOURCES FOR DRAWING LANDSCAPES. We will make several small studies of landscapes in which we will use the following graphic features: diagonal compositions, roads that guide the eye through the landscape, tilled land, rivers, and fences.

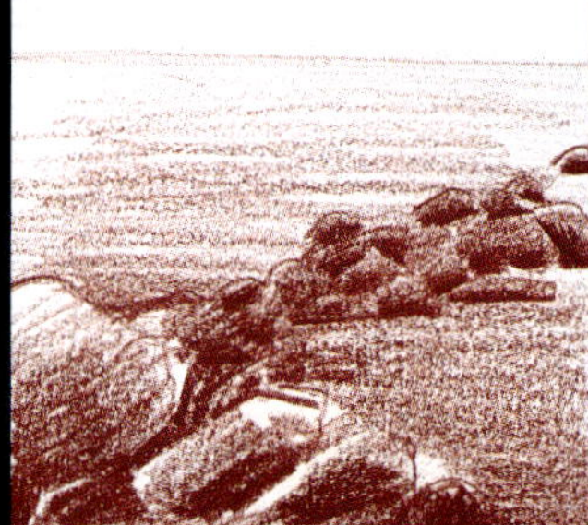

A diagonal composition projects the elements to the background, enhancing the effect of depth.

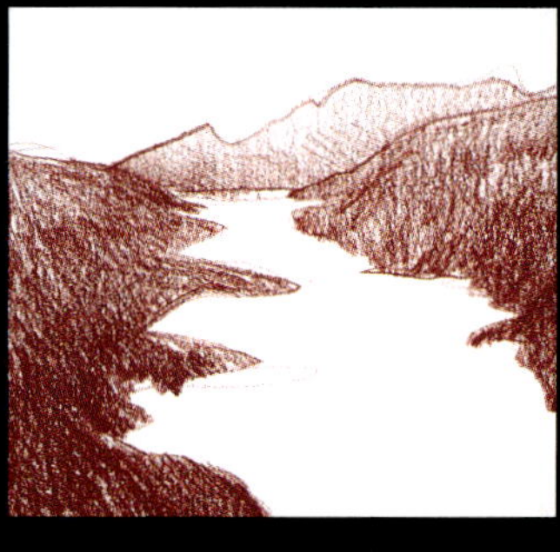

A meandering river directs the viewer deep inside the drawing.

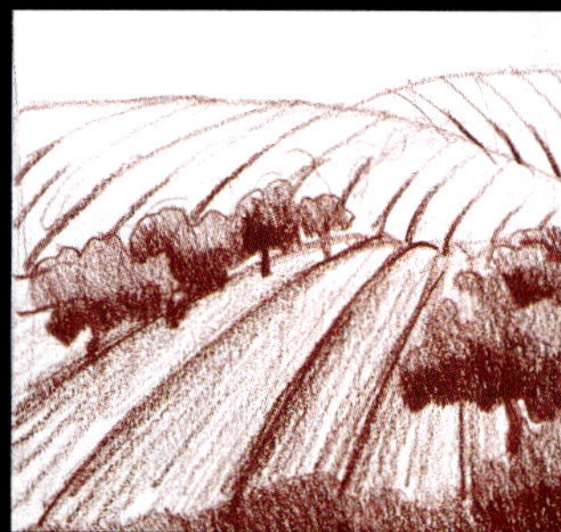

A way to enrich vast spaces is by adding details, such as furrows on the surface that show the direction of the land and thus emphasize perspective.

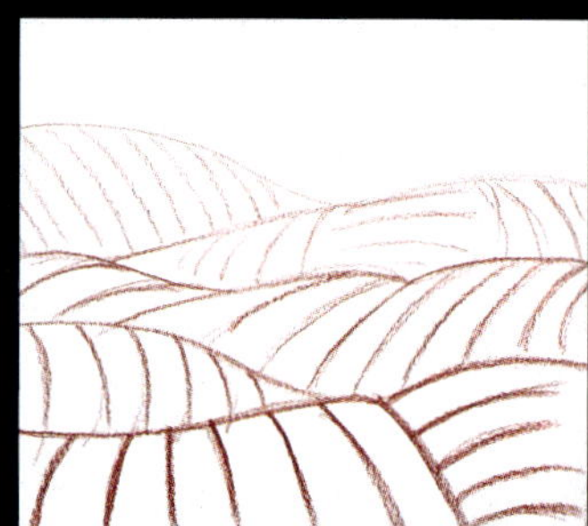

It is a good idea to try out different designs and line directions to find out how effective they are.

A ROAD IN PERSPECTIVE. The illustration shows how to draw a path or a road with curves. After each curve, the road has a new vanishing point, provided both sides of the road are parallel to each other. Naturally, all the vanishing points are found on the same and only horizon line.

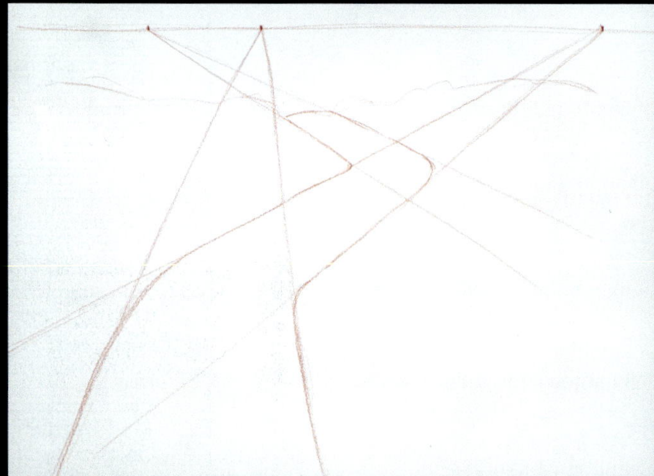

If we have difficulty drawing a road that cuts through the landscape, we must keep in mind that each change of direction requires a new vanishing point on the horizon.

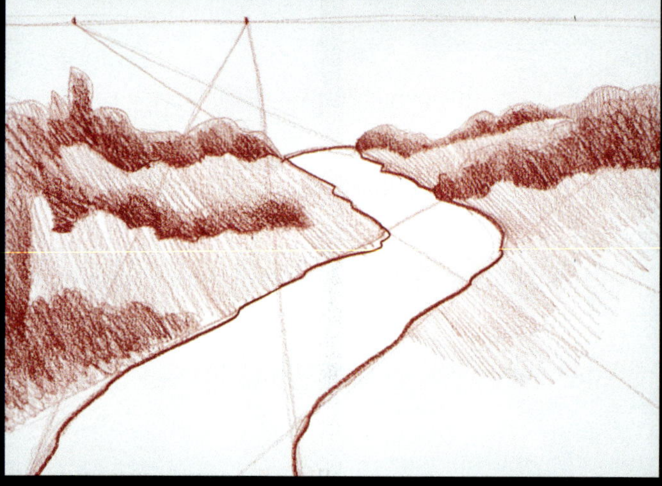

After laying out the different elements, the vanishing points disappear to give way to thicker lines and to shading.

COMPOSITION AND DEPTH IN LANDSCAPES. Some compositional resources enhance the effect of depth. So, properly drawn roads that recede into the landscape create the effect of depth in a painting.

POSTS AND TREES AS REFERENCES. Electrical posts and trees define a road and help the artist portray its depth or ruggedness. If we look at this drawing carefully, we will notice that the trees become smaller as the road recedes; one tree is even partially hidden in the background, which indicates that, behind that hill, the road goes down and turns right.

The fence and the trees that are located at the edge of the road establish its depth and ruggedness.

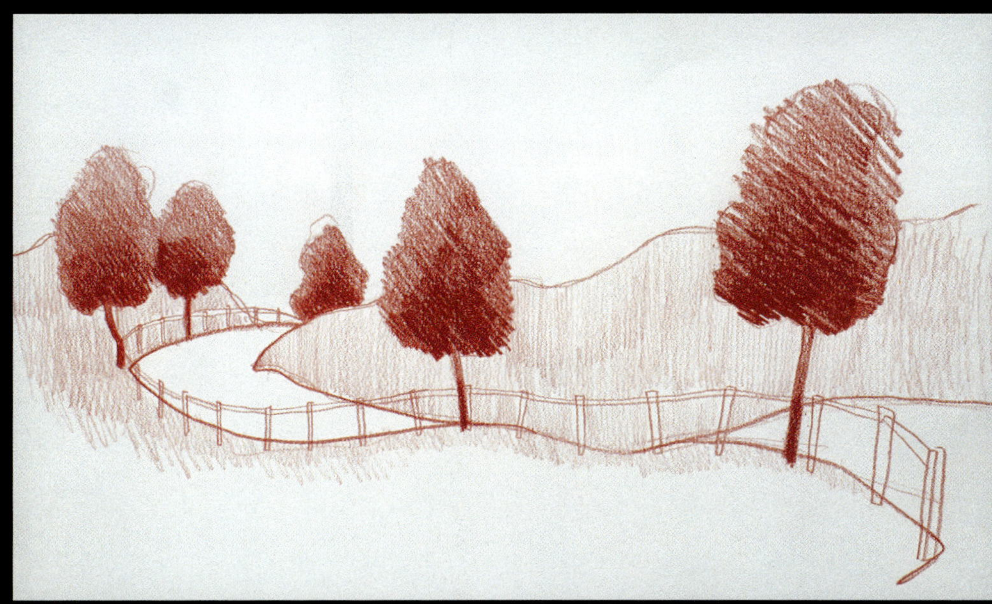

UPS AND DOWNS. Another way of emphasizing the effect of depth, while portraying the terrain, is to describe its ruggedness with a road that cuts through it. This way, the changes of slope and direction in the road portray the changes in the terrain.

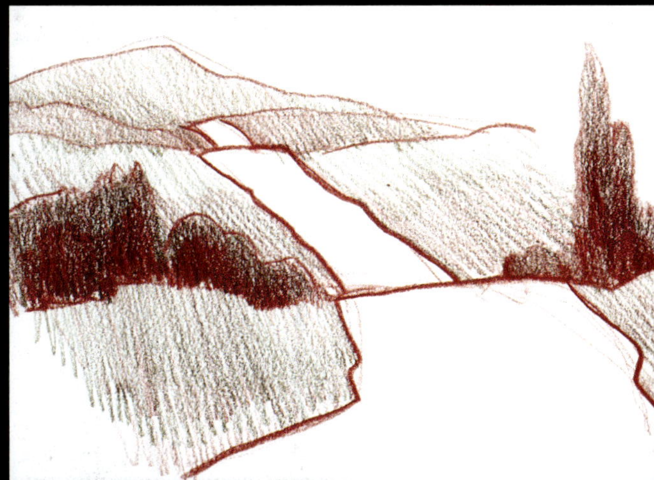

These slope changes are portrayed through cuts, together with slight changes of direction, in the road.

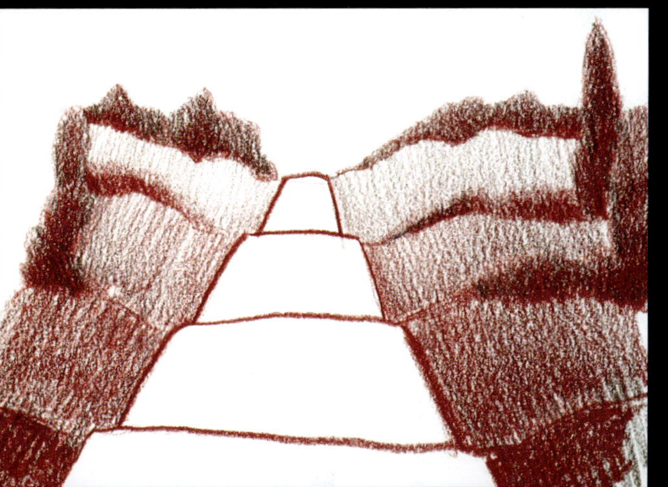

When the road is straight and is located right in front of the viewer, the rising of the slope is portrayed with cuts that fragment each section.

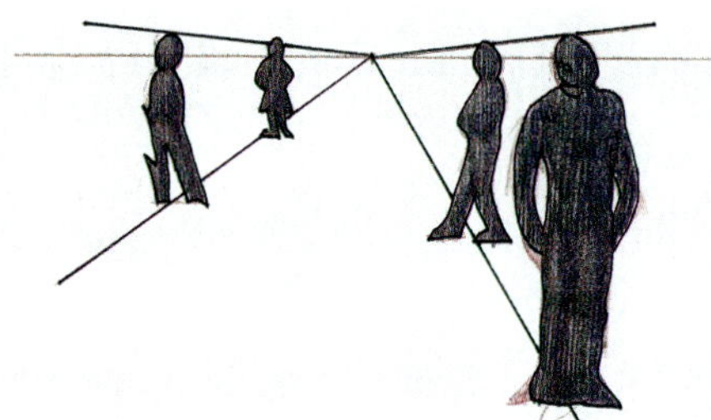

To better control the shortening of the figures—in general—with distance, we project the imaginary lines that connect the lower extremities and the head of the figures, until they reach the vanishing point located on the horizon line.

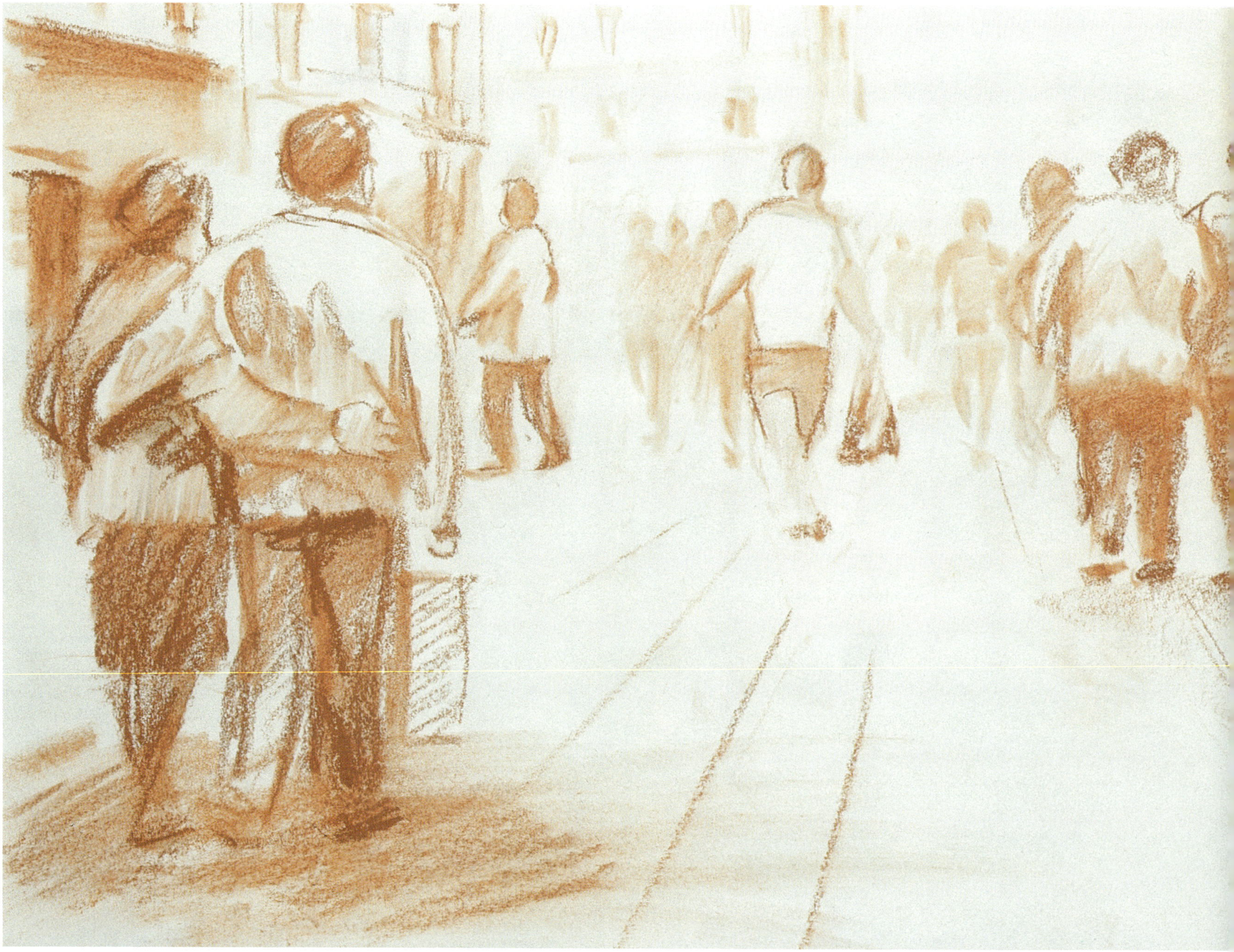

THE HUMAN FIGURE IN THE DISTANCE. Drawing people strolling in the streets is always challenging. They are not much different from any other object, though. Since we are so accustomed to seeing them all around us, the artistic license that we may take in drawing them will become very obvious.

Nothing prevents us from changing the size, the shape, or the placement of a tree, a mountain, or a house, but it is different with people because any mistakes will be very obvious and easy to identify.

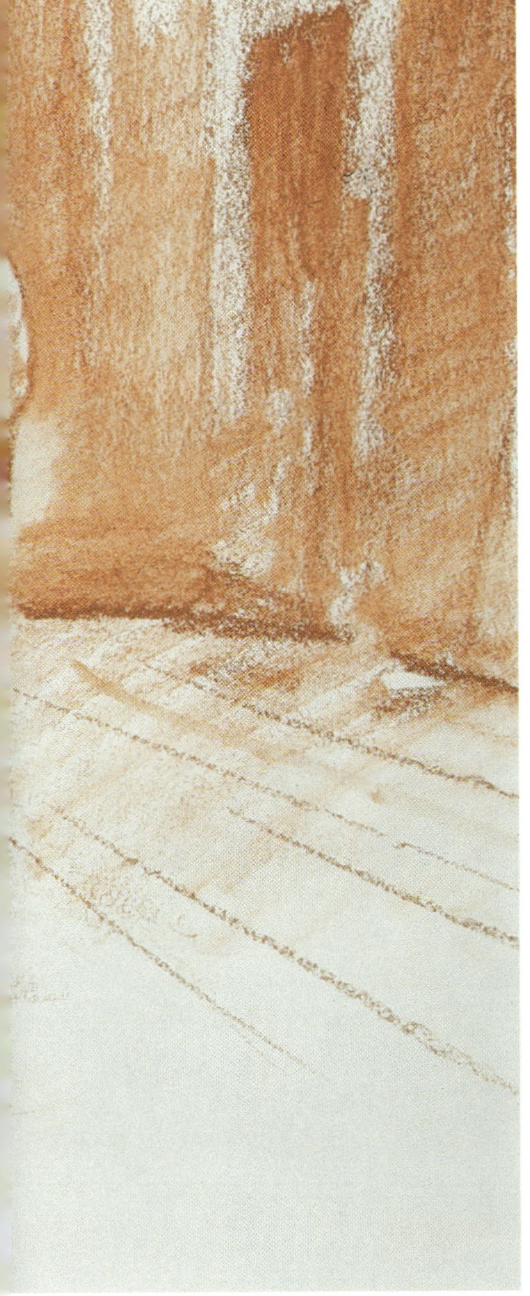

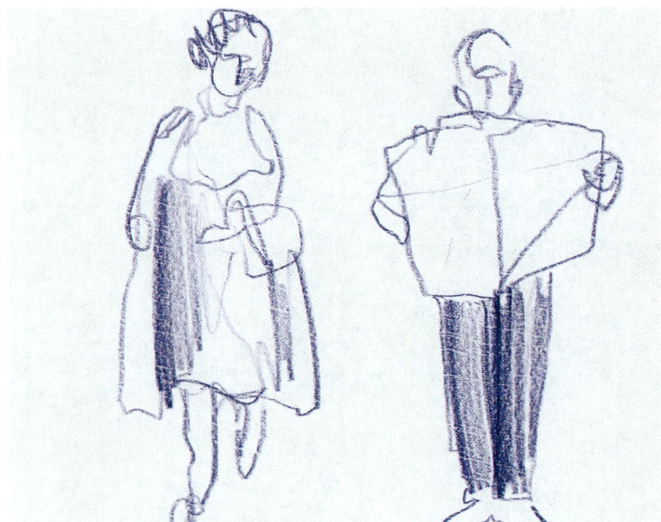

It is difficult to draw life figures because they are in constant motion. In these cases, we must reduce the physical features with a quick, spontaneous sketch.

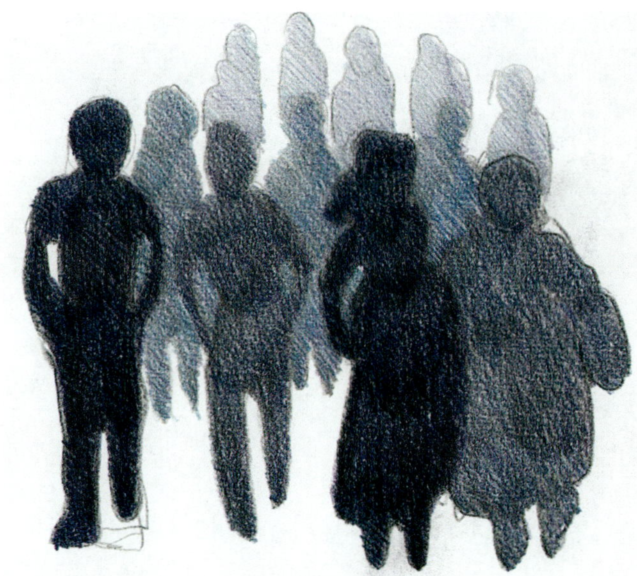

The artist is able to differentiate the figures located in the background from those in the foreground by making the former lighter, as with atmospheric perspective.

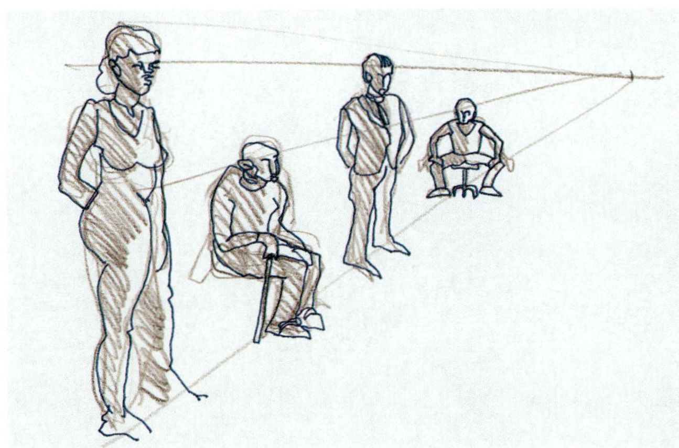

To draw figures by combining different poses—for example, standing, sitting on a chair or on the floor—all we need to do is to reference the head of the figures that are not standing against the ones that are standing to establish where the head of the former would reach if both figures were together.

LANDSCAPE WITH CHINESE PERSPECTIVE. Chinese art uses a variety of atmospheric perspective that blurs out the most distant colors and forms. Therefore, the peaks of the mountains located far away appear to float in the sky, while its base disappears completely due to the effect of the fog. Drawing by Gabriel Martín.

18.1

VOLUPTUOUS AND ROUNDED FORMS. The line drawing shows a design with rounded profiles, aiming at capturing the rhythm and voluptuous effect that provides an arabesque style, especially in the fore- and middle grounds. The drawing is done with a dark gray pencil.

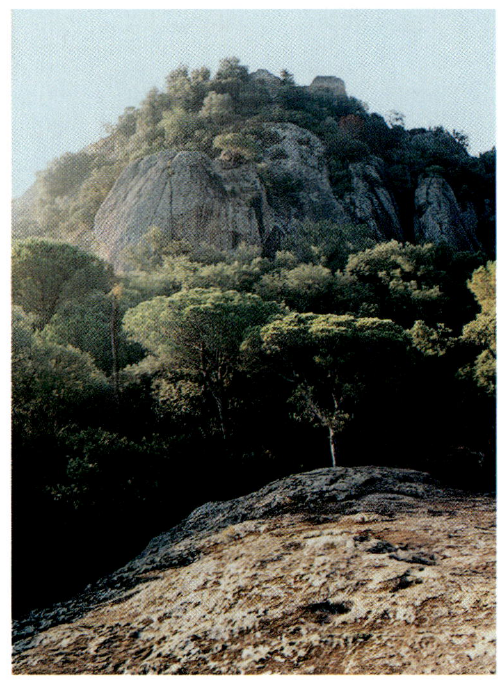

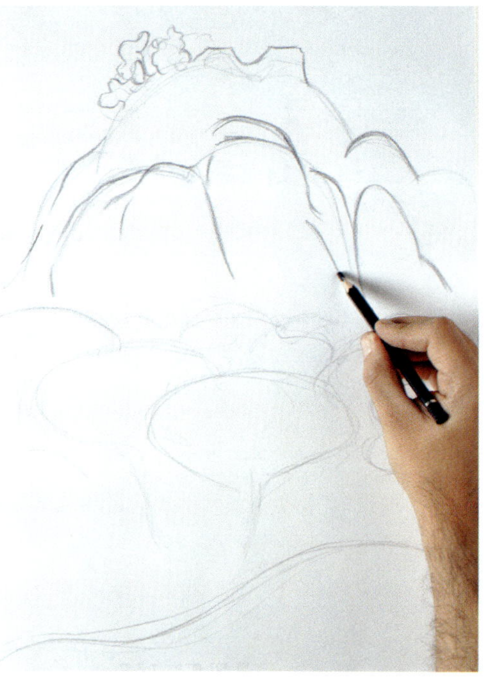

We interpret the model with voluptuous and rounded lines. The mountain appears higher and more majestic than the real one, and the area of the rocks in the foreground is reduced.

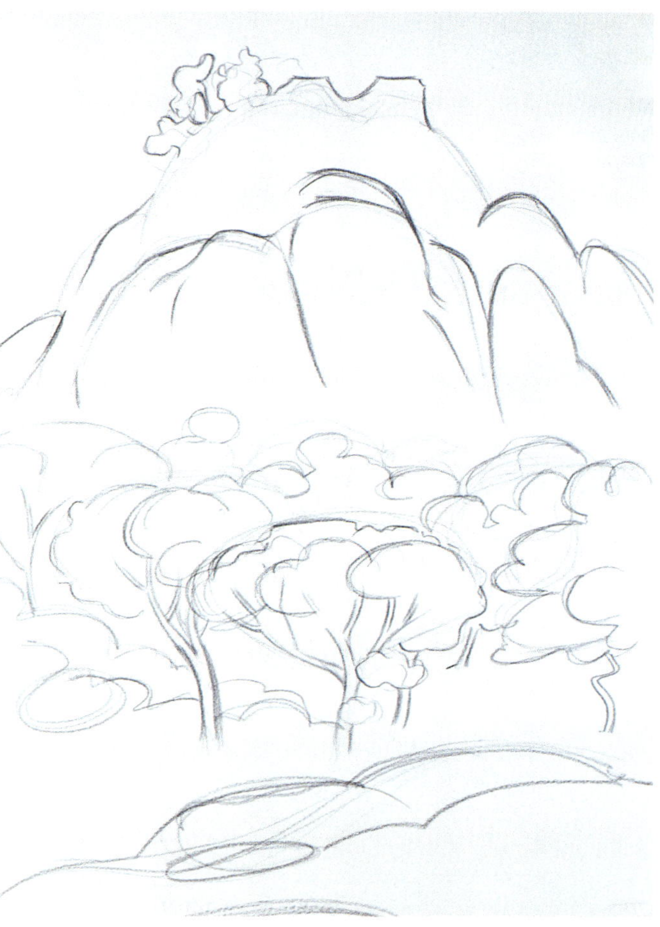

The arabesque and rounded shapes, in zigzag, direct the eye of the viewer from the bottom of the drawing to the mountaintop. The idea is to modify the shapes of the actual subject to suit our needs.

It is not necessary to erase the sketch lines, since these will be concealed behind a layer of shading.

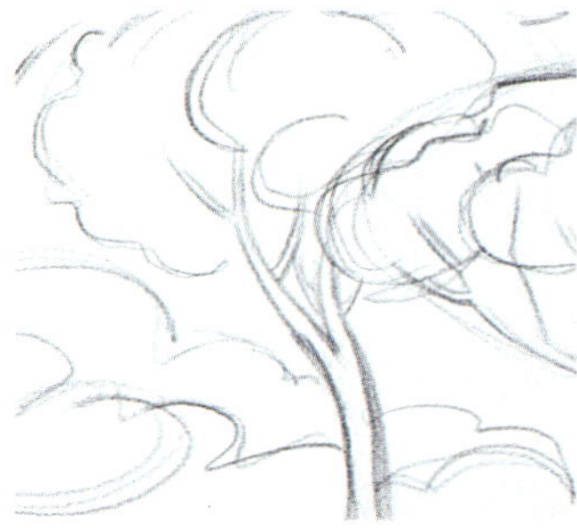

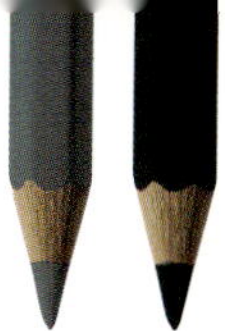

18.2

MAKING GRADATIONS FOR THE MOUNTAIN. We shade the landscape, beginning with the background and moving to the foreground. The rocky mountain should have a darker gradation of shading on top. The bottom of the mountain is white, bathed by imaginary light.

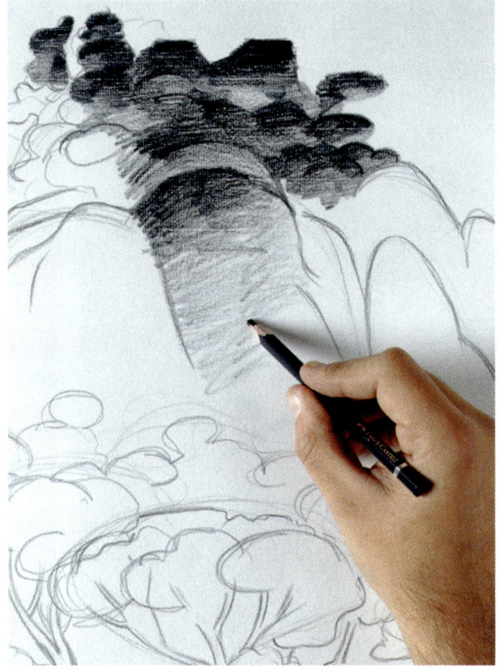

The mountaintop is shaded with dark black by holding the tip of the pencil slightly at an angle. Each form and each volume (trees and rock features) must be represented with gradations.

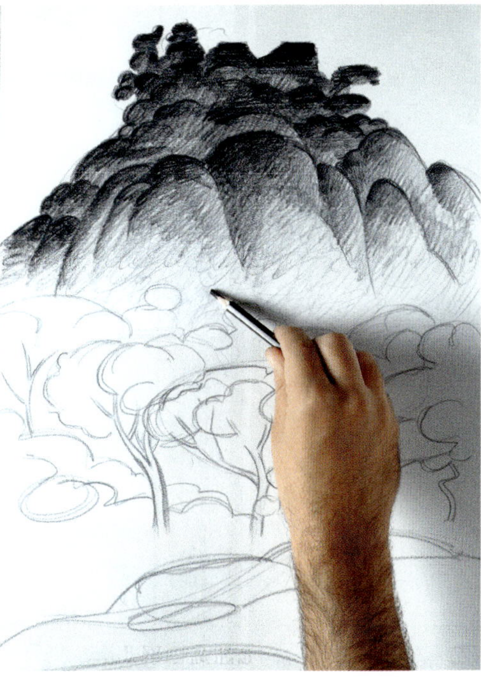

Each area represents a contained gradation, but all these areas put together give the mountain an overall feeling of shade progression. The pressure applied on the pencil decreases as we reach the bottom.

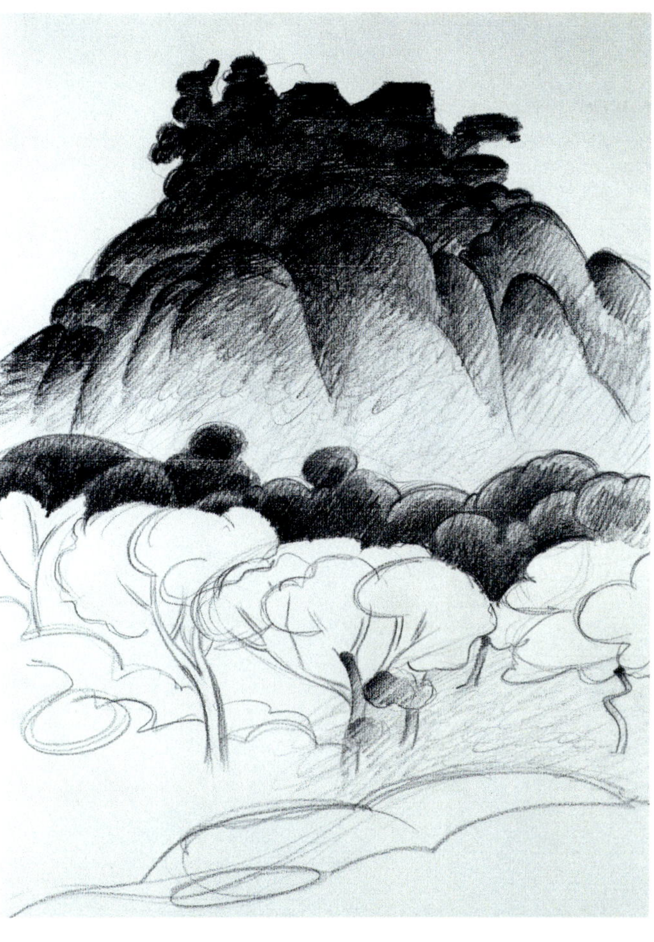

When we reach the bottom, we continue with the vegetation in the middle ground, producing a sudden tonal change between planes. The light that bathes the base of the mountain gives it a poetic and magical feeling.

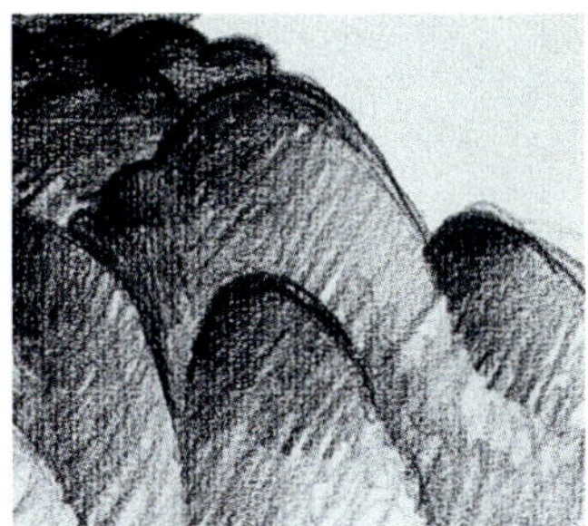

To understand the graduated volumes correctly, we must create constant contrast, superimposing dark contours over light backgrounds and vice versa, even if that means departing from the real model.

18.3

THE IMPORTANCE OF UNPAINTED AREAS. The empty spaces that appear in the lower part of each area enhance the effect of depth. The goal is to construct each plane with graduated shading; this way, the mountaintop, the trees, and the rocky ground are emphasized vividly, while its base appears blurry due to the effect of the imaginary fog.

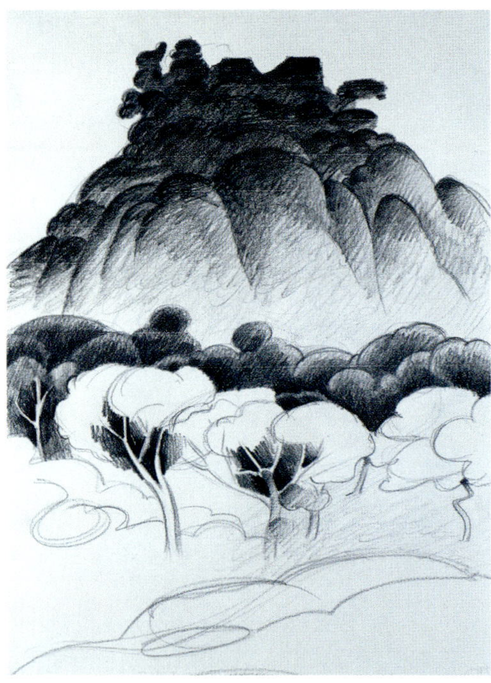

Carefully, we recreate the foliage of the forest with gradations. The shapes have been simplified by making them rounded, which makes shading easier. It is a good idea to shade the trees in the background first, followed by the ones closer to the front.

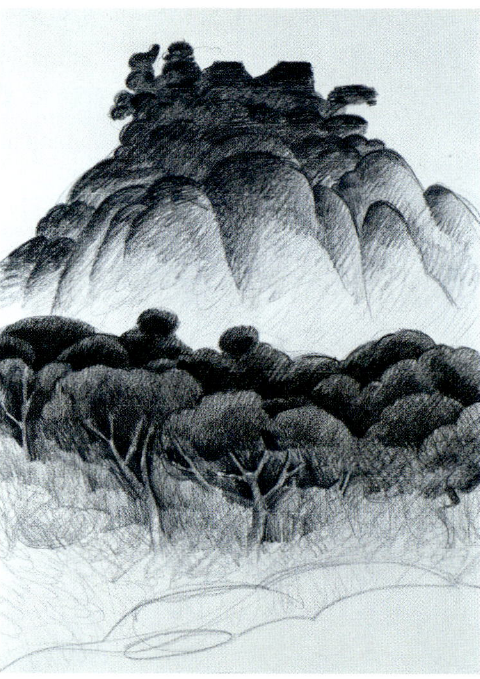

The foliage of the trees in the foreground is of medium gray, while the ones in the background are drawn with a black pencil, adding very dark shading to enhance the gradation. The tree trunks require more detail.

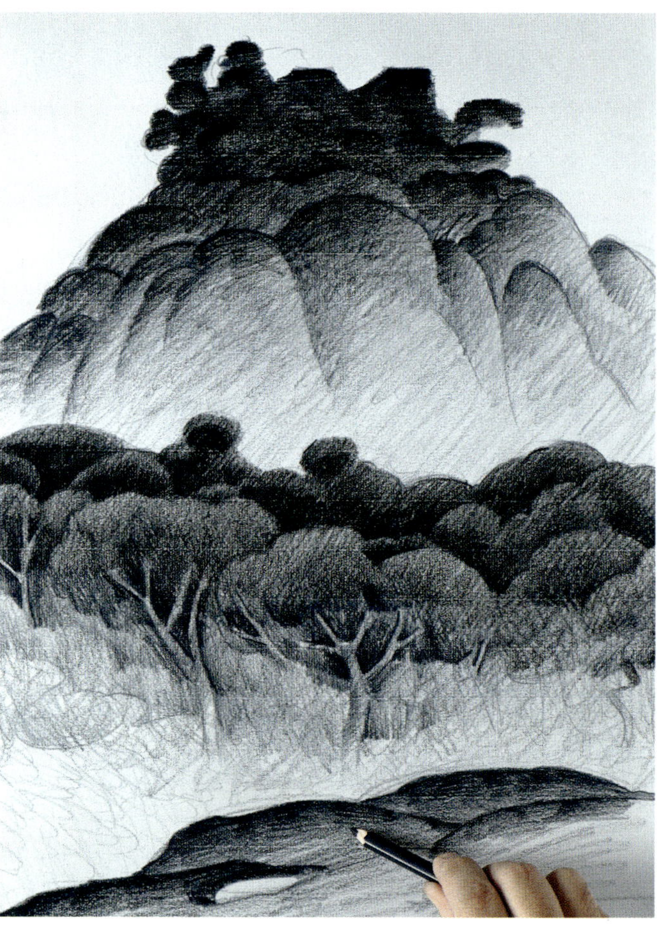

The lower part of the trees is drawn with gradations until we reach the white of the paper. The foreground is represented with a sudden jump in color, which occurs when we draw the upper profile with a black pencil.

It is a good idea to go over the shading of the treetops, so each color mass stands out in contrast against the one below. To achieve this, we superimpose black lines over the gray shaded areas.

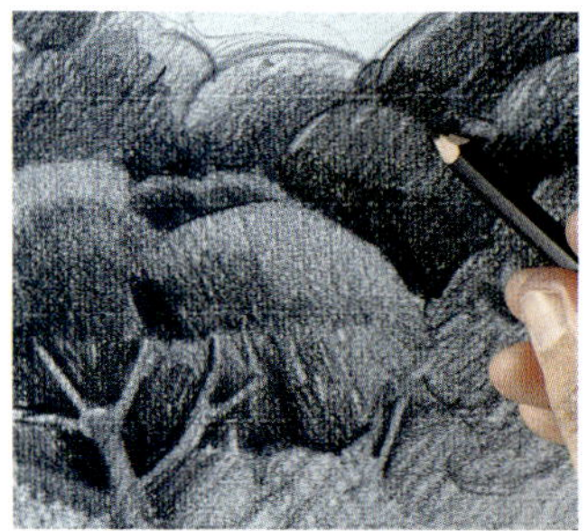

The tree trunks and their branches are represented using contrast. Basically, we darken the background with black, and the branches stand out against it in contrast.

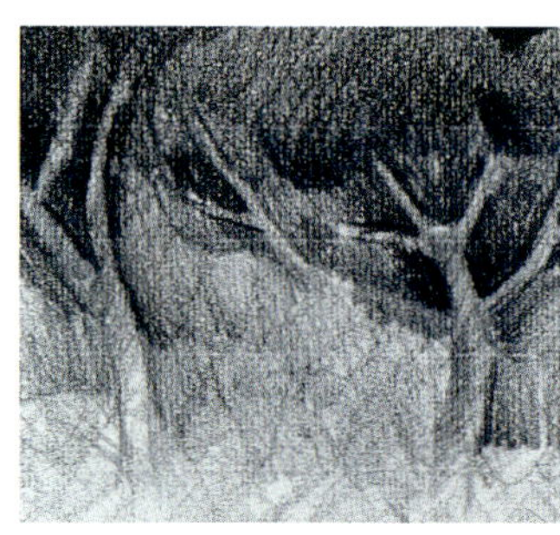

When every plane of the landscape has been established, the distance is suggested either by the absence of color, with white spaces covered by fog, or through the clear and sharp presence of the different heavily shaded elements of the landscape.

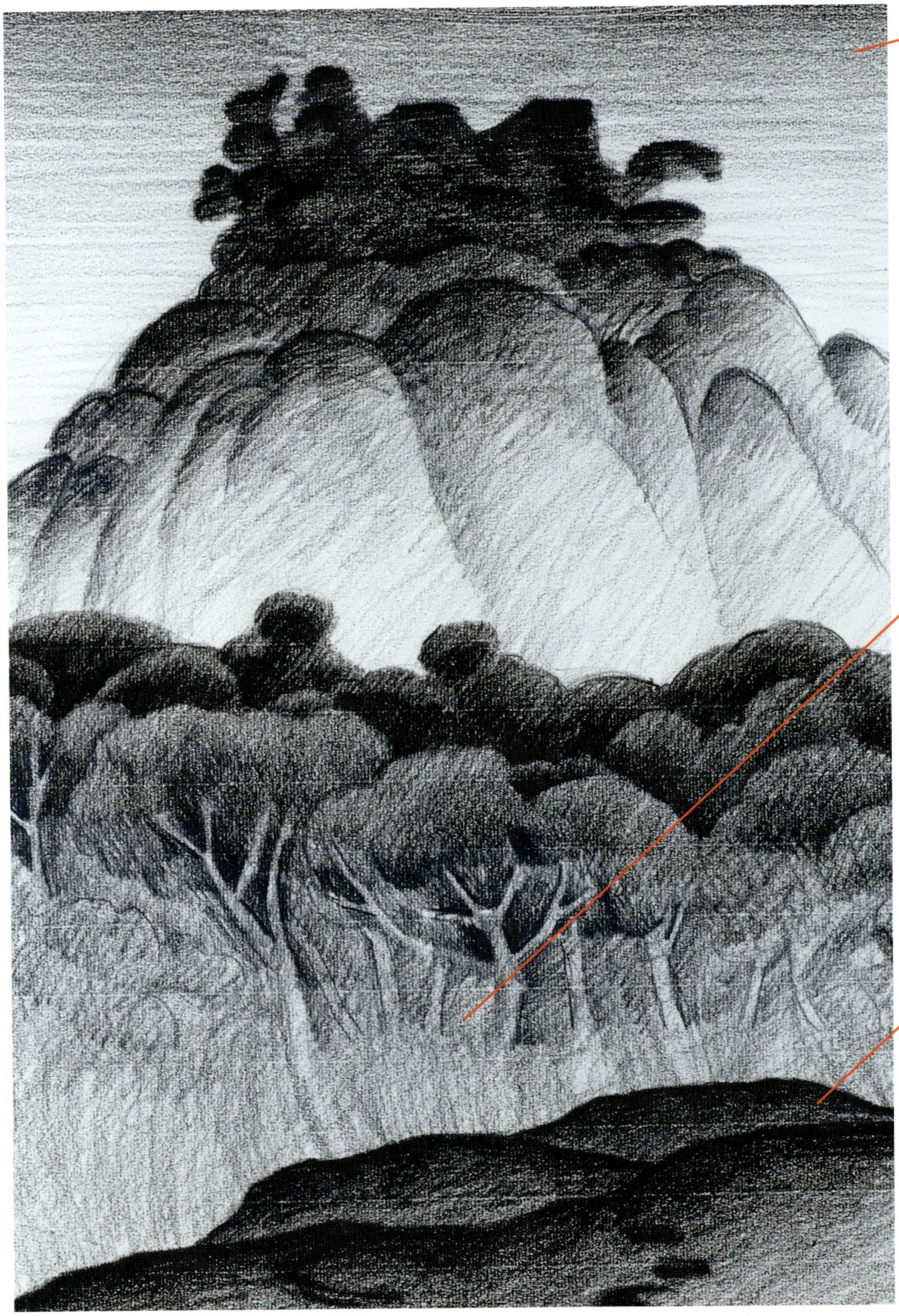

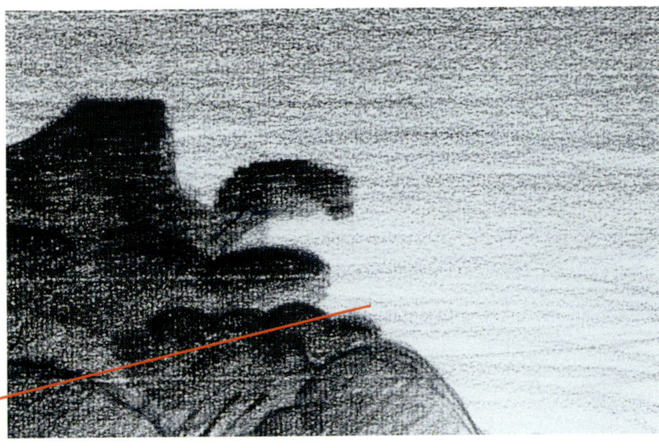

We finish the sky with a gradation applied with horizontal strokes, without applying too much pressure on the pencil.

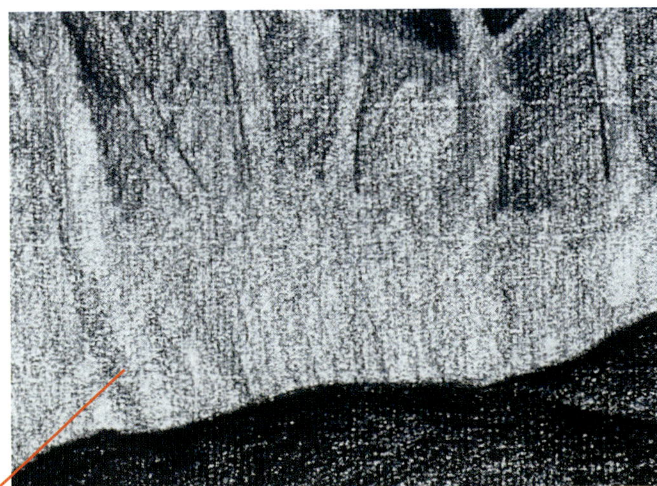

Leaving areas unfinished, shaded with very light tones, almost white, is important so that the viewer can complete the drawing mentally, and also to create contrast in this Chinese-style approach.

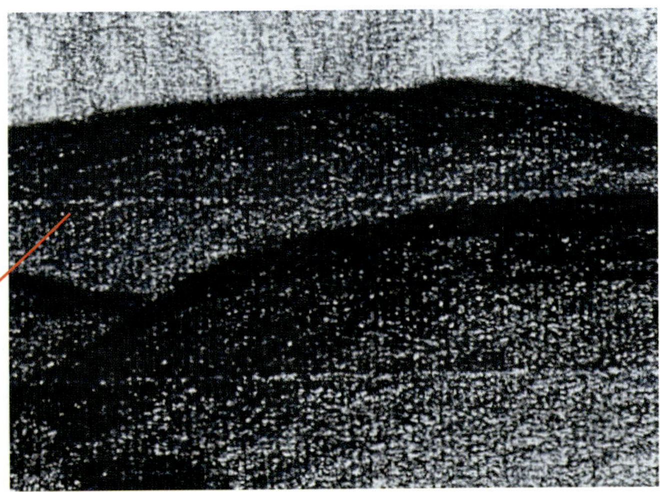

When the drawing is finished, we go over the upper contours of each plane, shading them with a black pencil. We apply a little more pressure so the forms become sharp and distinguishable.

ATMOSPHERIC PERSPECTIVE. This perspective is based on gradations of light, saturation, definition, texture, and even shading. In nature, this phenomenon is due to the density of the atmosphere through which we see the objects.

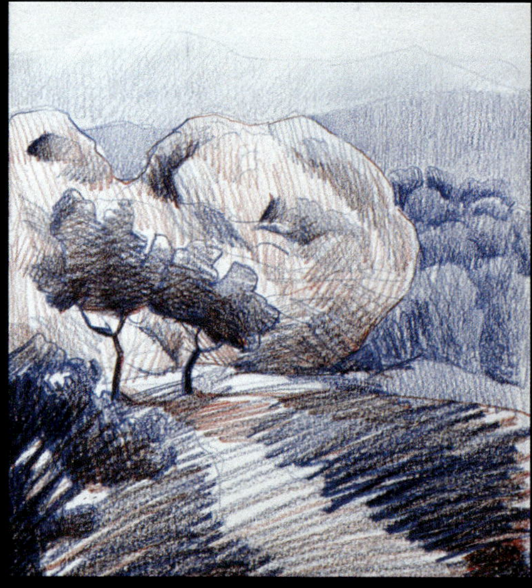

Atmospheric perspective dictates the degree of coloration for the different planes of the landscape. Colors fade away as the objects recede.

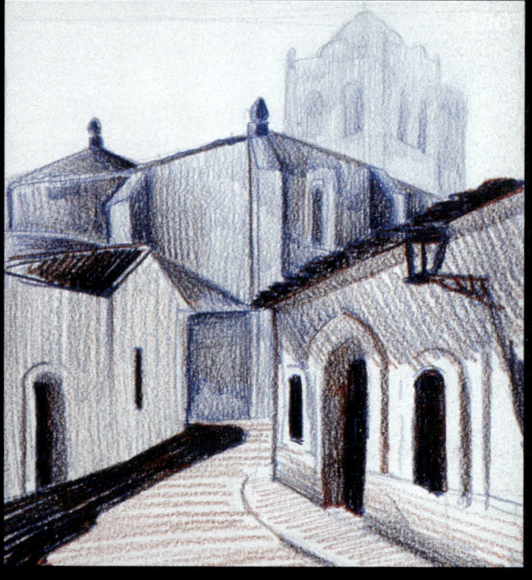

The atmospheric effect is not exclusive to landscapes; it can also manifest itself in an urban setting. We can observe here the way the tones have been applied on the façades in the foreground and the bell tower in the back.

CONTOURS AND VALUE IN THE DISTANCE. Careful observation of a large landscape will help us confirm that with distance the contours get blurry and tonal values decrease. The opposite is true for close-ups, where each object is sharply defined and easily visible.

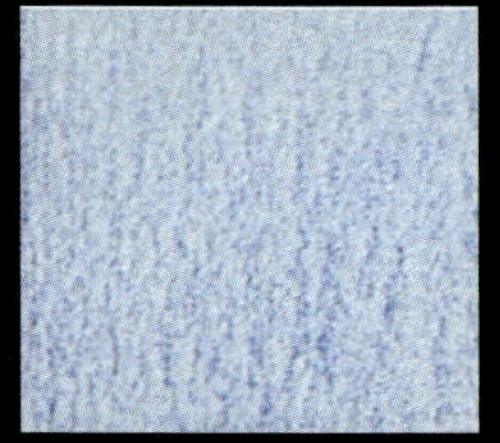

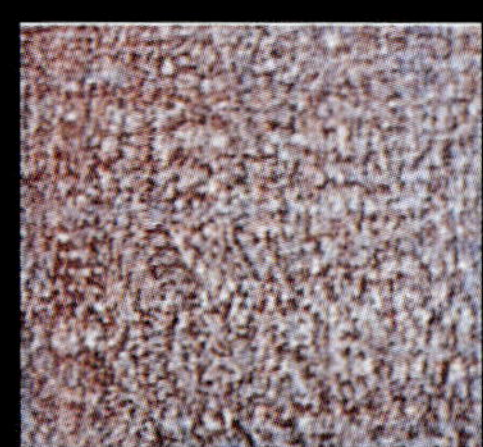

Looking at these two illustrations, we will notice that the one on the left appears to be farther away since it has lighter colors.

A TREE IN THE DISTANCE. The values of a tree in the distance are very soft and airy, which gives the form a supernatural look. These drawings capture the mist in the air, a phenomenon that fades the light and makes the sky and the ground merge together. The effect of depth is more obvious if we compare it to trees nearby that have more defined lines and different shading gradations.

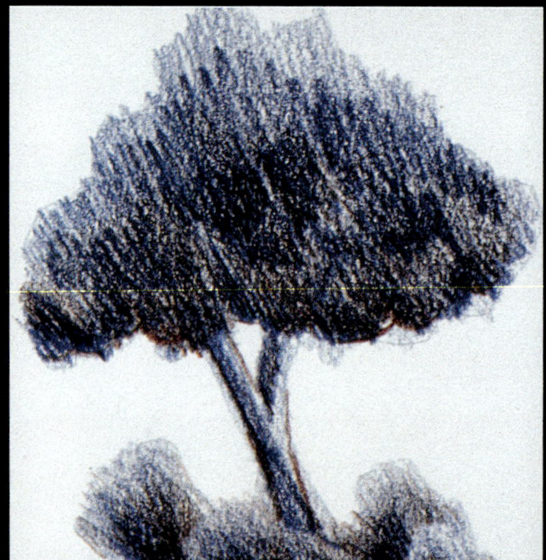

A tree at short distance has well-defined contours and visible degrees of shading.

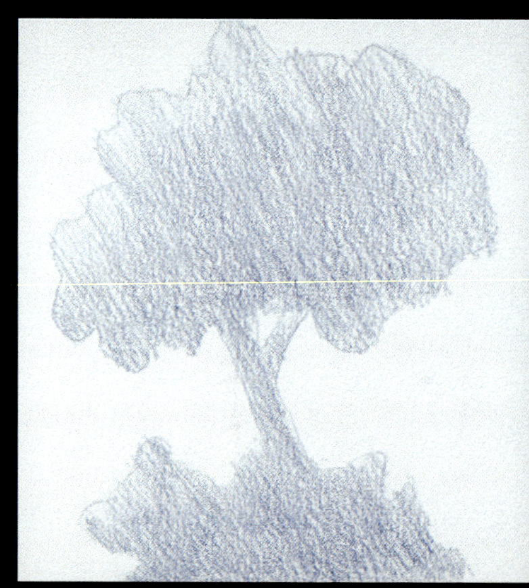

The same tree in the distance has a ghostly appearance; there is no contrast, and its

ATMOSPHERIC EFFECT IN THE DISTANCE. Atmospheric perspective is based on the optical effect produced by the light absorbed and reflected by the atmosphere (a foggy layer of dust and mist). This fog dilutes the light and makes the receding colors lose their contrast. For centuries, artists have mimicked this natural effect by using light and soft tones in the horizon.

FOREGROUND WITH CONTRAST. When we use the atmospheric effect, the objects that are well defined appear in the foreground, where there is greater contrast. Light and dark colors and the outlines of illuminated and shaded areas are sharper than in the distance. The inclusion of an object in the foreground thus enhances the feeling of depth.

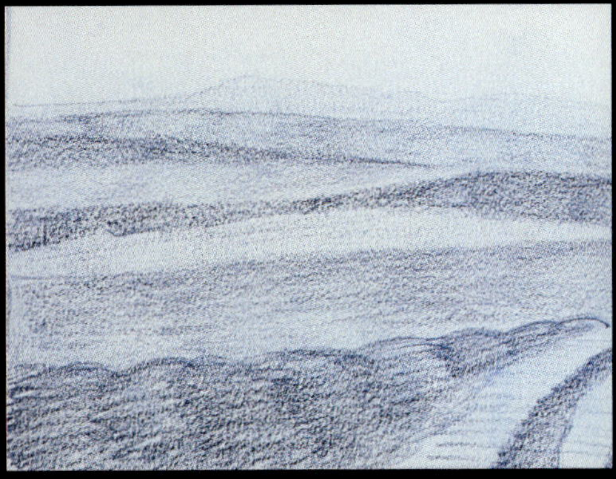

We will look at the importance of contrast in the foreground by studying this model of a diffused landscape.

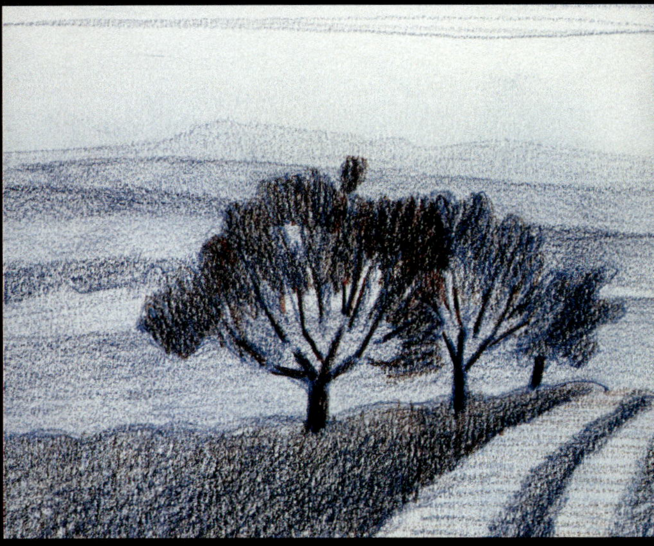

By including a close-up view of a group of trees, the effect of depth is maximized through contrast.

VERTICAL PERSPECTIVE. Asian art showed Western artists that vertical perspective could also provide an interesting approach to space. In vertical perspective, the farther away an object is, the higher it is represented. The culmination of this effect was Chinese perspective, which introduced thick fog at the base of mountains.

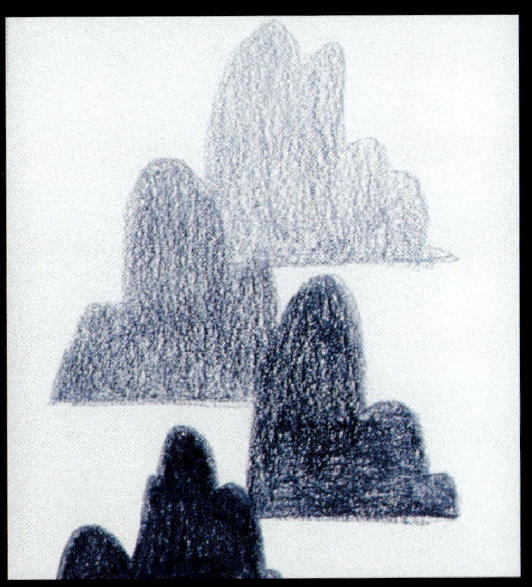

Asian vertical perspective is very clear; the higher the plane, the farther away it is.

Chinese perspective combines the verticality concept with soft gradations that create a mysterious fog at the base of the mountain.

LEARNING BY DOING

LANDSCAPE WITH GRADATIONS. The simplest and most direct way to represent distance with atmospheric perspective in landscapes is through gradation using any of the usual techniques: hatching, sfumatto, lines of different thicknesses, and so on. Drawing by Gabriel Martín.

19.1

SURFACES WITH GRADATION. In this exercise we will observe that a graduated effect applied to a surface automatically provides a feeling of distance. It helps explain how the color of a surface becomes lighter as it recedes.

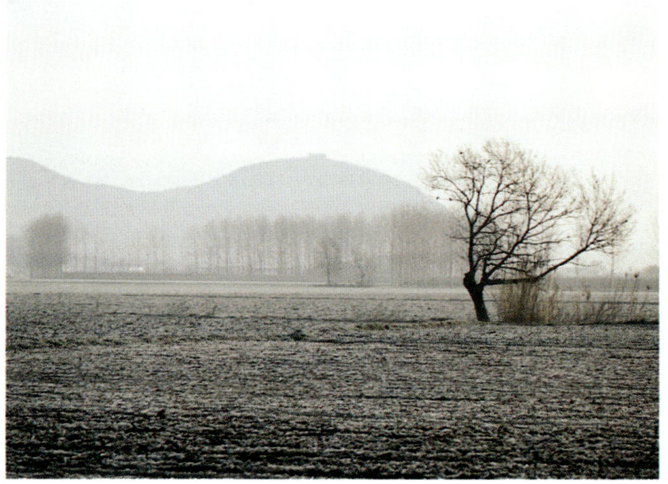

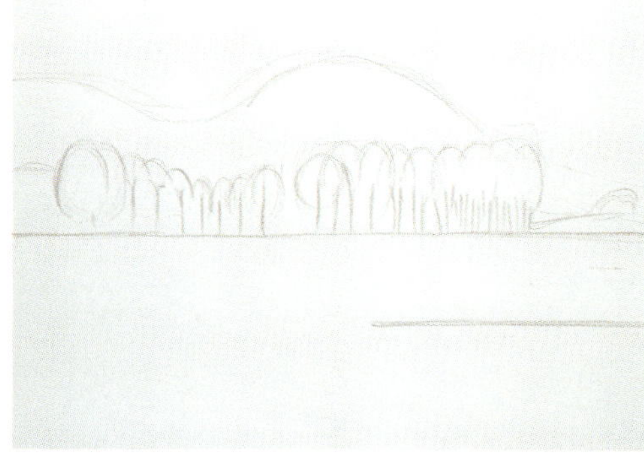

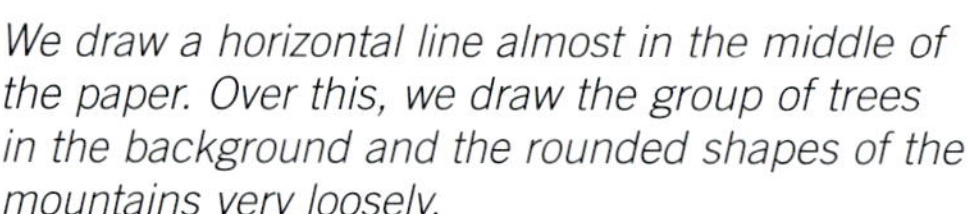

We draw a horizontal line almost in the middle of the paper. Over this, we draw the group of trees in the background and the rounded shapes of the mountains very loosely.

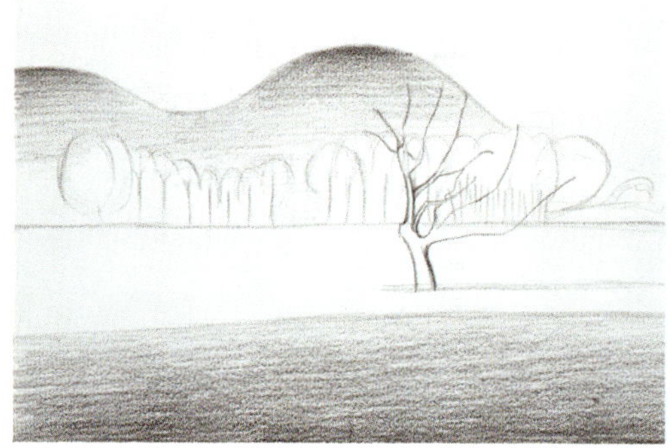

We shade the mountain with a gradation, making the top darker. A second gradation is applied to the terrain in the foreground, although this time we invert the tonal intensity. We sketch the tree with thin lines and careful consideration.

To apply the gradation, the pencil is held at an angle to avoid exercising too much pressure. This way, the line is very soft and does not create too much contrast.

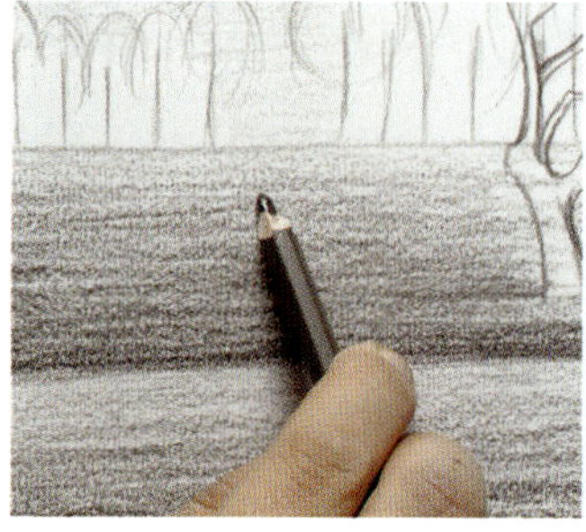

19.2

CONTRAST WITH GRADATIONS. We shade each area of the landscape with gradations. It is a good idea to change their intensity and direction to increase the contrast between the different areas—in other words, to make sure that the profiles are visible as a result of the color contrast.

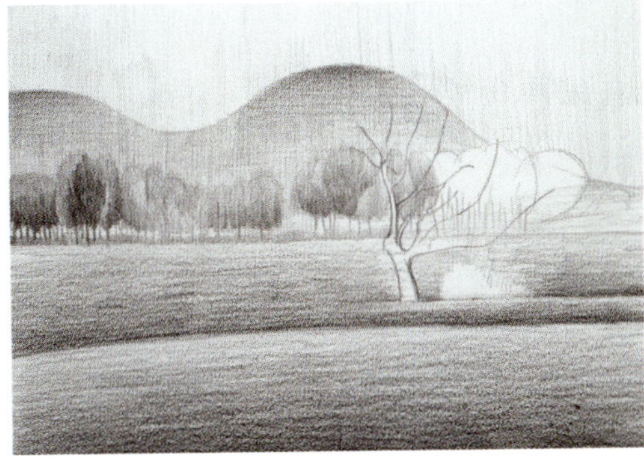

We shade the sown fields in the middle ground with an ample gradation. Each tree in the distance is drawn individually and shaded with a gradation, making sure their outlines and forms become clearly distinguishable from the mountain in the background.

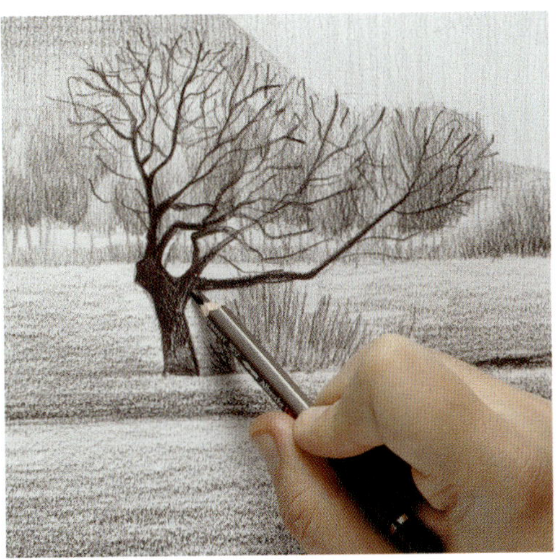

After covering all the areas with soft to medium intensity, we focus on the tree in the foreground. We draw it by applying a lot of pressure with the pencil, so the brown is very dark.

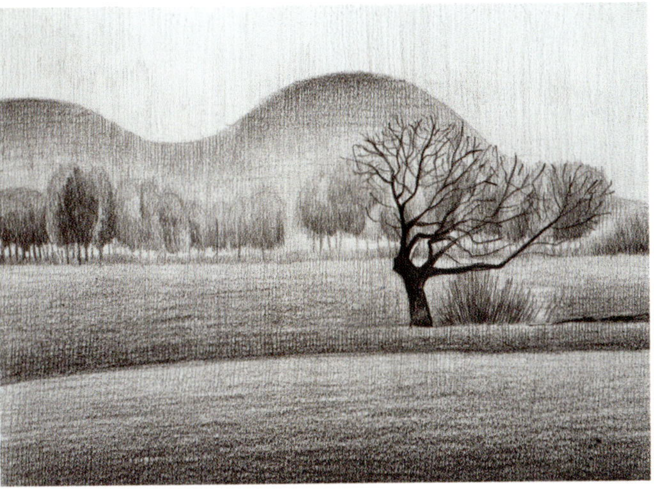

As we can see in this finished drawing, gradations provide the necessary elements to suggest the effect of depth.

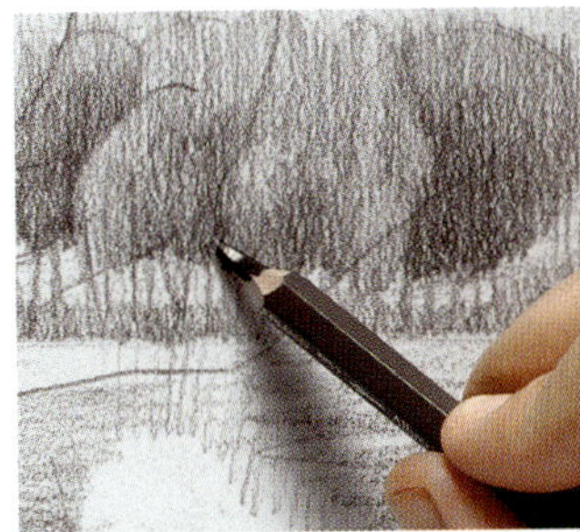

The absence of lines forces us to construct the trees with tonal contrasts; therefore a light profile is superimposed over a dark one and vice versa, to create a layer of objects.

TEXTURES IN PERSPECTIVE. To represent different surfaces that have the same texture in perspective, the intensity of the graphic elements that are used to recreate these surfaces is gradually reduced and summarized. Drawing by Esther Olivé de Puig.

20.1

PERSPECTIVE LINES. Before we begin drawing a surface or texture, it is a good idea to construct the different architectural planes that form the drawing with perspective lines. This procedure is done with a stick of sanguine Conté crayon because it makes softer and thinner lines than black chalk.

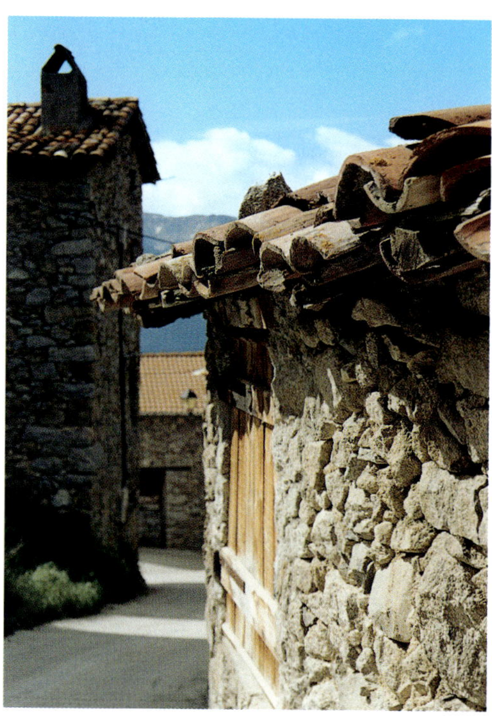

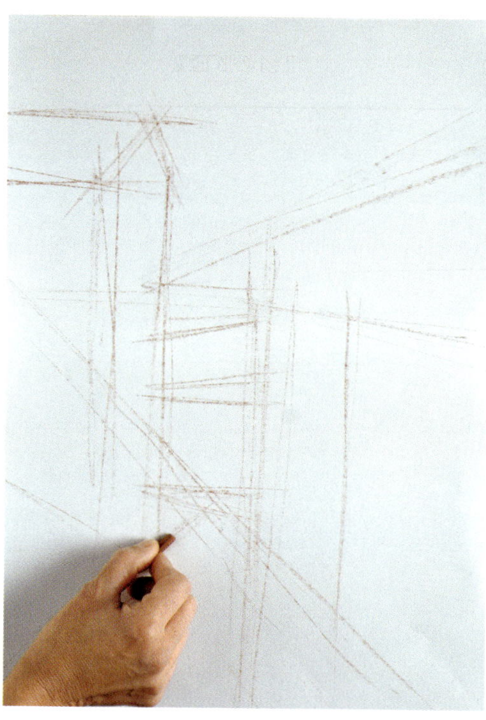

We locate a vanishing point at a midpoint on the left side of the paper to project lines that define the angle of the window and the roof of the building in the foreground.

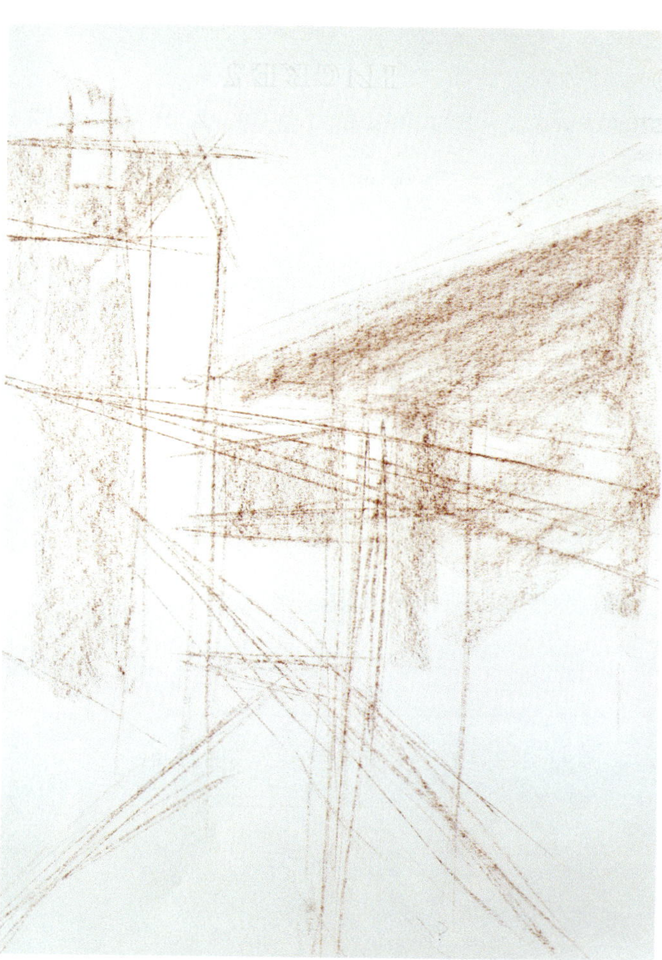

The buildings in the mid- and backgrounds do not create any perspective issues, since they are parallel to the painting's surface. Once the line sketch is finished, we apply the first shadows with the sanguine bar placed flat against the paper.

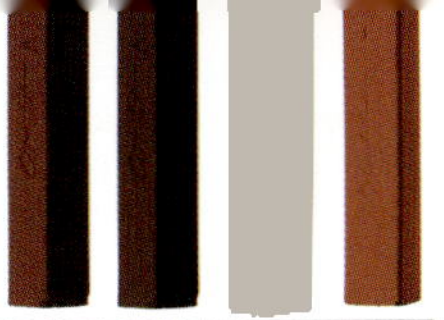

20.2

STONES AND SHINGLES MADE OUT OF CLAY. Now we draw the stones and arrange and form the clay tiles of the building in the foreground. The dark line and tonal contrast are key to represent texture, so black chalk takes the place of sanguine.

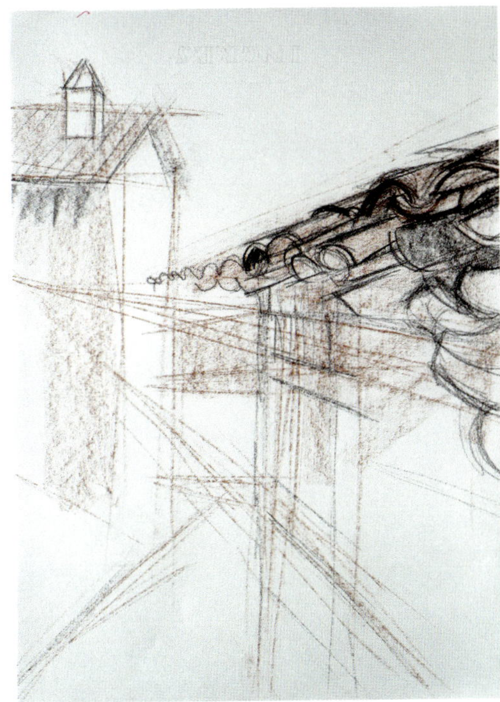

The profile of each shingle is drawn with black chalk, defining its characteristic rounded shape carefully, making sure that the idea of layering and a certain spontaneity in the arrangement are conveyed.

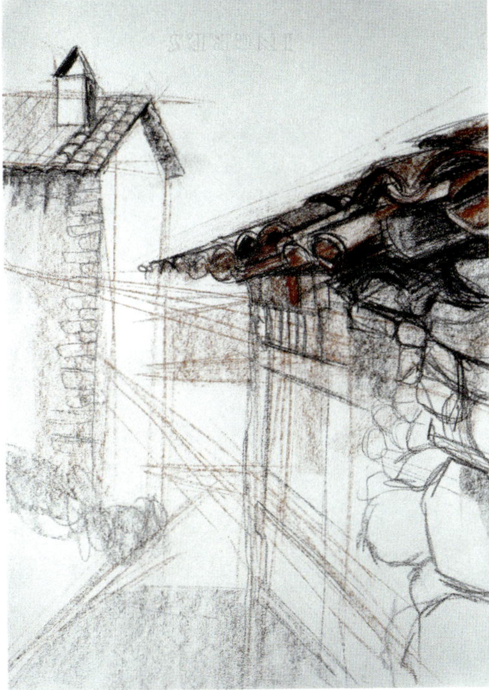

Combining black and sanguine chalk, we shade the shingles repeatedly and with contrast to emphasize their proximity and volume. The shape of the stones in the wall is sketched out with soft lines.

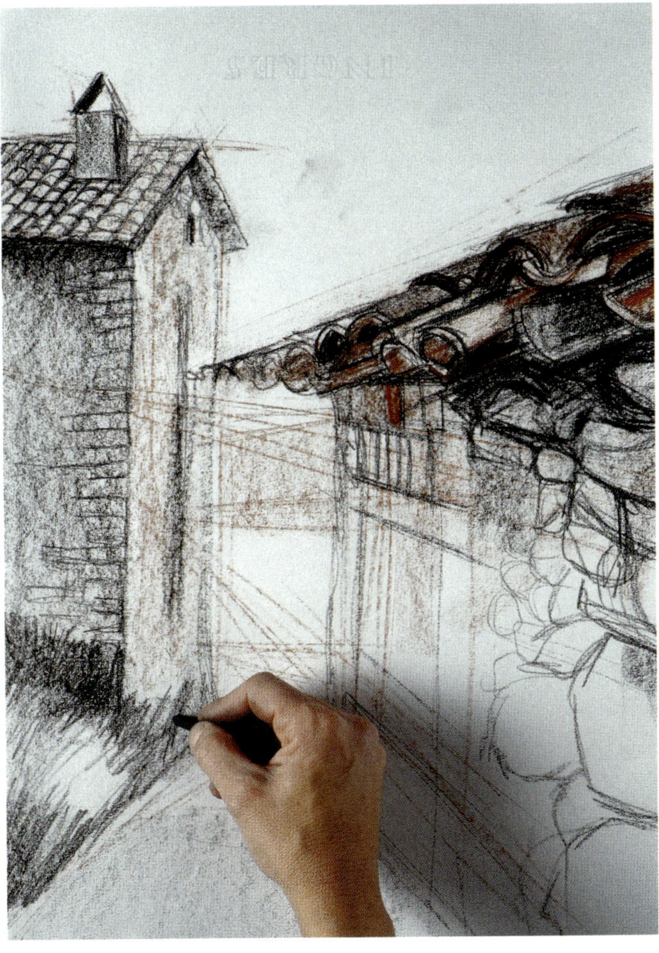

The profile of the house in the midground is drawn with the tip of the black chalk, applying very little pressure. The roof's texture is created with diagonal lines, more or less parallel, and the texture of the stone is suggested only at the corner of the building.

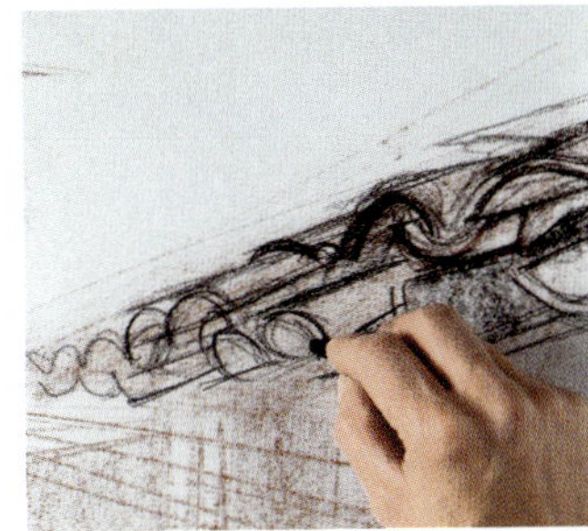

To sketch out the shingles we can use short diagonal lines to help us define and establish their position and angle.

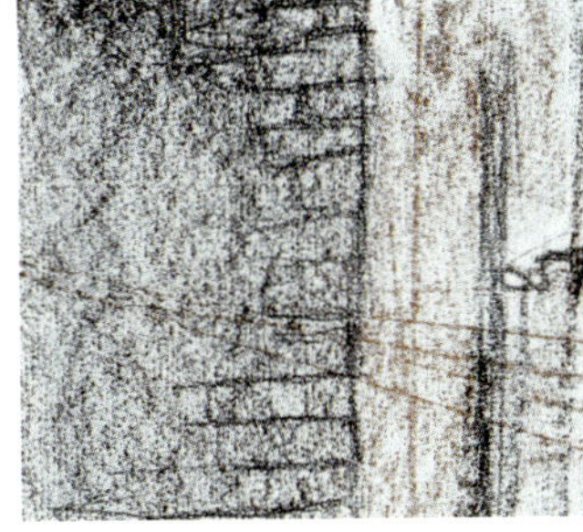

The texture of the stones in the wall of the house in the midground should be drawn with soft lines; they are combined with reflections and unpainted areas.

20.3

ENHANCING THE FOREGROUND. When an object is located very far away, it is very difficult, sometimes even impossible, to see its texture. However, with the resources used in drawing, the artist can create the feeling of depth by adding detail to the foreground and reducing it as the subject recedes.

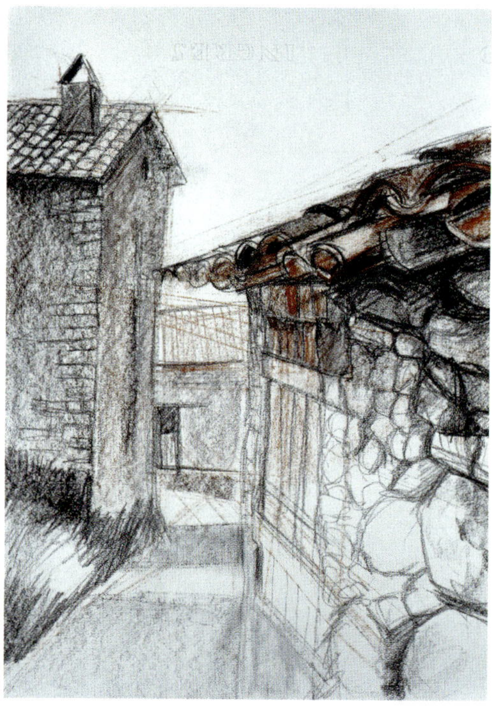

We go back to the wall in the foreground. We emphasize the shape of each stone by drawing a dark outline, which is darker on the upper part of the wall and somewhat lighter at the bottom, due to the incidence of light.

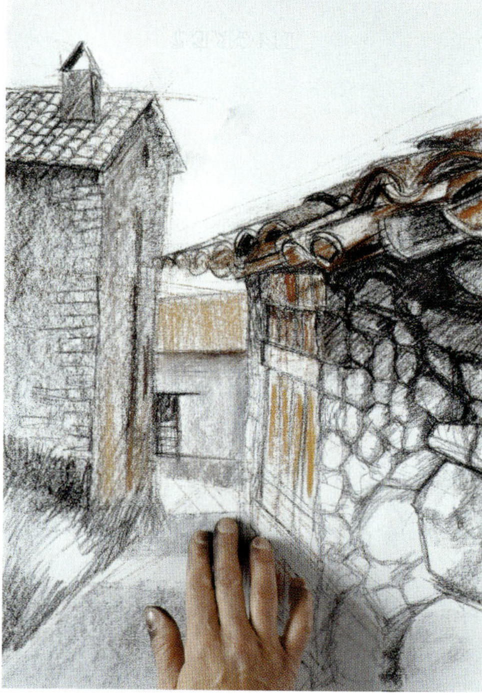

We continue defining the texture of the objects in the foreground. The wall of the house in the background is smooth, without any texture. At the same time that we draw the lines, we shade with black and sepia chalk. We blend the areas with the hand.

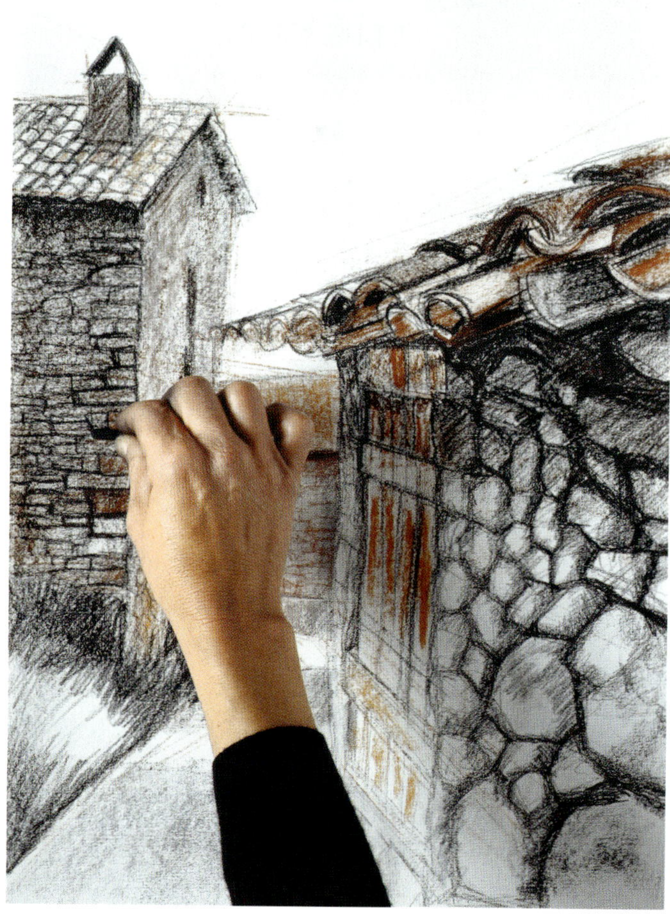

With the last application we emphasize the gradation on the texture that is far away. We go over the lines of the stones in the foreground again, paying special attention to their shape. We darken the façade on the second plane; here the stones look squarer and somewhat diffused.

The stones of the façade in the second building are shaded with black and sanguine chalk. Gradations are avoided to prevent them from becoming three-dimensional; they should look flat, in clear contrast with the foreground.

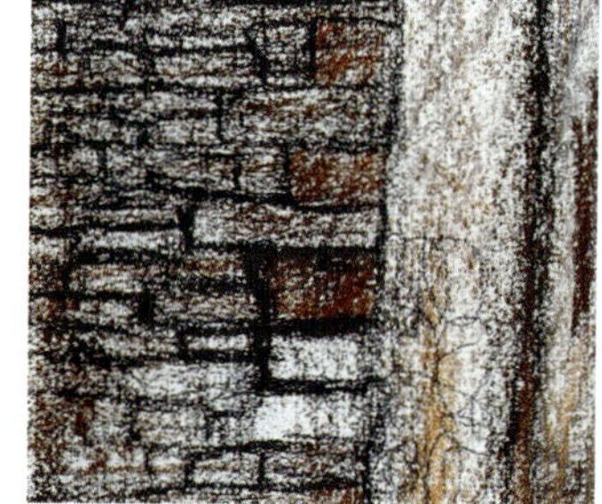

The final drawing shows three different treatments for each of the façades. Lack of definition plays an important role in creating depth. The greater the distance, the lighter the lines that define the texture of a surface.

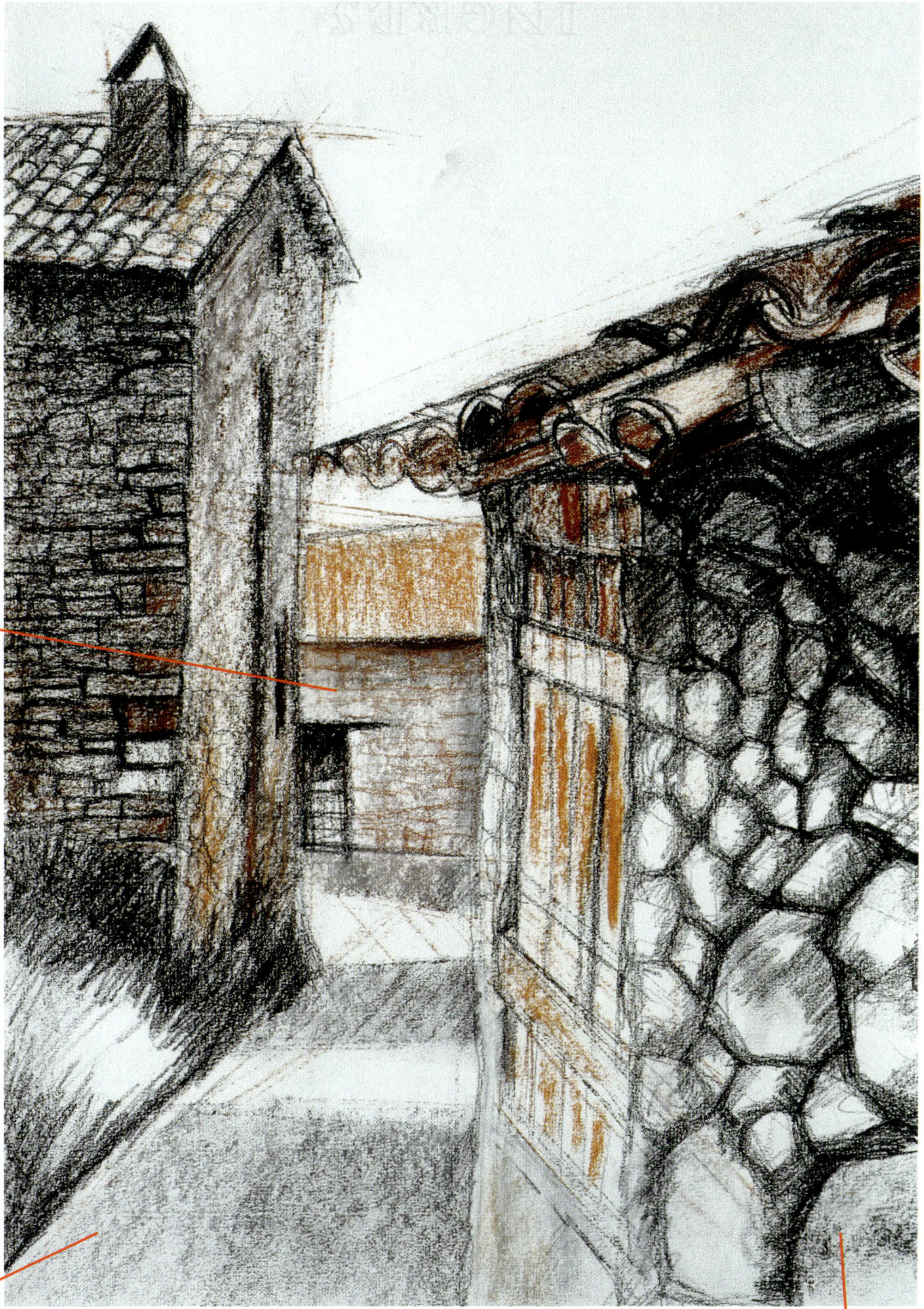

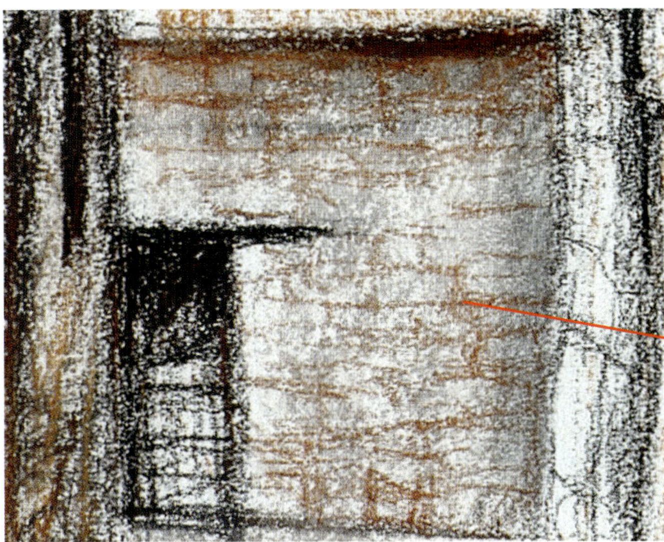

The façade in the background hardly has any texture. It is drawn simply with a few lines of sienna.

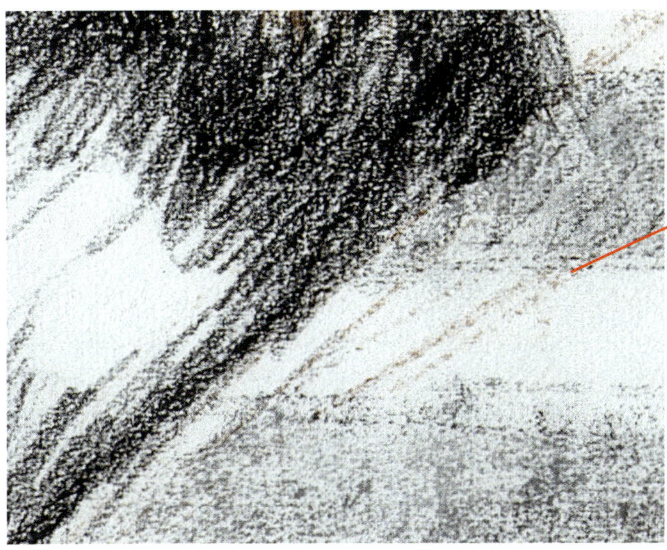

Each texture requires a different type of shading. The ground is created with flat shadows blended with the hand, while the edges are covered with gray hatching.

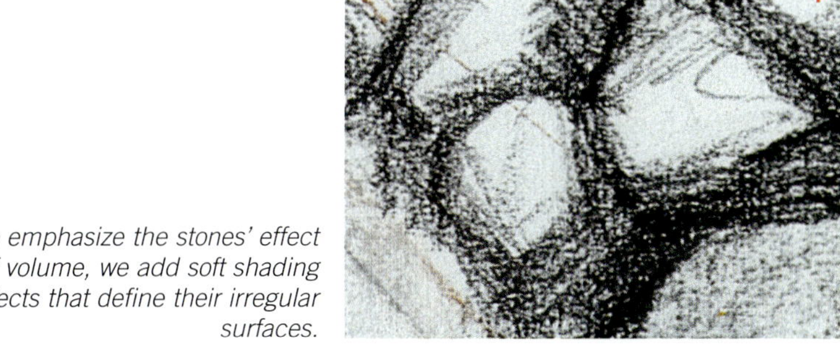

To emphasize the stones' effect of volume, we add soft shading effects that define their irregular surfaces.

GRADATIONS. The graduated shadows best portray the loss of color effect experienced by receding spaces. It is therefore the most commonly used method in atmospheric perspective. It enhances the three-dimensional effect when applied to any surface, since it portrays, very effectively, the changing quality of light.

A simple gradation by itself explains the effect of losing color saturation that the landscape experiences with atmospheric perspective.

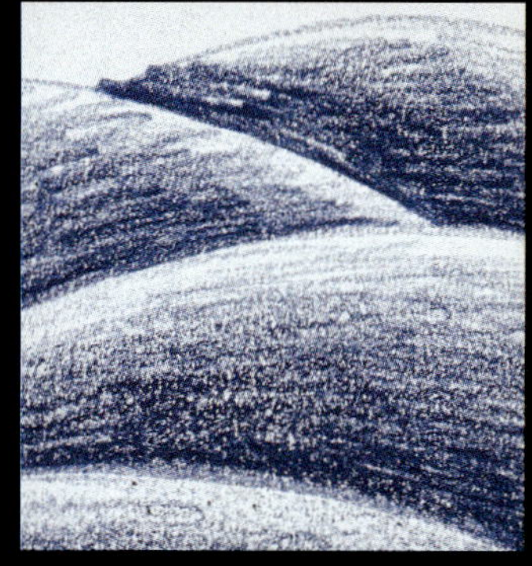

Gradations can be applied over each plane to enhance volume and to give the terrain a more rounded look.

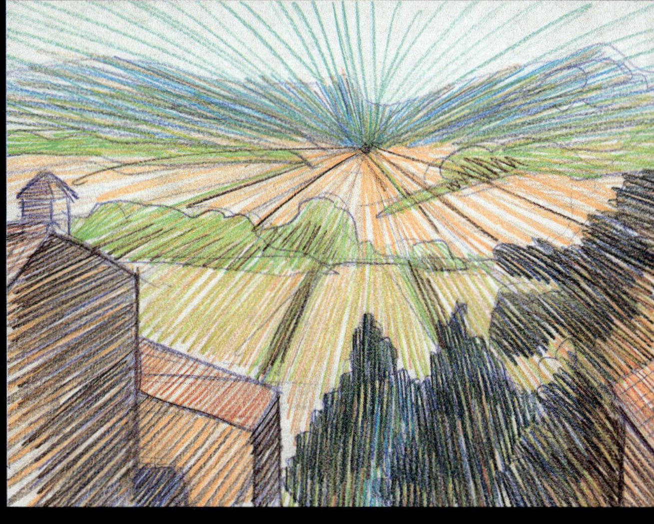

RADIAL LINES. When we use cross-hatching for drawing, radial lines can become very handy. These lines converge at a single point on the horizon line; this way, all the lines look as if they were drawn in a circular configuration around that point.

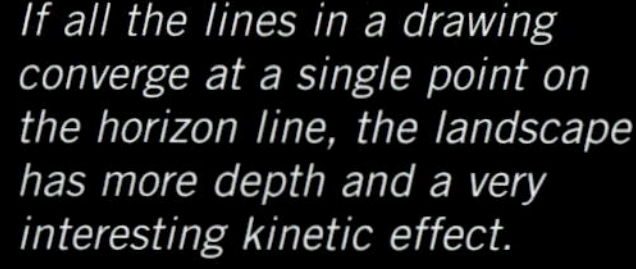

If all the lines in a drawing converge at a single point on the horizon line, the landscape has more depth and a very interesting kinetic effect.

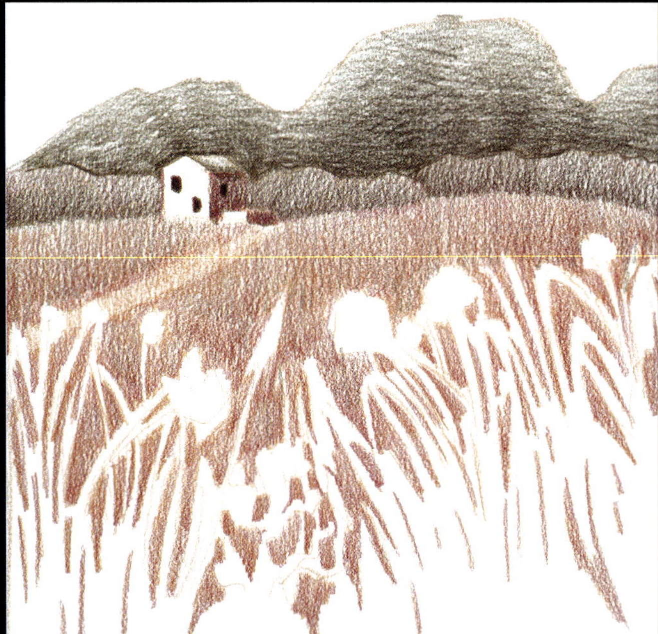

FOREGROUND OUT OF FOCUS. Often, with atmospheric perspective, we try very hard to show detail in the foreground of the painting, even when that is not the most important thing. There is no logical explanation for it, because if the area we want to focus on is in the center of the piece, the grass below our feet or a branch that cuts through the surface is not important.

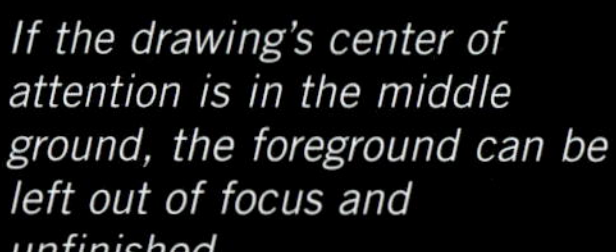

If the drawing's center of attention is in the middle ground, the foreground can be left out of focus and unfinished.

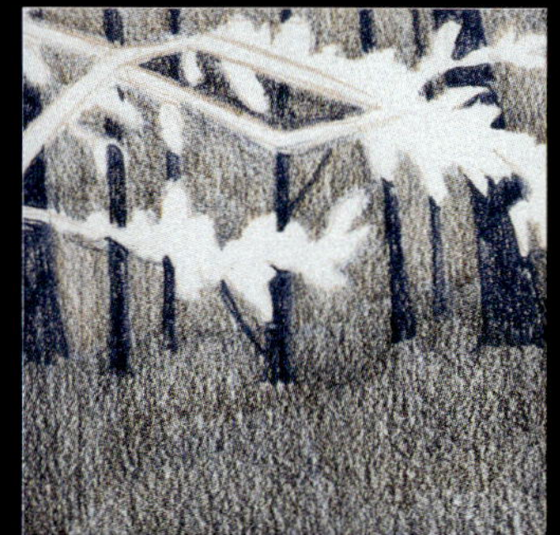

A branch drawn out of focus, without details, that springs out in the foreground can enhance the effect of depth.

GRADATIONS, LINES, SOFT FOCUS, AND TRANSPARENCIES. There are several ways to ensure the continuity of the space and to make it coherent, for example, the use of gradations or radial hatching in perspective, as well as other approaches that help break down the physical quality of an object, such as drawing an element out of focus to create an imaginary space, or using transparencies. Let us look at how these resources can be used.

DEPTH AND TRANSPARENCY. A special case for overlapping elements is through transparencies. Here, the occlusion is only partial since the layered objects can still be seen. The light of the transparent area creates an imaginary space that differentiates the foreground from the background, enhancing the effect of depth through overlaying. The sun rays, the mist, the filters, the haze... are physically transparent.

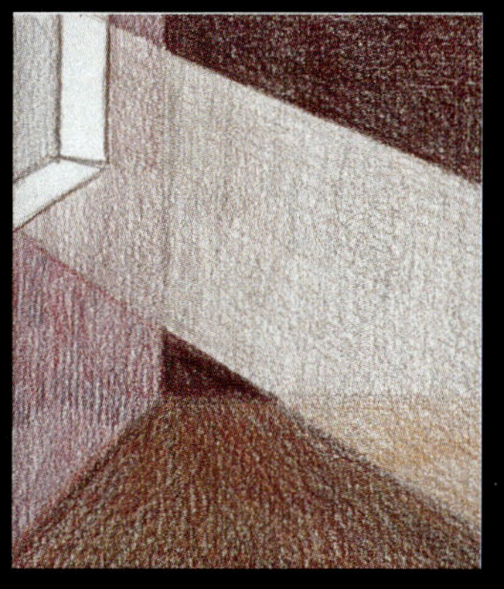

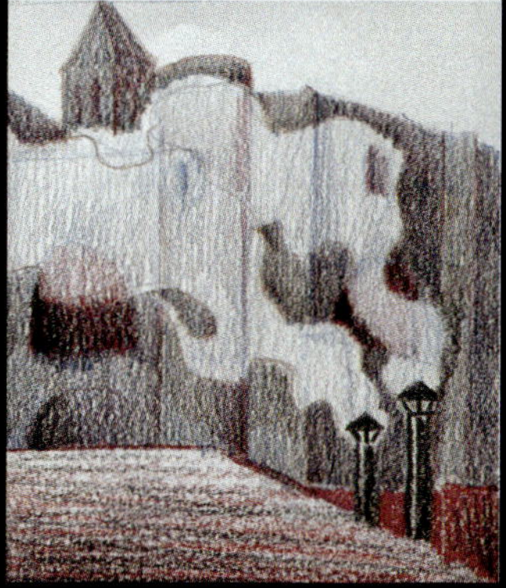

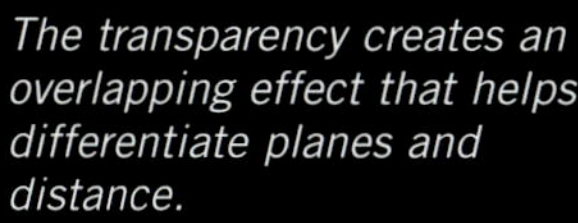

The transparency creates an overlapping effect that helps differentiate planes and distance.

A transparency is achieved when a surface lets sufficient light through for the element below to be visible.

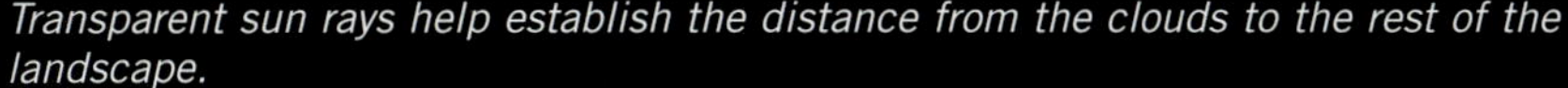

Transparent sun rays help establish the distance from the clouds to the rest of the landscape.

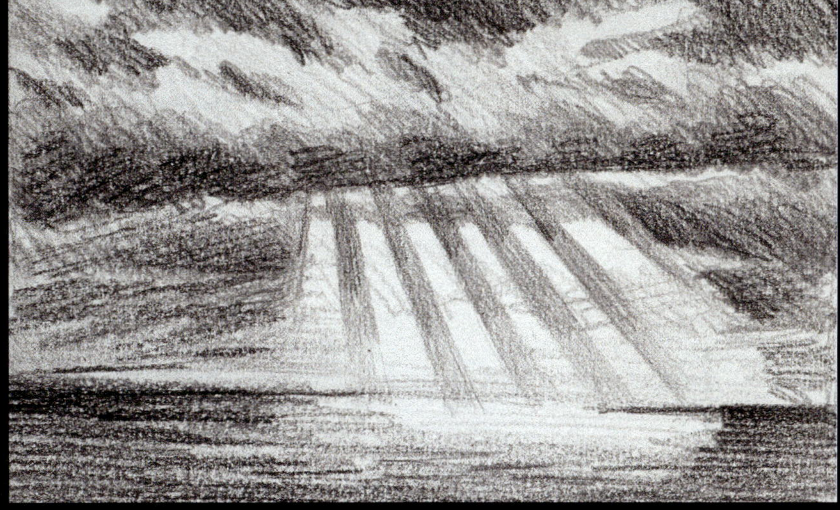

THE CONTRIBUTION OF TRANSPARENCIES IN LINEAR PERSPECTIVE. Transparencies are very helpful in linear perspective, especially in urban scenes. In this case, drawing transparent cubes and rectangles helps represent dual surfaces at once, as well as differentiating the front from the back.

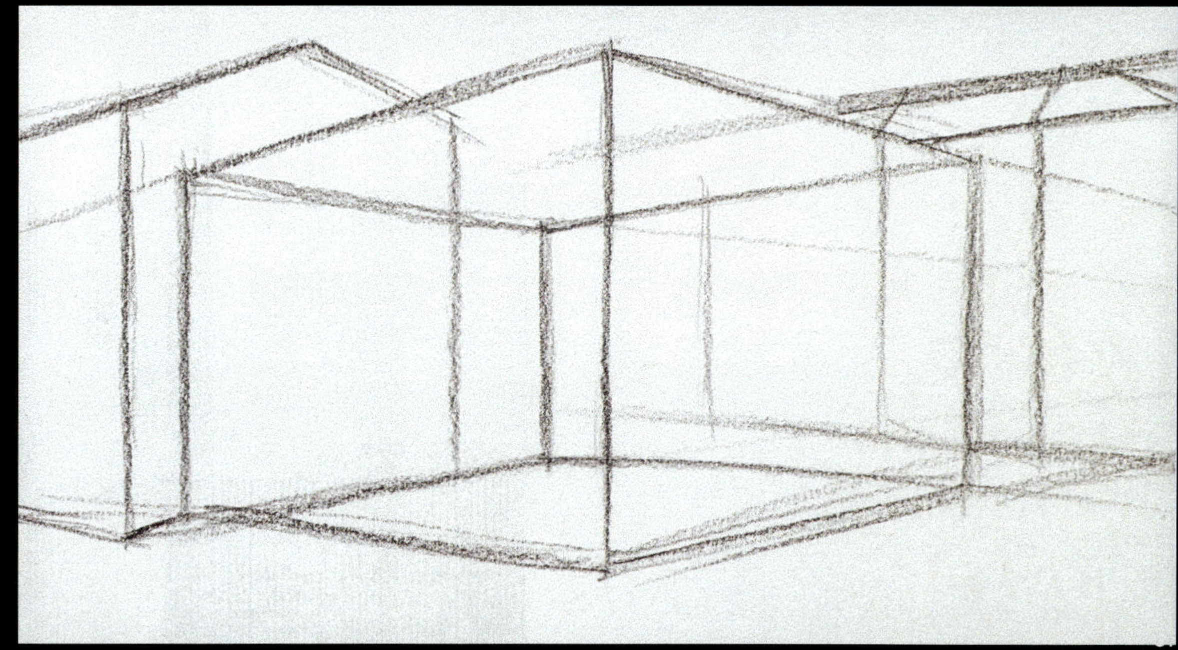

Drawing urban elements as if they were transparent geometric shapes helps understand the subject.

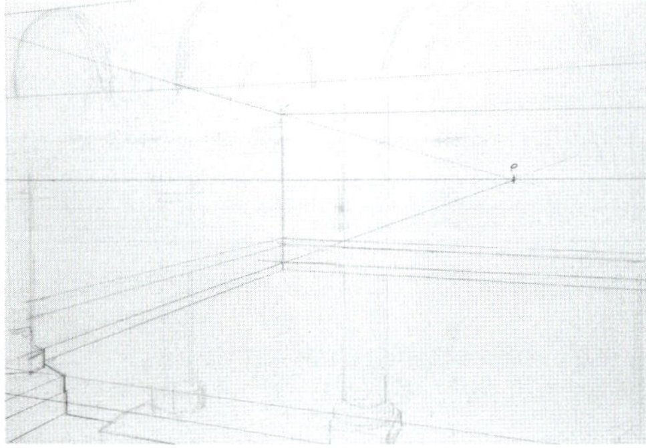

We use a series of lines to block in the cloister and the placement and sizes of the arches. There is also another indicator of depth: the shadows, which are darker in the foreground and lighter gray in the background.

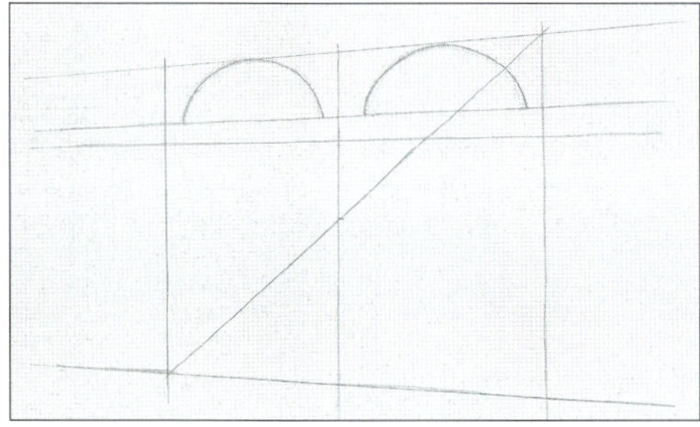

To draw the arches in the foreground, the width of each one of them is established with the texture gradient technique. Then, we project a diagonal from the upper part of the first line, which crosses the second one through the middle, and it is projected across the previous vanishing line. We draw a new perpendicular line from this point.

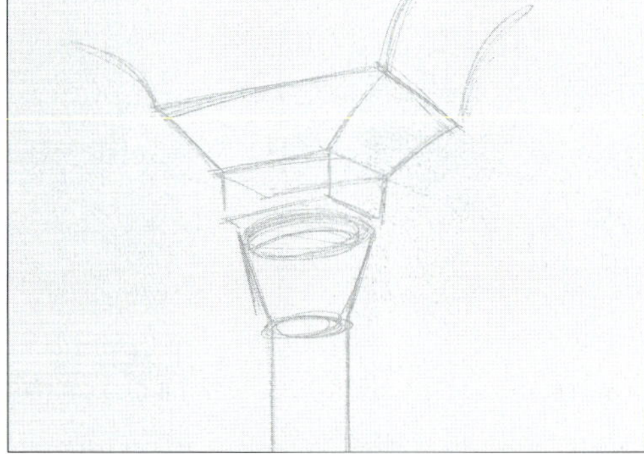

The easiest way to resolve the capitals is by combining different simple geometric shapes, as if it were a series of stained glass pieces that fit together.

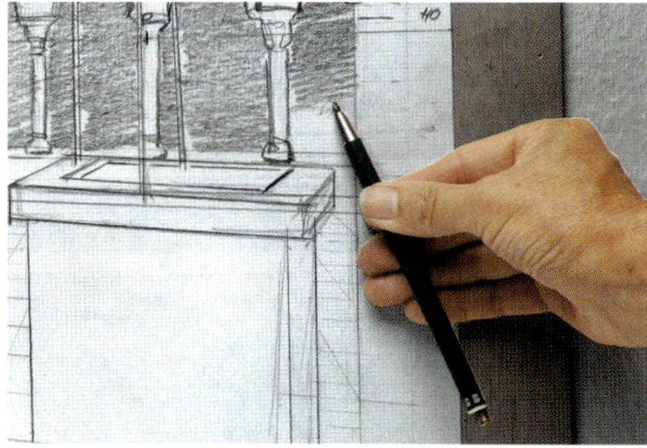

Shading is another important factor that gives the work a feeling of depth. It is a good idea to work with a 4B pencil or mechanical pencil. The background is shaded softly and lightly.

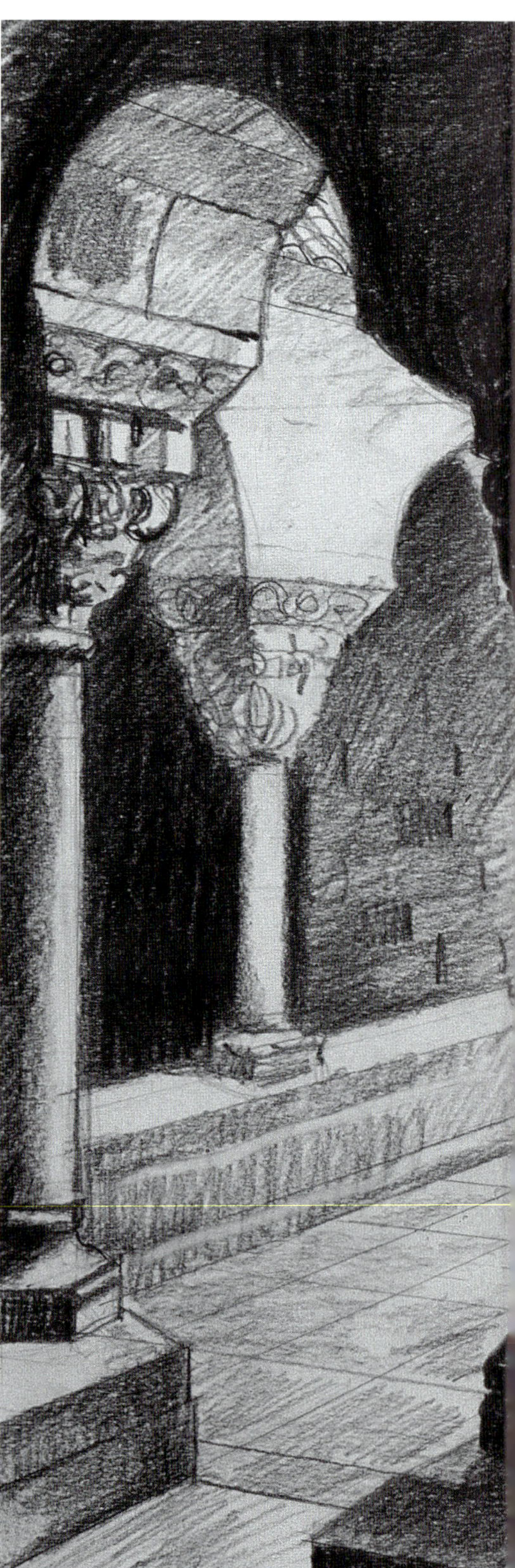

When a model presents some degree of architectural complexity, it is necessary to break down the space into very simple shapes. To begin with, it is a good idea to draw the vanishing lines of the walls in the cloister with a two-point perspective: the first one on the paper, and the second one, very far away, outside of the surface of the drawing.

PERSPECTIVE OF A CLOISTER. A cloister full of architectural features and elements may look like a daunting task for an artist. However, knowing how to break down the space from the beginning makes the process very easy and very pleasant.

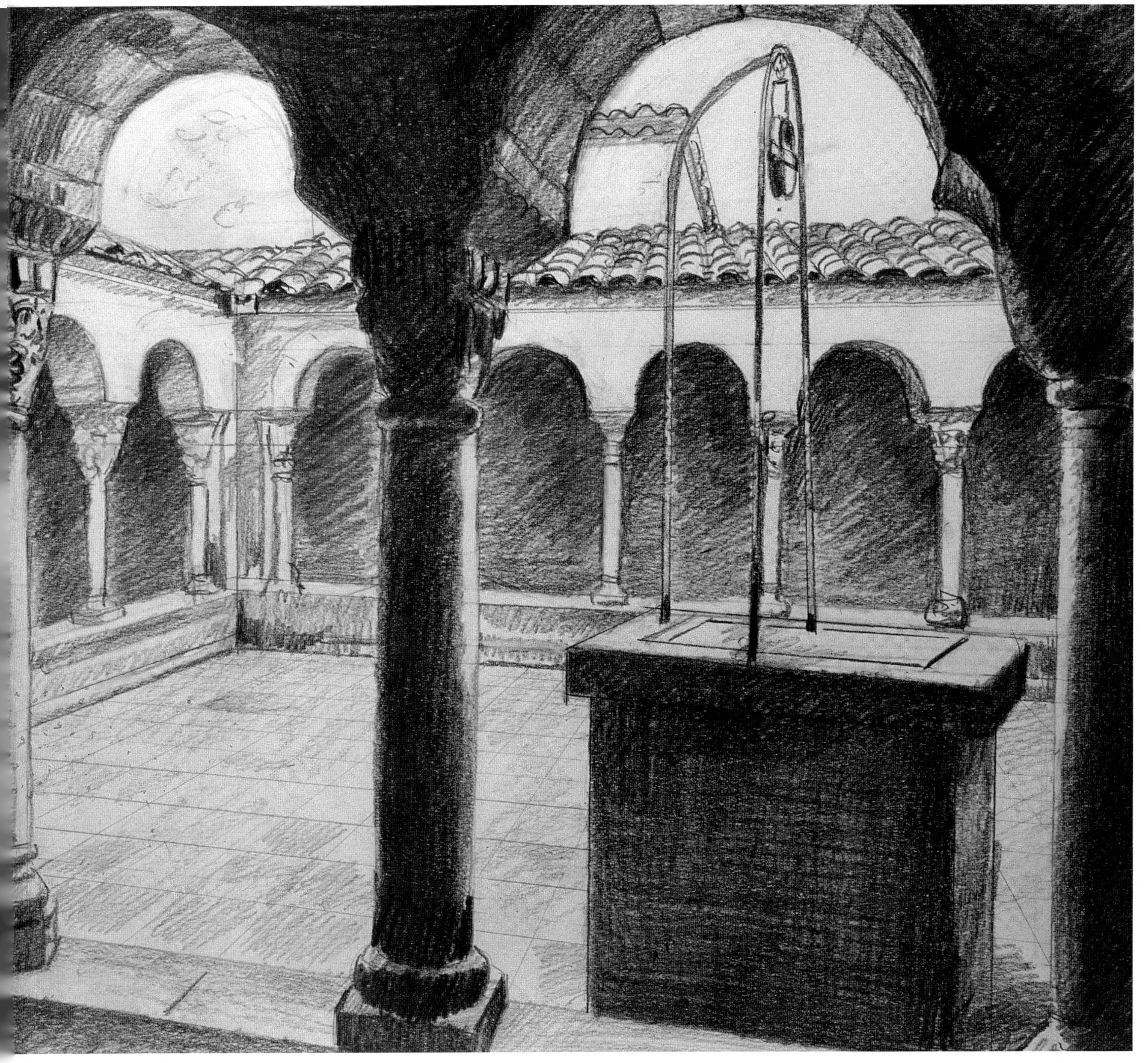

THE *COULISSE* EFFECT. The term is a French word that makes a reference to a theater's stage set. It consists of representing each plane with a solid color that becomes lighter as it recedes. When the *coulisse* effect is used to represent depth in a landscape, it is important for the progression of values to be decreasing and orderly; this way, all the forms that belong to the area in the background are seen as if they were a continuous backdrop.

In a landscape with a coulisse effect, each plane is treated with a uniform color that lightens as it recedes.

ELEVATION IN PERSPECTIVE. To draw this, we create a floor that is divided into regular squares, drawn in perspective. Beginning with the grid, we project the objects in perspective. This approach is very useful for drawing interiors with their furnishings.

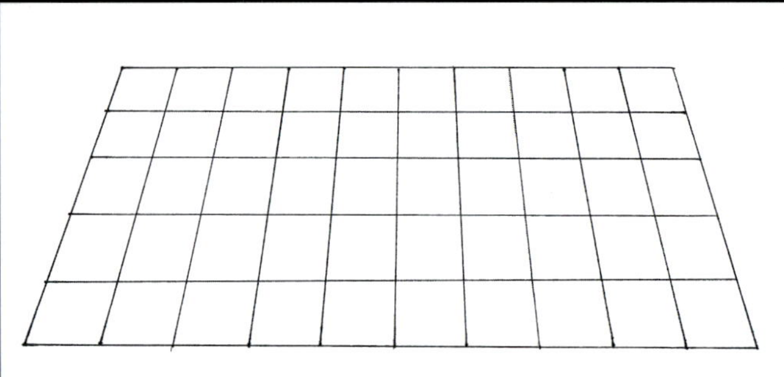

We draw a tiled floor. The grid in perspective helps us project the volumes.

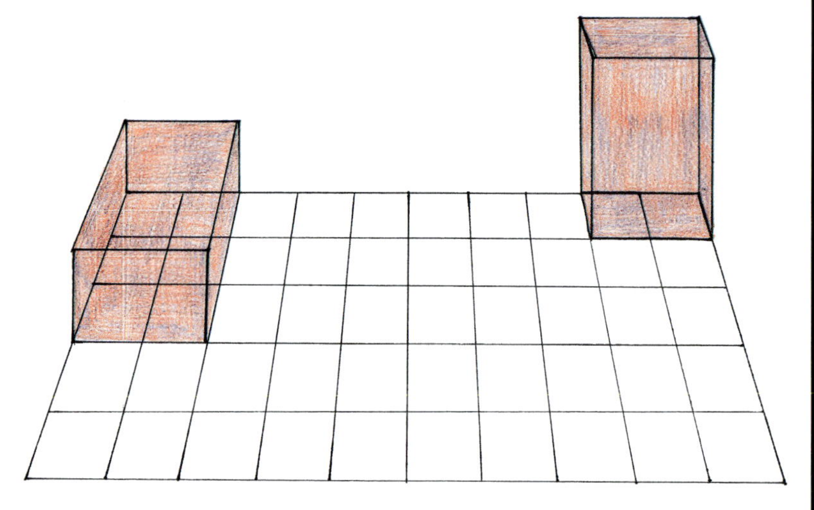

Using the grid as reference, we project the rectangular geometric shapes.

SCENIC PERSPECTIVE. Theatrical perspective is often compared to an auditorium or a stage set, complete with an offstage area and a backdrop. Perspective resources are drawn from elevation techniques, from creating depth with stage sets, from angling the floor, among other techniques. The goal is to create the optical illusion that the limited stage is a landscape with unlimited depth.

ASCENDING FLOORS. Often the artist wishes to create a greater feeling of depth than is physically possible. If a stage designer builds a regular space, with horizontal floors and rectangular walls, the viewer arrives at specific conclusions. If, on the other hand, the floor gradually goes up toward the back, the ceiling descends and the trapezoidal walls converge. A physical slope combined with perspective slopes results in a projection.

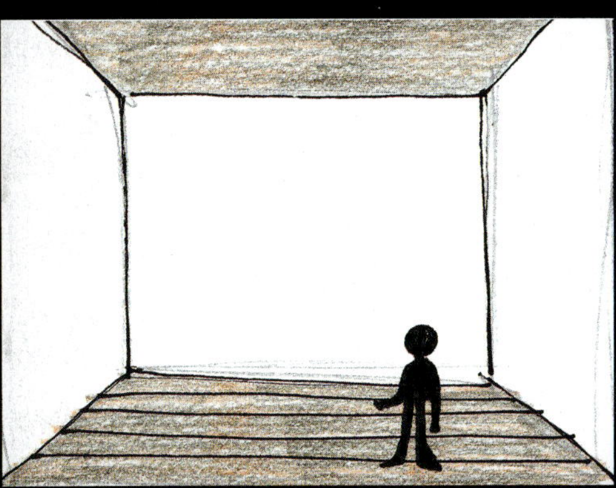

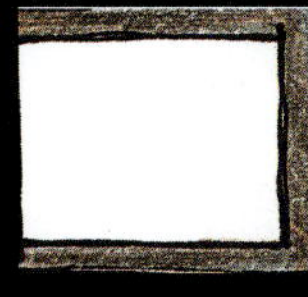

If an interior has a regular shape, with the corners meeting at right angles, the effect of depth is limited.

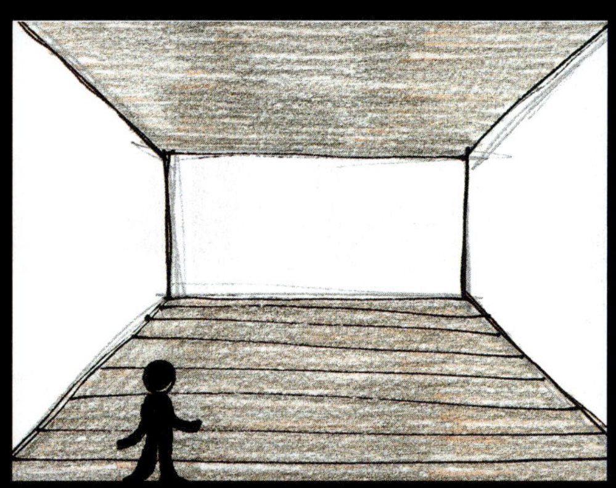

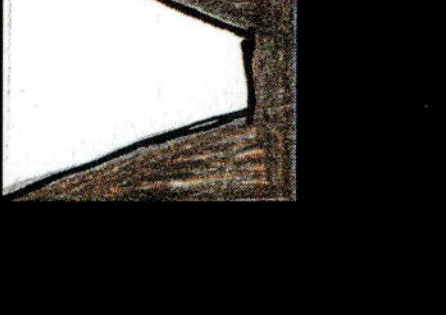

The perception of depth in a stage or a room is increased by placing the ceiling and the floor at an angle to force the perspective.

DIVERGENT PERSPECTIVE. Converging perspective conceals the sidewalls; diverging perspective reveals them. It reveals the sides of a cube, and in doing so gives it more volume. The visual advantages of this procedure are so obvious that modern artists (Fauvists, Cubists, and Futurists, among others) used this method to represent façades, buildings, and still life.

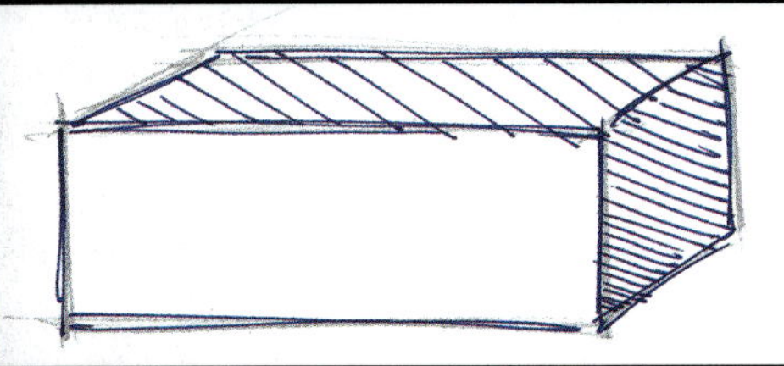

An example of a geometric shape in converging perspective.

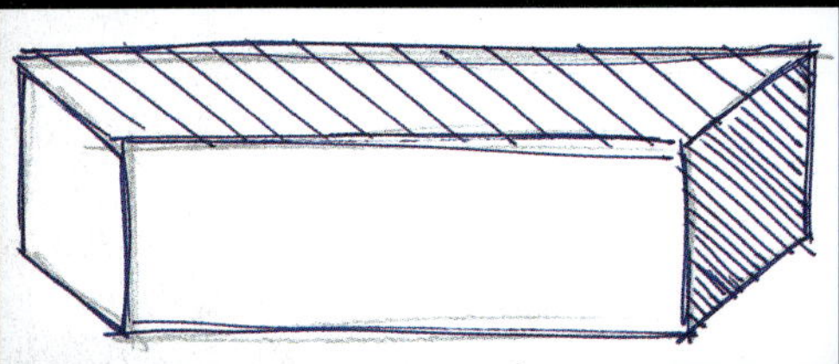

The same geometric body in diverging perspective.

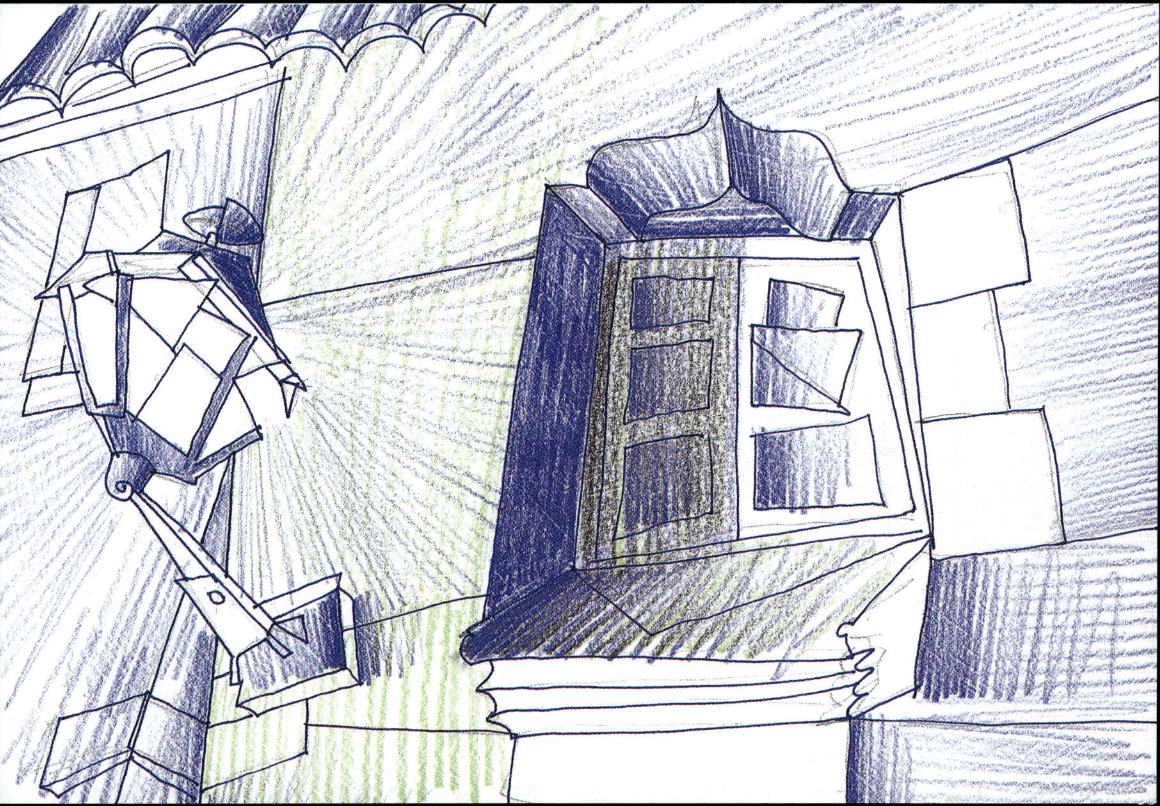

Diverging perspective has always been a source of inspiration for Cubist artists.